LOUIS BOUYER, of the Oratory
Dom JEAN LECLERCQ, monk of Clervaux
Dom FRANCOIS VANDENBROUCKE, monk of Mont-César
and LOUIS COGNET, professor at L'Institut Catholique, Paris

A HISTORY
OF
CHRISTIAN SPIRITUALITY

III
ORTHODOX SPIRITUALITY
AND
PROTESTANT AND ANGLICAN SPIRITUALITY

ORTHODOX SPIRITUALITY AND PROTESTANT AND ANGLICAN SPIRITUALITY

LOUIS BOUYER

THE SEABURY PRESS • NEW YORK

Second paperback printing

1982
The Seabury Press
815 Second Avenue
New York, N.Y. 10017

Originally published as *La Spiritualité orthodoxe et la
Spiritualité protestante et anglicane*
© Editions Montaigne 1965
English translation by Barbara Wall
© 1969 Burns & Oates, London
and Desclée Co., Inc., New York

Library of Congress Catalog Card Number: 63-16487
ISBN: 0-8164-2374-1

Printed in the U.S.A.

TABLE OF CONTENTS

Part One

RUSSIAN SPIRITUALITY AND THE REBIRTH OF GREEK SPIRITUALITY

PART ONE

Russian Spirituality and the Rebirth of Greek Spirituality

INTRODUCTION

AFTER the fall of Constantinople and the total subjection of the Christian East to Turkish domination, the evolution of Byzantine spirituality seemed to have come to a standstill in the countries where previously it had been so productive. It was then that an illusion of Byzantine stagnation came into being, or the illusion of a corpse superimposed on an extremely vital past. We say "illusion" advisedly—for the stagnation in fact, far from concealing death, marked the often heroic continuation of a hidden life that was to blossom into a magnificent new birth in its own good time.

Meanwhile, at the very moment when Christian Byzantium seemed thus immobilized by the inroads of Islam, the Slav peoples, to whom she had brought Christianity, as if by an arrangement of Providence became spiritually adult, so that the temporary halt to the development of Byzantine spirituality coincided with an upsurge of Russian spirituality which showed as yet undreamed-of potentialities within the tradition that it had received. And then in the second half of the eighteenth century, when Russian spirituality seemed weary in its turn, there was a rebirth of Greek spirituality, as it delved back into its own sources while becoming receptive to new influences.

But hardly had this rebirth taken shape at Athos than it led to a parallel revival, though a strongly individual one, in the Slav world.

This is the story that we hope to trace in our essay. The fact that it is so little known to Westerners is even more surprising than their massive ignorance of medieval Byzantine spirituality. It is true that its source-books occur in the less familiar languages and, though they have been fairly widely published, are not easily found in libraries on this side of the Iron Curtain. Yet work on Slavonic mysticism has already taken many shapes, and owing to the exile of Russian scholars caused by the Bolshevik Revolution a good number of books have been translated into our languages if they were not written in them in the first place. This is the case with

1*   3

such crucial works as several of Professor Fedotov's.[1] Moreover, there are Westerners who deserve to be placed in the front rank of researchers in this field, for instance, and first and foremost, Pierre Pascal.[2]

We should like to help our readers to become aware of the importance of this tradition whose vitality has been extending and renewing itself right up to our own time. If we give the facts and let the texts speak we shall hope to show that the term "Orthodox", by which all these spiritual writers are known, is not only not an empty word but signifies something very different from the mere conservatism with which we too often associate it, though with fewer and fewer possible excuses. As a result of the tragic and yet providential fact of Russian emigration, we can say of these things too that "they did not happen in a remote corner, but in our midst".[3]

[1] See primarily *Sviatije drevnej Roussi*, Paris, 1931, whose essential message has been summarized by Mme E. Behr-Sigel in *Prière et Sainteté dans l'Eglise russe*, Paris, 1950. For the origins of Russian spirituality, G. Fedotov has given us an incomparable account in English in *The Russian Religious Mind: Kievan Christianity, the Xth to the XIIIth centuries*, Harvard, 1946 (re-issued in The Harper Torchbooks in 1960—our quotations follow this edition). We are equally indebted to him for the most important selection of translated texts, with masterly introductions: *A Treasury of Russian Spirituality*, New York, 1948. In French, Fathers Stanislas Tyszkiewicz and Theodore Belpaire have given us a shorter selection but a very valuable one, *Ascètes et moralistes russes*, Namur, 1957.

[2] See primarily *Avvakum et les débuts du Rascol*, Paris, 1938, and also two articles that appeared in the *Revue de psychologie des Peuples*, 1947, Nos. 2 and 3, on "La religion du peuple russe".

[3] For a general bibliography, see Pierre Kowalevsky, *Saint Serge et la spiritualité russe*, Paris, 1958. More details on the sources and on modern works can be found in Father Ivan Kologrivof's *Essai sur la sainteté en Russie*, Bruges, 1953. This excellent book is a mine of texts and valuable pointers, even if it needs to be checked and completed.

I

ANCIENT RUSSIAN SPIRITUALITY

The Princely Saints

RUSSIA became reflectively aware of the special value of her spiritual tradition through the school of nineteenth-century thinkers and writers called Slavophiles who were not without links with our Romantics.[1] These thinkers who were won back to Russian Orthodoxy were in some ways the counterpart of their Western contemporaries who were won back to Ultramontane Catholicism. Whereas the latter saw as typically Roman many things that were merely Catholic and that Rome had received from elsewhere, the former inclined to see as typically Russian what more objective historians would attribute to an Orthodox tradition coming from Greece. There is no field in which these fluctuations are more striking than that of iconography. Many ikons regarded as typical of Russian spirituality and aesthetics are now recognized to be either Greek exports, or the product of Greeks working in Russia. The very ikon which people once saw as the most perfect expression of Russian spirituality—the Trinity attributed to Rublev—is today suggested by critics to be a typically Byzantine work, and with this additional point: that its peculiar characteristics seem to derive less from Russian soil than from Sienese painters.[2]

Such suggestions should by no means lead us to underestimate the very real individuality of Russian Christianity, but rather to look for it where it really is, and where it is natural that it should be at the heart of an authentic Christian tradition: not in any creation *ex nihilo* but in the particular emphasis given to an eternal truth by a new experience. And for this we should go to the spiritual books dating back to the origins of Russian Christianity, the lives of the saints who converted Russia. There are early

---

[1] Concerning this school see Abbé Gratieux's studies devoted to Khomiakov, and also the relevant chapters in the *Histoire(s) de la philosophie russe* by Nicolas Lossky and Basil Zenkovsky.

[2] See Gervase Mathew, *Byzantine Aesthetics*, London, 1963, p. 168, n. 2.

5

chronicles that date this conversion from the baptism of the people of Kiev on the Dnieper in 988, and show us St Vladimir the Prince, and his grandmother St Olga, in a convention that is exactly that of Byzantine panegyrics as applied to Constantine, the Emperor "equal to the apostles", and to his mother, St Helena.[3] However it is worthy of note that the Russian chronicler even at that early date, and unlike Eusebius in *De Laudibus Constantini*, makes no attempt to gloss over the previous somewhat unedifying conduct of his two characters. Quite the reverse; he shows us Olga's brutality and Vladimir's dissolute life—and this is not due to naivety. He shows us two people who, in bringing Christianity to Russia, were not prefabricated saints but needed conversion just as much as their people.

From the first it was a feature of Russian Christianity that it was a Christianity of penitents, and penitents who found no difficulty in confessing their grossest sins. This was to mark it with an evangelical character of striking consistency, though there would be distortions in which the excesses of penance were barely distinguishable from morbid complacency (whence Gide's remark that Russians are incapable of sinning with simplicity). Yet we would be more than unjust if we did not see what lay behind the distortions: the candour and true and humble humanity with which so many spiritually minded Russians have seized on the phrase, "I have come to call not the righteous but sinners . . ."—a phrase that our over-civilized Christianity has some difficulty in digesting.

The old chronicles then give us the lives of St Boris and St Gleb, and this takes us a step further. Sons of St Vladimir and slaughtered by reason of a brother's jealousy, they were not penitents nor, strictly speaking, martyrs, for they did not die for their faith.[4] Yet they were canonized the first of all the Russians, well before their father and Olga, and what won them their extraordinary popularity was the simple fact of having accepted unjust suffering with total resignation. This does not mean that they consented to it gladly, like Corneille's Polyeucte. On the contrary, Gleb in particular quailed before the idea of a painful and untimely death. Yet he submitted to it without resistance, following the example of Christ.

Behaviour of this kind impressed the Russian soul so early and, again, so consistently, that we shall see examples of children and other innocents becoming objects of a cult solely on account of their unmerited suffering—to such an extent, indeed, that ecclesiastical authorities hesitated to ratify these canonizations on the

---

[3] See E. Behr-Sigel, *op. cit.*, pp. 39 *et seq.*
[4] See Fedotov, *The Russian Religious Mind*, pp. 94 *et seq.*; E. Behr-Sigel, *op. cit.*, pp. 42 *et seq.*; I. Kologrivof, *op. cit.*, pp. 27 *et seq.*

grounds that the voluntary, personal element of sanctity was insufficiently in evidence.[5] However, these facts testify to the hold exercised over the Russian people by the figure of the humiliated Christ, such as the "Songs of the Servant" help us to understand.[6] This is another feature with its roots in the Gospel, although its literalism at times degenerated into a turbid masochism of which the *klousty* and *skoptsy* sects were the best-known examples.

The Monastic Saints: Antony and Theodosius Pechersky

But in Russia, as in the ancient East, spirituality was soon to centre mainly on monasticism.[7] So let us study the way in which monasticism was introduced into ancient Russia and how it developed there.

Monasticism was already in existence in Russia before the conversion of the Kiev princes, but in its first phase its influence spread from the monastery to which princely interest and generosity was pre-eminently extended, namely the Petcherskaia Lavra in Kiev, or the Monastery of the Caves. Its founder, St Antony, seems to have started his monastic life on Athos. But our knowledge of him links him more closely to Syrian monasticism and to an almost exclusive insistence on penitential asceticism of a kind we are tempted to regard as inhuman.[8]

Born at Liubitch in the province of Chernigov, he was unable to settle down in any of the existing monasteries on his return from Athos. After wandering from one to another he finally established himself in a cave in the side of the hill overlooking the city of Kiev. There, we are told, he lived in total solitude on bread and water, digging out his cave with his own hands, watching and praying. Disciples from all sections of society soon gathered round him and proceeded to enlarge the caves and build a church. He welcomed them, but when there were too many he withdrew further up the hill and finished his life in total seclusion. When he died in 1073 (?) the monastery was under the direction of one of his followers, Theodosius, very different from himself and Russia's second canonized saint after Boris and Gleb.

[5] See notably the cases of Julienne de Viazma, Basile de Mangazira and Dimitri Rurikovich in Fedotov, *op. cit.*, p. 109.
[6] See Nadiejda Gorodetzky, *Le Christ humilié.*
[7] For a factual history of Russian monasticism, see Father Rouet de Journel, S.J., *Le monachisme russe et les monastères russes*, Paris, 1957. On the evolution and ideals of Russian monasticism, the best study is still Igor Smolitsch's *Russisches Mönchtum, Entstehung, Entwicklung und Wesen (988–1917)*, Würzburg, 1953.
[8] See Fedotov, *The Russian Religious Mind*, pp. 154 *et seq.*; Kologrivof, *Essai sur la sainteté en Russie*, pp. 37 *et seq.*

We have a biography of Theodosius[9] written shortly after his death,[10] but it is doubtful if any similar document was written about St Antony, who was not canonized until much later. The paradoxical thing is that, in spite of Theodosius's much greater immediate popularity in the Church, he established a less durable school in the monastery than Antony his predecessor, though Antony was lost in the obscurity in which he purposely buried himself.

Born at a date unknown in the city of Vasilkov, Theodosius came of a fairly well-to-do family that moved shortly afterwards to Kursk. He lost his father when he was thirteen and was thus under the thumb of a mother who is depicted as a veritable virago whose one passion was to dominate her eldest son. She was horrified when he began to show pity and love for the poor. He worked in the fields with the serfs, regularly gave his best clothes to the destitute and dressed in rags himself, and one of his favourite occupations was to bake the bread used for the eucharistic liturgy. Once he tried to leave home with some pilgrims bound for Jerusalem, but he was caught by his mother, punished and taken back by force. However, this only increased his longing for a life dedicated to asceticism and prayer. He wore chains under his clothes like the ancient Syrian ascetics, and finally, when his mother was away, he ran off to Kiev. There he vainly sought admittance into various ancient monasteries—poor and without recommendation as he was—until at last Antony took him into his caves and gave him a habit. When his mother managed to get on his tracks she went straight to the Superior and, affecting anxiety regarding the culprit, soon melted Antony's heart. Good and simple man as he was, he unwisely allowed her to see her son, so once again there was the classical scene, though this time violence was replaced by emotional blackmail. But to no avail. Theodosius gave her no further chance of seeing him unless she herself became an enclosed nun in a convent in the city. This in fact is what finally happened.

Shortly after Theodosius's entry into the monastery, Antony, while in principle remaining its spiritual father, went off to a more distant cave and handed over the direction of the community to the monk Barlaam. But Theodosius won the esteem of the other monks, not so much by the rigour of his asceticism (though we are shown him exposing himself to mosquito bites at the entrance of the cave while spinning and singing psalms) as by his humility; so

[9] Fedotov, *op. cit.*, pp. 110–131; Smolitsch, *op. cit.*, pp. 61 *et seq.*; Kologrivof, *op. cit.*, pp. 35 *et seq.*
[10] The life of Theodosius, by the monk Nestor, is translated by Fedotov in his *Treasury*, pp. 15 *et seq.*

that, when Barlaam was summoned by the Prince to govern the monastery of St Demetrius, the brothers told Antony that they wanted the new recruit for their abbot.

Barlaam had already begun to lead the growing community out of the caves by building a small church. Theodosius built a larger one and surrounded it with cells and a cloister. In 1062 they transferred to these buildings, and the caves were hardly ever used except as places of more or less temporary withdrawal before becoming tombs. Into the monastery thus transformed Theodosius introduced the Studite cenobitic rule, so close to our Benedictine rule in its moderate application of St Basil's ideal. Here we are plainly very far from Antony's ideal, for Antony himself seems to have been totally uninterested in these innovations (unless he was already dead when they took place).

But Theodosius did not altogether abandon either rigorous asceticism or the longing for total solitude. Though we are no longer told of the extreme austerities of his youth, it appears that he never slept except seated and that he returned every Lent to the caves where he had ordered that he should be buried. On the whole, however, monastic life as he lived it found its whole meaning in the ceaseless opportunities it offered for humility closely bound to charity, and for his own personal deprivation for the sake of others. As Superior of a monastery whose prestige had grown almost overnight, and as one soon to be the intimate of Kiev princes, he nevertheless continued to dress like the poorest of beggars and was indifferent to the scorn that this provoked (or rather, he provoked it on purpose). He preached to his community by example rather than precept. When the cook complained that the brothers had not brought in a fresh supply of wood, it was he who quietly set himself to the task while the others were at table. They were so dismayed on coming out of the refectory to see him with a hatchet in his hand and surrounded by logs that they all soon set to work. But things did not always turn out so well, and it is obvious (we only have to read his exhortations to regularity to be convinced of it) that the brothers took things easily where discipline was concerned, knowing that nothing would be said, however much they trod on their Superior's toes. Deserters, if they returned, were always sure of being welcomed back like prodigal sons even if they ran away several times. When he heard monks chatting in their cells as he did the nightly rounds, when they should have been asleep or at prayer, he contented himself with tapping gently on their door as a warning. And if he summoned them before him next day, he reprimanded them by means of a parable that they were free not to understand.

On one point he was intractable: poverty. If he discovered superfluous provisions he had them thrown on the fire at once. But in the ordinary way the cellarer hardly had the opportunity to put much on one side, for the monastery was a centre of charity where almost everything that came in was promptly given out again. And when this deliberately improvident economy resulted in shortage, we are told that Theodosius solved the situation by an unobtrusive miracle—a gold piece brought by an angelic visitor, for instance ...

Otherwise he seems to have impressed the brothers especially by the serene continuity of his prayer, and by the way he repelled the assaults of both devils and brigands by the angelic presences he drew to the monastery. An episode in which the saint's prayer and humility came together with his delightful simplicity occurred once when he was praying in his cell. On hearing someone coming to awaken him he stopped singing and answered only at the third knock so that the caller might think he had been asleep.

The same simplicity characterized his relations with princes. Not only did he receive them without being any more impressed by their splendour than irked by their importunity, but he accepted their invitations with good grace. That did not prevent him from censuring their pagan recreations which he was able to observe on such occasions, nor from boldly denouncing their extortions. When Sviatoslav dispossessed his elder brother Isviaslav, Theodosius consented to resume relations with him, but he never hid from him that he looked on his brother as the lawful sovereign and exhorted him to the end to put him back on the throne.

We can understand how this Gospel-like humanity immediately made Theodosius a popular saint. But it remains none the less true that his type of cenobitism, which we feel to be much nearer to the Palestinian Lavras such as St Sabas's than to Studium for which they were a source of inspiration, was to have less influence on the later tradition of the Petcherskaia Lavra than St Antony's fierce Syrian asceticism. St Theodosius died in 1074 and was canonized less than thirty years later. But the *Paterikon* of Kiev calls attention—in the twelfth and thirteenth centuries—only to the crazed disciples of Antony among the monks worthy of note.[11] It seems that the cenobitism of the Lavra, where Theodosius himself had not imposed a very firm discipline, relaxed still more after his death, while more and more gifts poured in from princes and boyars; so that the more serious monks were tempted to go back to Antony's example while being held in check by his successor's spirit of prudence and sense of measure. Later that brake was no

[11] See Fedotov, *The Russian Religious Mind*, pp. 142 *et seq.*; E. Behr-Sigel, *op. cit.*, pp. 57 *et seq.*; Kologrivof, *op. cit.*, pp. 53 *et seq.*

longer there, or no longer operative, so that free rein was given to the horrifying ascetic exploits of, for instance, John the Sufferer who was buried alive, or Pimen the Sickly who was perpetually and intentionally diseased. The constant thought of death, symbolized to a macabre degree by the life of Mark the grave-digger, consumed them, together with the struggle against devils whose hallucinating aspects were more and more emphasized. One outstanding figure in this tradition should be mentioned—a contemporary of Antony and Theodosius. A disciple of Antony and a recluse like him, Isaac sank into madness, from which state Theodosius rescued him. He thereupon took over the vilest tasks of the kitchen and, when he saw that his brothers regarded him as a saint, simulated a relapse. He was probably the first example of a type of humble saint that was to become common in Russia: the "fool for Christ".

A literary vulgarization inspired by modern thinkers has tended to present Orthodoxy in general, and Russian Orthodoxy in particular, as a Christianity of the resurrection, as opposed to Western medieval Christianity centred on the cross.[12] The Kiev monastic tradition gives us pause with regard to this over-simplification of the facts. If the notion of affective co-suffering with the suffering of Christ was expressed less often in the East than in the West (but we shall see that it was by no means absent, especially in Russia), the vision of the risen Christ, far from obliterating that of his cross —or, more generally, that of necessary death—went hand in hand with it. In the monastic tradition in particular, and ever since the emergence of a peculiarly Russian spirituality, this last aspect has been stressed with a vigour and rigour that should not be underestimated.

Abraham of Smolensk and Eschatology

In the following century and in a different form, the personality and work of another monk testified to the importance of this aspect. This was St Abraham of Smolensk, who died in 1221[13]—the only monk besides St Theodosius of whom we have a biography dating from before the Mongol invasions. Like Theodosius, he was initially attracted by evangelical poverty, but once he was a monk he developed a passion for study and was one of the first preachers and writers of old Russia. It was the Bible that interested him, with such commentaries of the Fathers as he could get hold of, and

---

[12] Basil Zenkovsky says of Dostoievsky in vol. I of his *Histoire de la philosophie russe*, Paris, 1953, pp. 457 *et seq.*: it is a Christianity of the Transfiguration, but without Golgotha.

[13] Fedotov, *ibid.*, pp. 158 *et seq.*; Kologrivof, *op. cit.*, pp. 64 *et seq.*

among these (also a persistent characteristic in old Russia) the apocrypha of the first centuries seem to have particularly claimed his attention. Their apocalyptical mysticism fascinated him. His preaching, like his most personal prayer, seems to have been dominated by the fear of God's imminent judgment and an impatient expectation of eternal life.

If we are to understand these various characteristics and the significance they had for him, we must place them in their context. Christianity had barely penetrated the pagan masses when heretical gnoses, such as the Neo-Manichaeism of the Bogomils, came to mingle with the faith. Against this background it was not surprising that St Abraham's knowledge and speculations caused him to be suspected of heterodoxy, the jealousy of his unlettered brothers seizing too easily on what was unusual in his reading and preoccupations. Yet it was a very authentic biblical vein that he had recaptured in his exalted expectation of the judge and the saviour. The vision of imminent judgment in fact gave way to an anticipation of the heavenly city and a longing for its luminous beauty, to which his taste for the liturgy and for iconography bore equal witness. If, as Mr Fedotov suggests, the sermon on the judgment, generally attributed to St Cyril of Turov, should by rights be ascribed to him,[14] then he seems to have been very close to those pilgrimages of the soul that had fascinated the Irish monks and thereafter never ceased to nourish the vein of apocalyptic mysticism in the West, from Guillaume de Digulleville to Dante. But with St Abraham it seems clear that the Russian vision of a transfigured world, linked to Christ's resurrection, was very consciously also that of the world beyond death, as being the only one that is or could be beyond sin.

If we take the fascination felt so early by popular Russian Christianity for the image of Christ as the humbled Servant (as we saw it in the cult of SS. Boris and Gleb), together with the Gospel-like asceticism enshrined in the person of St Theodosius, and the eschatology—or more precisely the apocalyptic thought—of St Abraham, we cannot avoid being struck by the echoes of the Bible to be found in all these different aspects. It is certain that the Bible, with the liturgy, various great ascetic texts and some of the apocryphal writings in which the most primitive Christianity is expressed for long constituted almost the only literary stock of knowledge in this corner of Christendom. It was only slowly and always very sporadically that it would be influenced by the more intellectual forms of Greek Christianity. But one must believe that there was a particular affinity between the Slav soul and the Bible. This

14 Fedotov, *ibid.*, pp. 169–170.

soul was frequently to give a renewed vision of Christianity—and one very close to the Gospel as to the prophets—precisely because of this providential concentration on the Bible, illumined by the contemplative effects of Greek patristics on the Byzantine liturgy and an instinctive predilection for Syriac patristics: Ephraem was a major source for Abraham's sermon cited above, and Isaac of Nineveh was always to remain one of the most popular spiritual authors in Russia. The relationship of the man of God with the prophets of the Bible, in whatever guise the man of God would take in Russia, was to remain a striking feature. Whether monks or bishops, the ancient teachers of the Russians in the faith all had a freedom of utterance and an inspired and spontaneous mode of expression, whether they were addressing common people or princes. We have already noticed this in St Theodosius. The martyred Metropolitan of Moscow, St Philip (who died in 1569), gave it perhaps its last but most expressive realization in a hierarch at the time of the formation of the Muscovite Empire in the middle of the sixteenth century. Addressing Ivan the Terrible during Divine Service in the cathedral of the Dormition, he said: "Sire, we are offering here a bloodless sacrifice while the blood of Christians is flowing behind this sanctuary." The angry prince tried to silence him, but he went on, "I cannot keep quiet, for I cannot obey your command rather than God's. I am fighting for the true and the good, and I shall continue to do so even if I forfeit my dignity and suffer the cruellest wrongs."[15] Not long after this the leaders of the Church were throttled by the temporal power in Muscovite Russia which had become the Third Rome, just as they had been in Byzantium, the Second Rome. And this quasi-prophetic role passed to those "fools for Christ" of whom we shall speak again, before it again took on a more clerical but no less "charismatic" form with the modern *startzy*.

Lay Spirituality and the Admonition *of Vladimir Monomach*

Ancient Russian spirituality, like its Latin or Byzantine counterparts, was mainly monastic spirituality. Yet it would be a mistake to think that it therefore neglected the problems specific to lay spirituality, that is to say spirituality conformable with the tasks and responsibilities of a layman. In this Russia was different from our Western Middle Ages, and even the Middle Ages of Byzantium, and the reason for this was first and foremost the strongly evangelical direction of at least one part of Russian monasticism since its very beginnings. Just as it had been with primitive

[15] See Kologrivof, *op. cit.*, pp. 93 *et seq.*

monasticism, the monk in Russia was not so much someone who had a vocation apart as someone who had a particularly intense vocation to fulfil the simple basic Christian requirements. This was also probably why the layman saw monastic life less as an ideal life impossible of attainment than as a positive incentive to transpose into his own conditions the aspiration to be found there at the height of its purity.

Were we to judge by the penitential books for laymen which in Russia expanded those of Byzantium, then we would underestimate this fact—except that they were already characteristic by reason of the large place given to the practical requirements of charity, side by side with a ritualism still more stressed than in their models, and an obsession with sex hardly less in evidence.

But it is a different picture that emerges from a treatise written by a layman for his own sons, the *Admonition* of Prince Vladimir Monomach.[16] Though the reflections of a prince and stamped with his personal experience, it is so deeply meditated that it could easily be applied to all men with professional and family responsibilities. The simplicity of the Kiev princes' life and the community that they still formed with their boyars—in contrast to the Muscovite Emperors who gradually isolated themselves in a super-Byzantine autocracy—contribute no small part to the book's overall humanity. This is one of the features that distinguish it from the Byzantine *Mirrors of the Prince* with which Vladimir was familiar and which served him as model, others being, let us repeat, the biblical depth and the directly evangelical character of its Christianity. Fedotov has made an extremely detailed analysis of this book, and we can do no better than follow him.

The religion expressed in it, like that of the Sapiential books, is founded explicitly on the fear of God. But we do not have to read far to see that this fear should be understood in the deepest biblical sense of a religious reverence wholly penetrated by Christianity. God, the book says, is the just judge, and a judge who does not wait for the next life to mete out the retribution fitting to our actions, but uses our actions to bring retribution here and now. But he is also an infinitely merciful Father who waits only for repentance to bestow forgiveness, and calls it forth by this same forgiveness.

> Verily, my sons, understand how merciful and overmerciful is the loving God; we, men, being sinful and mortal, if someone wrongs us, we wish to lacerate him and shed his blood; but our Lord, master of life and death, endures our sins which are above

[16] See Fedotov's analysis in *The Russian Religious Mind*, pp. 244 *et seq.*

our head, over and over, until the end of our life, as a father, who loves his child, beats it but draws it to him again.[17]

Furthermore Vladimir shows a deep awareness of the creation, in which we find something of the age-old poetic depth of the Slav pagan soul such as it appears, for instance, in the marvellous story about Prince Igor's campaign. But in Vladimir this element is wholly Christianized in the vein of an entirely biblical thanksgiving.[18]

We should be totally mistaken if we imagined that these outbursts of religious lyricism, coming so unexpectedly from a realistic politician and war-chief, were some form of emotional compensation sought in a vague aestheticism. On the contrary, the theme of his layman's religion is the necessity for work, for patient and persevering work and study brought to bear on all the tasks for which he is responsible. Indeed, reversing the dictum to which we are accustomed, he says admirably that prayer has value only in so far as it is a higher form of work.

On the other hand he has a deep sense of the reality of sin, shown in his numerous quotations from the Lenten liturgy and the prayers of repentance proper to it. Repentance, tears and alms are the three weapons by which every man should ceaselessly combat the enemy he carries within himself. Vladimir gives this specific advice to his sons: "If God softens your hearts, shed tears because of your sins, saying: 'As Thou didst pardon the harlot, the robber and the publican, likewise pardon us sinners.' "

He does not insist on the recitation of set prayers morning and evening (although he did his best to take part in mattins and vespers as often as possible) but on a short prayer when getting up and going to bed, such as: "Enlighten my eyes, O Christ-God, who gavest Thy beautiful light", or "Add to me, O Lord, years to years that I may praise God, having repented of my sins and justified my life." We know he made constant use of his psalter, for he quotes from it frequently. He advises that free time occurring during the day's occupations be used for a simple return to God:

When you are riding on horseback and have no business conversation with anyone, if you know no other prayers, call: "Lord, have mercy," unceasingly and secretly: that prayer is best of all, better than thinking of nonsense while riding.[19]

He insists with particular force on the elimination of all pride from the heart, and Fedotov remarks that he calls God a terrible judge only in the context of the commandment of love for men.

[17] *Ibid.*, p. 246.   [18] *Ibid.*, p. 246.   [19] *Ibid.*, p. 250.

Generosity, not excluding (far from it) firmness, seems to him the essential duty of the prince, with absence of all avarice which meditation on death should bring about. In the list of lay works that he is always mentioning he includes, naturally, war and hunting. But we should note that he inculcates the duty of avoiding all other killing and makes no secret of his opposition on principle to capital punishment.

It would be difficult to find elsewhere, and at that time, such a complete and high ideal for the Christian layman.

St Sergius of Radonezh and St Cyril of Belozersk

The Tartar invasion (1227–1240) produced a general collapse of the political, economic and cultural life of Russia, and mainly in the cities where Christianity—as in the West—had known its earliest developments, and moreover where monasteries—as in Byzantium—had been early established. When some form of national life was resumed in the fourteenth century, centred on the principality of Moscow, the rebirth of religion was closely linked to the rebirth of monasticism. But the monks of this period, at least the most fervent and influential among them, took to leaving the cities and settling in the vast forests of the centre and the North.

This trend has for long been attributed to the man who was to become the patron of Moscow and all Russia, St Sergius of Radonezh (who died in 1392).[20] In fact the trend was general and spontaneous, and St Sergius no more than an outstanding representative of it; but we can study it more closely in Sergius and his follower St Cyril of Belozersk (White Lake), as two very remarkable biographies were written about them soon after their respective deaths—Sergius's by Epithanius the Wise[21] and Cyril's by Pachomius the Logothete.

People have conjectured whether this new type of monk had been influenced by their contemporaries on Mount Athos, whom they resembled not only in their taste for solitude but in the intensity of their inner prayer, in which a mystical aspiration now showed itself for the first time in Russia. Such an influence is all the more probable in that the monks of the following centuries, who could be regarded as their continuators, had an undoubted interest in Byzantine Hesychasm.

Sergius (Bartholomew in the world), born of a noble family of Rostov which later settled in Radonezh, established himself in the

---

[20] See Pierre Kowalevsky, *Saint Serge et la spiritualité russe*, Paris, 1958; Smolitsch, *op. cit.*, pp. 79 *et seq.*; E. Behr-Sigel, *op. cit.*, pp. 68 *et seq.*; Kologrivof, *op. cit.*, pp. 95 *et seq.*

[21] This is translated by Fedotov in his *Treasury*, pp. 54 *et seq.*

solitudes of a forest immediately after an encounter with a monk who opened his mind to the things of God. He built himself a chapel with a cell, but only formally became a monk through the intervention of a neighbouring priest-monk, Abbot Metrophanes. At first he lived entirely alone, in familiarity with wild beasts and taming a forest bear. Then companions joined him. When Metrophanes, who had visited them more or less regularly, died, they forced Sergius to become Superior of the Lavra they had set up. In the end he had a vast monastery around him, with a church, dedicated to the Holy Trinity; and soon a village started to grow up around the monastery. Like Theodosius, Sergius applied, or tried to apply, the rule of Studium. But as he also had Theodosius's humility (he insisted on wearing rags which brought endless contempt on his head as no one could believe that such an insignificant-looking man could be a renowned Superior) as well as his concern for individual and collective poverty, he does not seem to have been any more successful in imposing authority on his monks. Finally, when his own brother entered the community and conspired against him, he withdrew into total solitude once more until he was entreated to return. Yet his influence outside the monastery was extraordinary. The Metropolitan of Moscow, Alexis, who was for some time regent of the Muscovite state, employed him to go on political missions. Some of these concerned reconciliations between warring princes or cities, but others which foreshadowed a new conjunction between Church and State were not always so beneficial—as when he laid the city of Nijni-Novgorod under an interdict because its prince refused to submit to Moscow. But his national glory was due primarily to the blessing and encouragement he gave to Prince Dmitri Donskoi on the eve of the first great Russian victory over the Tartars at the battle of Kulikovo (1380).

However, if the Lavra of the Trinity became a centre of charity with social works more highly developed than those of any Basilian or Studite monastery, and even a centre of national renewal, it remained first and foremost a sanctuary for the most fervent prayer. We are not told that Sergius practised any other form of asceticism than the most humble work and the most complete self-abnegation; but the fervour of his prayer is brought out by his biographer, manifested in certain luminous visions that surrounded his person (such as an angel concelebrating with him, or the radiance of the chalice he had just consecrated), or of which he was the object (such as a vision he had of the Virgin with the apostles Peter and John; this was the first occurrence of the kind in Russian hagiography). At the end of his life he shut himself up in total silence. But, of this man of prayer and solitude—a solitude peopled with the crowds who flocked around him—it is an impression of radiant sweetness and matchless goodness that will endure. His grave is the most frequented and the place of most fervent pilgrimage in all Russia.

St Cyril's life (1337?–1427)[22] resembled his in some respects. Equally the son of boyars, Cyril began his monastic life in a typical urban monastery, that of Simonov in Moscow. He chose the humblest tasks and sometimes had to feign madness to escape his brothers' notice—St Sergius himself singled him out when visiting the monastery. He became Superior nevertheless, but resigned his trust so as to live in solitude. One day he saw a vision of the Virgin and felt irresistibly drawn to the Great North. There he settled in a forest on a hill almost entirely encircled by the White Lake. But it was St Sergius's story all over again: a progressive influx of disciples, the building of a small Lavra, then of a vast monastery, and these in their turn becoming the centre of a village (the present town of Cyrillov). Though he insisted on collective and individual poverty as much as, if not more than, St Sergius, his monastery became one of the richest in Russia shortly after his death.

Here are two lives about which we have first-hand knowledge, but—let us repeat—they were but typical of many others at the same period. Indeed the very success of these new monasteries, with their enormous influx of recruits and their rapid enrichment due to their influence outside, was soon to provoke a prolonged decline, aggravated by the general decline in ecclesiastical life similar to what was happening in the West for analogous reasons at the same time. There were similar sectarian reactions, too, like those of the *strigolniky* or the Judaisers, in whom disaffection from a secularized Church went hand in hand with neo-pagan, gnostic and rationalist currents. The religious revival in general, and the monastic one in particular, that was to come in the sixteenth century was primarily the work of two great saint-monk figures: St Nil Sorsky and St Joseph Volokolamsk. The drama of Russian spirituality and the Russian Church was that they would enter into a conflict not unlike that of Cluny and Cîteaux in the West, but with much greater radicalism on both sides.

[22] See Smolitsch, *op. cit.*, pp. 95 *et seq.*; Kologrivof, *op. cit.*, pp. 134 *et seq.*

II

RUSSIAN SPIRITUALITY FROM THE SIXTEENTH TO THE EIGHTEENTH CENTURY

St Nil Sorsky

S T NIL SORSKY,[1] though exercising great influence during his lifetime, underwent systematic oblivion after his death, so that we have no biography of him and may well doubt if there ever was one. He was not officially canonized until 1903. His rediscovery in the nineteenth century was linked up with the spiritual renewal born of Païssy Velitchkhovsky,[2] and he was then accorded enthusiastic adulation in intellectual circles of a very different inspiration, and for reasons largely based on a misapprehension. People sought quite artificially to build him up as a man standing aside from the general tradition of Russian monastic spirituality. But though he was certainly the most intellectual and refined of the ancient Russian saints, he was a far cry from the amiable humanist and liberal dreamer that people thought they found in him. Even when brought back to its true dimensions, however, his personality loses none of its charm—in fact very much the reverse.

Originally from Great Russia and born about 1433, he seems to have had no connection with the family of Maïkov boyars whose name he bore, for he himself tells us that he was of peasant origin. He entered early St Cyril of Belozersk's monastery and was initiated into monastic life by the *staretz* Vaïssy Iaroslavov. In the well-stocked monastery library it seems that he exercised the gifts of transcriber, and at the end of an unknown length of time he, like many other Russian monks of the period, left for a pilgrimage to Mount Athos. He stayed there long enough to assimilate fully and on the spot the riches of the hesychast tradition and to experience and evaluate the type of life that always remained his ideal: the life

---

[1] See Smolitsch, *op. cit.*, pp. 77 *et seq.*, E. Behr-Sigel, *op. cit.*, pp. 76 *et seq.*; Kologrivof, *op. cit.*, pp. 187 *et seq.*

[2] See further on, pp. 44 *et seq.*

of two or three in a *skit*, that is to say a tiny monastic society depending to a greater or lesser degree from a large neighbouring monastery. On his return to Cyrillov and a period in an isolated cell which he built for himself near the monastery, he went off in total solitude. He penetrated ten miles into the forest and settled on the winding banks of the river Sora, from which he got his surname. Companions soon joined him. Though he turned them away at first, he finally decided to welcome them, but always refused to build a monastery. They lived in small groups in huts, according to his ideal, near to a very modest wooden chapel.

He never allowed them to call him Master or Abbot, reminding them of Gospel teaching on this point, and he himself called them simply his friends. His life was extremely poor and hard-working. Ideally he wanted each man to earn his living by his hands. Not only did he prescribe no particular austerity apart from this, but the work he preferred was less that of land-clearance and building than of something peaceful, done at home, such as his own work of transcription. In this way he fostered and encouraged the spontaneous movement for translating and transmitting the Greek spiritual classics that characterized this epoch.

Though we have no biography of him, we have his own body of work, which caused a great stir, as many contemporary manuscripts testify. Here we find a plea for a new type of monastic life of which he was not the inventor, or even the initiator in Russia—for it was nourished by all the sap of a monastic tradition whose roots went back to the Fathers—but on which he set the seal of his own particular ideal.

His Rule,[3] as Fedotov has remarked, is less what would be ordinarily expected under this head than a co-ordinated body of advice on the spiritual life which deliberately sets aside all external organization, and at first we get the impression of a mere mosaic of quotations. But its secret lies in two complementary formulae. He tells us, "I examine first the Scriptures and their commentaries, then the apostolic tradition and the teaching of the Fathers: that which corresponds with my own understanding I copy out to please God and for the benefit of my soul, and thus I teach myself." But we must not interpret this in the sense of an arbitrary eclecticism, for he also tells us, "It is only when our own idea of God's Word corresponds with the commentaries of the Fathers and the Apostles that it can be held to be true." Nothing, then, could be more deeply traditional than his thought. But he had a very lively sense of the fact that tradition is not preserved outside a deeply assimilated experience.

[3] Fedotov has translated it in his *Treasury*, pp. 94 *et seq.*

He was the first Russian author to affirm the importance not only of personal reflection but of a keenly critical sense brought to bear on spiritual authenticity itself. "Without intelligence, even good can become an evil." And although he saw the Scriptures, together with all the ancient Russian authors and the most diverse traditional authors, as inspired writings, he was perfectly aware that the weight of their authority varied. "Many things have been written, but not everything that is written is divine. That is why we must test what we read, and only follow it when it corresponds with the requirements of truth." Collecting, comparing and transcribing the lives of the saints, he said again, "I consulted different manuscripts in my endeavour to arrive at authenticity. I noted many mistakes and corrected what my slender intelligence enabled me to correct." When he reproduced a text as it stood, he sometimes added critical comments in the margin.

His correspondence shows him as having been deeply responsive to friendship. In asking himself why the highest states of prayer do not endure, he gives an answer unlike anything else we are likely to come across: "It is so that we may have time to think of our friends and lavish on them words of help and support."

But we should be altogether mistaken if we were led by these characteristics to view him as a pious intellectual, sensitive and refined, rather than as a man of exacting spirituality, detached from the world. His rejection of strict regulation came from his lively sense of individual differences. His moderation was the fruit of a deep perception of the necessarily progressive character of spiritual ascent. But what he advocated in the place of traditional ceno-bitism was not sweet anarchy but the discovery of the way proper to each for arriving at absolute detachment. However keenly he appreciated spiritual conversation with friends undertaken in the search for God, he was vividly aware of the danger both of putting any affection in the place of the search to be alone with God, and of—quite simply—destroying interior silence by talk which, how-ever edifying, led to distraction. And the goal towards which he ceaselessly worked was the constant and total adherence of the whole being to God, who was not only within us but hidden.

Let us say it again: his eschatology, his aspiration to anticipate the celestial vision here below, were no less radical than that of the ancient ascetics. He was as convinced as they were that the resur-rection could not be anticipated except by complete death to self. For him, as for the strictest cenobites, it had its indispensable root in a total abnegation of the individual will. If he differed from them it was because he was more alive than any other spiritual master to the inner depth wherein each man, alone, and without anyone else being able to do it for him, must prolong this abnegation.

He was remarkable for his synthesis between the traditions of Evagrius and Pseudo-Macarius (a synthesis still more complete than in St Gregory Palamas, probably because, intellectual though he was, he was not a speculative but a purely spiritual man). From Evagrius he assimilated not only the analysis of the eight evil thoughts, but the idea of the purification of prayer by discarding all images or conceptual representations of God. But he fused this quite naturally with the purity of heart of Pseudo-Macarius, a purity sought in the loving humility of a silent adherence to Christ present within us, vital faith stripping us of ourselves so that we may be buried in him. In the same way we could not find a more flexible intelligence or one into which hesychast methods had been better filtered, with the Jesus prayer becoming the prayer of the heart. He made use of all the resources of Athonite experience without committing himself to any particular line of action.

Liberation had always been the driving force of ancient asceticism, and it also became his sole concern. Though he came at the end of a long tradition, he felt its requirements perhaps more keenly than anyone. There is no other explanation for his refusal of all monastic property, together with his distrust of even the most venerable liturgical forms—beginning with the intoned psalm—as soon as they became ends in themselves or a burden that encumbered the soul and hampered it in the realization of the only activity that should engross it: the most intimate and enduring prayer.

It was hardly avoidable that a conception of monastic life so interiorized and personalized should come into conflict with another reform that was simultaneously seeking, with all the resources already proper to Russian Christianity, to rediscover and spread the Basilian ideal of monasticism. This dramatic conflict brought Nil, and especially his disciples, up against a very different type of person, but one in whom it is difficult not to recognize a holiness as real as Nil's own: St Joseph of Volokolamsk.

St Joseph of Volokolamsk

If the success of the principles exemplified by St Joseph of Volokolamsk brought about a prolonged eclipse of St Nil's personality and influence, St Nil's resurgence was accompanied by a discredit thrown on his adversary which was unjust in its turn. There is no question that we owe to St Joseph some of the most solid and respectable traditions of modern religious Russia, and the veneration in which he was held by the Old Believers was something quite different from mere obstinate fanaticism. Fidelity to a very lofty ideal, and one that was deeply healthy and virile at the same time (despite certain narrownesses), could not have attached itself to a more suitable patron. The image of "Holy Russia" could become shrouded in illusions or sink into decay, but it remains none the less worthy of admiration. Not only was St Joseph its creator, but no one struggled more persistently and effectively to bring it down to earth.[4]

John Sanin, a young nobleman born in 1439 of Lithuanian origin, who entered the monastery of Borovsk so as to attend the school of the holy igumen Paphnutius, certainly does not emerge from early biographies as the dark, scheming inquisitor presented by so many modern authors. His strong personality, which had early sought the yoke of obedience, joined to his virile beauty and brilliant intelligence, exerted a very different attraction from that of St Nil, if no less compelling.

During the eighteen years he spent under Paphnutius' guidance he became a monk, took the name of Joseph, and was finally elected by his colleagues to replace his master. But in trying to introduce a stricter form of cenobitism he came up against the opposition of the majority. He resigned without putting up any resistance and for a year visited the most famous monasteries *incognito* in order to get to know their observances, during which time he accepted the most menial tasks. He found the monastery in Cyrillov the most impressive. Finally he returned to his native country and immediately founded a cenobitic community after his own heart in the nearby forest of Volokolamsk.

If we really want to understand him we must bear in mind that the decadence of the best monasteries, in Russia as in the Byzantine Empire, could seem to have been the outcome of what has been called idiorrhythmic life, that is to say the flexibility of a cenobitism that left each monk a little store of money and the right to organize his material existence more or less as he pleased within the framework of the community. The remedy according to Joseph, and unlike the hermits of the forests beyond the Volga who could have appeared, in their *skits*, to push the idiorrhythmic life to its limits, was to be found in a return not to large overcrowded communities but to authentic communities in the Basilian or Studite tradition. Moreover, the most complete individual poverty, together with the sanctifying exercise of the strictest obedience, would annul—or so he thought—the risks inherent in establishing these on more or less large estates. Besides, for Joseph more explicitly than for any other monastic legislator, these estates themselves would never dispense

---

[4] See Smolitsch, *op. cit.*, pp. 101 *et seq.*; Kologrivof, *op. cit.*, pp. 214 *et seq.*

the monks from hard toil; for they would find their only possible justification in being centres of social, charitable and cultural influence, which would be the realistic basis of a directly religious influence from which the whole Russian Church and Russian people would benefit.

The Rule, which he drew up only at the end of his life so as to codify his experience of his own community, was also based on what he had been able to observe elsewhere, and was informed by a learning exceptional at his epoch and in his *milieu*. It represents a full and detailed effort to realize his grand design.

It cannot seriously be doubted, whatever some have said, that it aimed directly at the personal sanctification of each monk. But, as a good Basilian, St Joseph saw this sanctification in terms of perfect integration in a type of communal life presumed to be the best. Such integration was the opportunity offered for obedience at every moment of the day, this being the very basis of asceticism, or rather asceticism itself. This led him to enter into the smallest details of regulations that did not leave the monk alone for a single instant, whether in church or in his cell, and the performance of these was the object of constant surveillance on the part of the Superior or his officials. But it has to be admitted that the vision of the whole into which these regulations were integrated—and they even touched on details of bodily attitudes—had nothing petty about it. It aimed at creating a community living in all its members solely for the communal service of God in charity. Moreover—a very remarkable feature—this charity was not confined to the particular community where it operated; it was explicitly understood that it should extend to the whole of society. Joseph could never consent to the restricted community of religious isolating itself and cutting itself off from society as a whole, and—a still more remarkable feature—he aimed at instructing and forming each monk in the realization and exercise of this limitless responsibility, to the measure of the capacity of each.

The monk should not only serve as an example to non-monks, but should become familiar with their needs and apply himself conscientiously to fulfilling them. In his work he should be motivated not merely by a concern for his own good, even his spiritual good, but by a feeling for the good of others, and to this he should dedicate himself. Likewise in his liturgical prayer in church, he should not only have his own and his brothers' edification in view, but that of the laity who might be present. This was one of the reasons why Joseph attached great importance to taking educated people into the community and encouraging humble recruits to receive all the education of which they were capable. In that way the monastery could become a seminary for the episcopate, and also supply competent men to the hospitals, charitable institutions and schools that were thought of as part of the integral whole. Furthermore, Joseph never hesitated to play his part in awakening the social sense of neighbouring nobles and rich men, and he preached by example, generously lending the monastery's agricultural equipment, horses or cows to the peasants who lived round about.

The heart of this collective life was the monastery church and the services held there. St Joseph wanted both church and services to be ordered according to traditional norms and to be as beautiful as possible. The spirit of generosity that should govern the monastery's social work applied equally to the church and all that went with it. Every monk must contribute his share to the perfection of divine worship. "Join your hands, put your feet together, close your eyes, and recollect your spirit." If the love for liturgical splendour that characterized the Russian Church dated from its very beginnings, certainly no one did more than Joseph of Volokolamsk to ensure that it remained one of its permanent features.

The idea that his aims in this respect were mainly formalistic, or at best aesthetic, is completely without foundation. He himself wrote:

> If for some reason you are unable to pray in church, you must pray all the same. He who has a pure heart and performs good deeds will see his prayers answered no matter where he prays. And you, wherever you may chance to be—at sea, on the road, or at home, whether you be walking or sitting—pray ceaselessly and with a pure conscience, saying, "Lord Jesus, Son of God, have mercy on me."[5]

In a more general way it shows a complete misconception to interpret his concern for minute external regulations as showing contempt for, or repudiation of, the interior life. Whatever one may think, no honest person can doubt but that this concern, in such a passionate educator, proceeded from a conviction that the inner man can only be touched and formed with the outer man as starting-point, and that there is no true spirituality that is not incarnate. Nothing shows this better than his insistence—in the matter of punishing negligent or guilty brothers—on the primordial necessity of leading them to face up to their fault and acknowledge it in the depths of their heart.

Behind all this he urged a deep sense of the solidarity of all believers, monks and non-monks, and of their need for each other in the process of salvation. Whence his vision of the whole of society

[5] Quoted by Kologrivof, *op. cit.*, p. 222.

as bearing the stamp of Christianity, and of the power of the prince himself as having no other end than to lead his whole people towards eternal life. Here, certainly, we find a heritage of the Byzantine notion of the Empire. But, here as elsewhere, we must recognize that the Russians communicated a vitality to concepts received from their Greek masters which the Greeks themselves had never given them, and this because the Russians took to heart with an almost naïve simplicity what the Greeks had often been content to develop as pure speculation.

Certainly there are grave omissions in St Joseph's achievement, and we can trace their origins in his writings. For in spite of his learning and thirst for knowledge, and his active conviction of the need for extensive religious culture in monks and the Church as a whole (his monastery was provided with a well-stocked library and a workroom for copyists where he himself worked), he showed no trace of St Nil's keen critical sense. He saw all "holy writings"— that is to say all traditional writings—as possessing equal authority. He quoted the most flagrant apocrypha without seeming to see that they posed any problems. This came from his integrism: for him authority was everything, and everything that was a vehicle for tradition imposed itself with the same weight. However, as happens with people who see things in this way (provided they are not imbeciles), an instructive common sense puts a check on the harm this type of mind can do. We must not forget that before he established his Rule he had for long practised it and worked on it, and that even before that he had made systematic research into all the monastic practices of his time and shown great discernment in seeking out the best.

But this cast of mind, combined with a determined institutionalism, goes far to explain the conflict with St Nil and his disciples in which he was soon to find himself engaged. The conflict was centred on various specific points, but it obviously originated in two types of mind, two spiritual orientations rendered mutually exclusive by the radicalism of each.

The Conflict between St Nil and St Joseph

The first difference of opinion arose with regard to the treatment of Judaizing heretics whose activities greatly increased towards the end of the fifteenth century. Here again St Joseph's attitude does not seem to have been so schematic as many modern writers have supposed. *The Illuminator*, the book composed of his writings against the heretics put together by his disciples after his death, shows that he underwent considerable evolution on the matter—an evolution impossible to explain except in the context of a supremely disillusioning experience. The first eleven chapters[6] consist of a discussion of the heretics' arguments followed by an exposition—often very liberal and lively—of the orthodox doctrine. There is no bitterness, and indeed in the fourth chapter we find the following:

> God himself is truth and love, and he brings all impious men to piety, not by the force of arms and violence, not by drowning in water or burning by fire, but by sweetness and patience, by humility, mercy and love.

But in the twelfth chapter the tone changes and Joseph ends by treating of these heretics in the most violent terms; he shows how civil authority ought to punish them by life-imprisonment or even death and not be swayed by any protests of repentance.

It is not hard to guess what had happened in the interval. The controversy with the Judaizers had revealed the extent not only of their estrangement from the Church and the faith but also of their infiltration into the Church and State—the disastrous result of their propaganda and the difficulty of stemming it, for they conformed in all superficial ways while not giving an inch as to fundamentals. St Joseph's reaction, when confronted with this situation, was not unlike St Augustine's in the Donatist affair. It was less one of cold-blooded cruelty than of pastoral anxiety giving way to panic before a situation whose grave consequences had not at first been suspected.

Certainly this does not excuse the extreme measures he came to justify and even to demand of hesitant authority such as Basil III, the Muscovite Prince. We are particularly disturbed by the "pious ruses" that he advocated, backed up by more or less tendentious biblical or patristic quotations, and by the extreme harshness with which he wanted the sectaries, even when penitent, to be treated. However, we must not underestimate his deep anxiety with regard to the ravages wrought among simple people, and the mortal threat to a society whose re-Christianization, after the Tartar invasions, still seemed so precarious. Critics not bowed down under the pastoral responsibilities of an Augustine or a Joseph are not really in a position to pass judgment on changes of policy such as theirs.

When St Joseph drew on the Old Testament to justify his dubious reasoning to the prince—for instance, "It is all one whether we eliminate the sinner or the heretic by prayer, that is by conversion, or by death"—the answer given by the monks from beyond the Volga was certainly irrefutable. In a collective letter in which St Nil's hand has been seen (but which seems rather to be the work of his disciple, the prince-monk Vassian Patrikeev), they issued the

---

[6] Kologrivof follows them step by step, *op. cit.*, pp. 237 *et seq.*

following pointed reply: "There was once a time when the Old
Testament was indeed the rule for all action. But as for us, we live
in the age of grace. Our Lord gave us a new bond, that of charity,
by which it is not allowed for a brother to judge his brother, by
which it is said that those who condemn shall be themselves condemned, and that God alone can judge the sins of man."[7] This did
not prevent St Joseph from retorting that their task was easy
enough, for they passed judgment on him from the depths of their
solitude whither they had fled the world. He himself, who was
vowed to saving souls within the world, would extricate himself
as best he could in face of difficulties about which they knew
nothing.

An acrimonious exchange started up again shortly afterwards,
this time concerning a question that appeared less inflammable but
nevertheless added fuel to the flames. Though the previous matter
had not yet been solved, nor the problems that had caused it, the
possession of property by monasteries was brought up and called
into question at the Muscovite Council of 1503, and especially of
property comprising whole villages with their serfs. St Nil, although
not an abbot strictly speaking, had been summoned to the Council
because of his immense influence with the hermits in the forests
beyond the Volga. There he submitted his brief motion: "Monasteries should not possess villages, and monks should live in solitude,
earning their bread by the work of their hands."[8] Feeling immediately ran high among the abbots of the large monasteries,
especially as the prince had not concealed his approval, for motives
which, it is easy to guess, were not entirely disinterested. St Joseph
had already left the Council at this point but promptly returned on
being told what had happened.

St Nil then drew on St Theodosius, of whom his biographer
Nestor had said that "he yielded [on this point] only because of the
weakness of faith of those around him". St Joseph countered with
an argument of some substance. Without property of this kind and
the educative work of the monasteries—in particular the preparation of candidates for the episcopate—social works would no longer
be possible. St Nil was certainly echoing a view that had frequently
been put forward by monks and bishops: that possessions were the
perennial cause of monastic decline. But when in his own Rule we
see him countering Joseph's arguments with the reflection that those
who are totally poor are thereby dispensed from giving material

---

[7] Quotations from Kologrivof, *op. cit.*, p. 227; cf. Smolitsch, *op. cit.*, pp. 114
et seq.
[8] On all this matter see Smolitsch, pp. 145 *et seq.*, and Kologrivof, pp. 195
et seq.

charity to others, we can hardly help finding the simplification excessive. If all those who vow themselves to perfection left the world to its own devices, even for so apparently legitimate a motive, can we deny that one part of the Gospel, and not the least one at that, would be for all practical purposes void?

Joseph was certainly not wrong when he perceived and denounced the over-facile evasion inherent in this purely interior and spiritual vision of monasticism, and the Council finally dismissed the motion. Nil returned to his hermitage where he died five years later after expressing the hope—which was not granted—that his grave would remain unknown. Joseph, after several years of grievous infirmity, died in 1515, to the plainchant of the "Trisagion" of the liturgy.

But open conflict was to be pursued among their respective disciples. St Nil's were accused not only of taking in persecuted heretics, but of compounding with their errors, or with others still, and this accusation was not entirely without basis, as in the case of the prince-monk Vassian. Vassian was condemned in a Josephite synod in 1531, and between 1553 and 1556 the independent *skits* beyond the Volga were progressively harried and dispersed by the bishops.

Other condemnations inspired by the same tendency were pronounced round about the same time, such as the one launched in 1525 at Maximus the Greek—that astonishing figure of a humanist monk, faithful both to the Byzantine tradition and to the idea of an eschatological monasticism, who refused to be circumscribed by any earthly city, even the Third Rome.[9] In 1551 the Council of the Hundred Chapters, as it was called, seemed to have assured by detailed legislation the absolute and definitive victory of St Joseph's spirit over St Nil's. In the event this legislation prepared the way both for the schism of the Old Believers which broke out in the following century, and for the sclerosis of the official Church, more and more bound to the State, that resulted from it.

St Cornelius of Komel

It would be a mistake, however, to see a clear-cut alignment on the part of all monks in this deplorable quarrel. Many of them made a more or less successful attempt to combine the spiritual legacy of both Joseph and Nil. The most interesting of these was certainly St Cornelius of Komel, who died in 1537.[10]

Born in Rostov like St Sergius, to a rich family related to Grand Prince Basil II, he became a monk when only thirteen at the

[9] See E. Denissov, *Maxime le Grec.*
[10] See Kologrivof, *op. cit.*, pp. 247 *et seq.*, and Smolitsch, *op. cit.*, pp. 96 *et seq.*

Cyrillov monastery—at the same time as an uncle who had first introduced him at court. But after some years he went off on a peregrination from monastery to monastery, seeking a more perfect life, until he finally established himself in the forest of Komel. After nineteen years of solitude he had gathered disciples, and these he established not in *skits* but in a cenobitic monastery. He always wanted it to be utterly poor—like St Nil, rejecting large properties—but, although orientated towards interior solitude, he welcomed all the physically or spiritually afflicted. He drew up a Rule for this community in which it could be said that there was a constant cross-blending of inspiration from the texts of both St Nil and St Joseph.

We have proof that the synthesis was difficult in practice by the fact that he twice tried to resign from his post and go back to the solitary life. Each time, however, he gave way before his disciples' entreaties and returned to his place among them. There he d⁻ ⁻⁴ to the plainchant of the Akathistos hymn, leaving behind him t! pression of a life steeped in contemplative charity. Nui monasteries tried to follow the inspiration of his example, ana many holy monks could be called his disciples.

Nikon and the Raskol

In spite of attempts of this kind, the Russian Church during the sixteenth and seventeenth centuries—with its ever-closer collaboration in the building up of Muscovite autocracy—became more and more marked with the legislation inspired by Joseph. But when the ideal of the Third Rome was at the height of its apparent triumph, it brought about an interior schism. This paved the way for the final submission, under Peter the Great, of a Church that had become subject to a State in process of de-Christianization. Many of the best and most popular elements of its religious life would take refuge in a schism which was savagely self-enclosed.[11]

Towards the middle of the seventeenth century religious and moral life was visibly in decline. A necessary reform was then sought in St Joseph's successors, but it rapidly diverged along two opposing roads. There was one current of opinion that tended to identify the reform with an ideal past, of which St Joseph and the Council of the Hundred Chapters appeared as the incarnation; this was centered around the archpriest Stephen Vonifiatovitch, the spiritual father of Tsar Alexis. Its positive elements were beyond reproach; they included an emphasis on preaching, on frequent

[11] See Pierre Pascal, *Avvakum et les débuts du Rascol*, Paris, 1938, and also his translation of Avvakum's *Journal*, Paris, 1938, of which Fedotov too has given an extract in his *Treasury*, pp. 137 *et seq.* Cf. Smolitsch, *op. cit.*, pp. 357 *et seq.*

confession, on prayer, fasting and a very pure moral life. But all this was conceived in terms of a return to the old Russian traditions which were judged to be in process of dissolution.

In the most cultivated circles such as those of the Patriarch Nikon, people were no less convinced that reform could only take place along traditionalist and ritualistic lines, but they considered it essential that Russia should open her windows on to the outside world, and first and foremost on to the Greek Church, the custodian of Byzantine traditions; Maximus had already advocated this in the previous century. From this would come a revision of the liturgy in conformity with contemporary Greek books, and the Patriarch was anxious to impose this. But he does not seem to have suspected the scandal he would thus arouse in certain fervent circles. Moreover, this neo-Byzantinism contained many of the illusions that we shall meet again in the nineteenth-century West—in the neo-Ultramontanism of a Guéranger. Just as the contemporary Roman liturgy was to be contrasted with the Gallican liturgies, without realizing that these contained—with many particularities of their own—many elements of the ancient Roman liturgy better preserved than in Rome itself, so similarly Nikon's revisers did not realize that a number of Russian usages were no more than archaic Byzantine usages better preserved than in Greece.

The leading reformers of the first group reacted strongly against what seemed to them merely the liquidation of the most precious Russian traditions at the very moment when they were attempting to revitalize them. In face of the high-handed attitude of the Muscovite authorities, the tension could only grow. Those who would later be called the Old Believers detected positive heresy in the most seemingly innocent patriarchial innovations, such as the sign of the cross made with two, instead of three, curved fingers.

Concerning this struggle, which rapidly degenerated into a blindly brutal repression on the part of the authorities, while it turned to fanatical exaltation in their adversaries, we have a memorable record in the autobiography written in prison by the archpriest Avvakum who was sent to the stake after fifteen years' solitary confinement. Side by side with an obstinate naïvety in his popular over-simplifications and an exaggeratedly apocalyptic mysticism, this book reflects a simple faith and warmth of heart that are truly evangelical. That members of a hierarchy of a superficial yet arrogant intellectuality could meet him with nothing better than authoritarianism and violence is obviously not to their honour, though the West offers too many examples of proud and uncomprehending intransigence among its religious leaders at about the same time for us to throw the first stone at Nikon.

However, if the Old Believers, ousted from the official Church, lost all possibility of broadening their outlook by a cultural revival, they certainly took with them in compensation all that was best in traditional Russian piety. This they have preserved right up to our own times, not as a dead relic but as an astonishing treasure though embedded within the most stubborn archaicisms. Their communities, for the most part peasant and turned in on themselves in lonely country, preserved a moral health and nobility of patriarchal flavour. Their ardent piety kept the rites, the ancient plainchant and the ikons of the greatest Slav period freshly intact, while all this degenerated in a matter of a few years in the official Church.

There have been numerous descriptions right up to our own time of the impression produced on the traveller who comes by chance on these little communities that have turned their back on the world but practise a Virgilian hospitality none the less for that. All the evangelical perfume of old Christian Russia seems concentrated there as if distilled in an imperishable essence.[12]

In spite of the apocalyptic currents that have always run through them, the *milieux* of the Old Believers should not be confused with the strange sects that were to wax and multiply from roughly the same date, that is to say from the seemingly definitive sclerosis of a Church entirely incorporated within the autocratic State. Under the persistent influence of pagan or gnostic currents, and sooner or later of sectaries coming from the Polish, Germanic and Anglo-Saxon West, these sects were to develop—more or less outside the authentic Christian tradition—all the deep spiritual anarchy of the Slav soul that had been brutally left on one side by a Church grown rigid with authoritarian formalism.

Yet it would be unjust to say that this hardening of the arteries left no place at all for spiritual spontaneity within the Muscovite Church. Parallel to Josephite regimentation there was a development of an old type of lay holiness, charismatic and unconventional in the extreme, and this is sufficient proof to the contrary.

The "Fools for Christ"

The "fools for Christ" (*yurodivy*, that is to say "odd") of Russian tradition have perhaps had an exaggerated attraction for the modern mind; and by seeing them through literary presentations, such as Tolstoy's Grisha and Dostoievsky's Muishkin, we have not altogether understood them.[13] Yet we should neither underestimate

---

[12] See the account of A. Anzerna, *Am weissen Meer*, Paderborn, 1938, summarized and commentated by N. Arseniew in *La Piété russe*, Paris, 1963, pp. 63 et seq.

[13] See E. Behr-Sigel, *op. cit.*, pp. 92 et seq.; Kologrivof, *op. cit.*, pp. 261 et seq.

their importance nor deny that they embodied highly characteristic features of Russian Christianity.

The type is not exclusive to Russia. The early life of Isidore recalls Syrian saints such as Simeon (sixth century) or Andrew (ninth century); and the same type of sanctity is to be found in the West, not only in antiquity with St Ulf (eighth century) but during the Renaissance with Blessed Colombini or St John of God, and even in the nineteenth century with St Benoit Labre (not to mention episodes in the lives of other saints, such as Francis of Assisi, Felix of Cantalice, Philip Neri or Thomas More, not forgetting Father Surin). Indeed it was from the West, by way of Novgorod, that the first Russian "fools for Christ" seem to have come in the thirteenth and fourteenth centuries. This was certainly so in the case of Procopius of Ustiug (fourteenth century). There is some doubt as regards Isidore, who died in 1474, but it seems certain of John the Long-haired who died in 1580 in Rostov (where a Latin psalter has been preserved among his relics). But the response that their lives and actions found in the Russian people, even when the eighteenth-century hierarchy refused to canonize them any more and they became the object of governmental suppression, is a phenomenon without parallel in other countries.

Although we should not press the point too far, three phases have been remarked in the evolution of this type of holiness. The earliest cases seem to have been purely ascetic: generalizing from episodes in the lives of several Russian saints whom we have mentioned, such as Isaac of Petchersk and Cyril of Belozersk, the first "fools for Christ" behaved as they did so as to expose themselves to the humiliation of men. We must also bear in mind the old theme of the *peregrinatio* which was so common in ancient monasticism and held such an important place in Ireland. We are told of Procopius of Ustiug that he went "from town to town, wandering through woods and fens ... in search of his lost country". Of him too, as of Isidore and John the Long-haired, we are told that "they had no roof over their heads". They went about more or less naked, sleeping on church steps or even on the village dung-heap.

Later on they were no longer content to feign madness and put themselves in the ranks of the proscribed. Like the Hebrew prophets who were the first to live the life of voluntary outlaws, they sent forth exhortations and apocalyptic warnings to their fellows. Frequently, too, they had recourse to parabolic acting, where satire shading off into indecent clowning had a large place. The first examples of this that we know of were the two "fools" of Novgorod, Nicolas and Theodore, who parodied the political factions of the town by means of burlesqued debates. It was in sixteenth-century Moscow that this second phase reached its apogee, faced with the autocracy of the first Tsars. When everyone, with the exception of the Metropolitan Philip, had been reduced to silence by Ivan the Terrible, Blessed Basil ridiculed him in public, saying that when he was in church he did not think about the prayers he was reciting but about the wonderful palace he was having built for himself. After the massacre of Novgorod Nicolas of Pskov offered Ivan red meat in the middle of Lent. To his reply, "I'm a Christian and I don't eat meat in Lent," Nicolas countered, "Then why do you drink the blood of Christians?"[14] It was Basil again who threw stones at the houses of the ostentatiously pious while kissing the houses of ill-repute, saying: "Devils lay siege to those, whereas angels weep over these." He became the most popular of these saints, and the cathedral in Red Square was rechristened after him by the people of Moscow after his burial there. A little later, and still in Moscow, similar acts were reported of John of the Large Cowl.

In the last phase, dating from the end of the seventeenth century, the type—having become too popular—degenerated into mere vaguely pious bohemianism: vagabonds wandering from monastery to monastery, "innocents" (or rather the "blessed" as the Russians called them) exploiting their disorders so as to attract pious compassion. A final striking example was St Xenia in Petrograd in the middle of the eighteenth century. Crushed by her untimely widowhood, she lived disguised as a man in her husband's clothes under the name of Andrew. She led the life of a tramp between the city and the fields, praying in the open air while carrying bricks for a church that was being built. Then she took her own name and her woman's clothes again but without abandoning her life of poverty, and she became famous for her prophecies. Her grave became a place of pilgrimage and Empress Maria Feodorovna, who attributed to her the unhoped-for recovery of her husband Emperor Alexander II, remained faithful to her memory right up to the last years of Tsarism.

It can hardly be doubted that the number of these strange saints and their extraordinary popularity gave expression to a love for Christ as the humiliated servant and to the prophetic sense of Christianity, both of which had been such striking features of Russian Christianity from the very first. And at the moment when the Church was developing hardening of the arteries through official conformism, it was supremely under this form that the

---

[14] A similar episode has been attributed to Blessed Basil, doubtless in imitation of this one, although he died in 1555, fifteen years before the sack of Novgorod.

charismatic and radical eschatology of Russian faith at its deepest made itself felt as if by instinctive compensation.

St Dmitri of Rostov and St Tikhon of Zadonsk

Though from the second half of the seventeenth century the Russian Church was marked by formalism and an increasingly narrow subjection to a diminishingly Christian State, it would be a great mistake to imagine that all its deep religious life had been extinguished. On the contrary, it was now that the hierarchy produced two of its greatest saints; and they should not be regarded as exceptions but as particularly eminent figures in an episcopate that included many fervent and zealous pastors.

Dmitri, Bishop of Rostov (1651–1709), and Tikhon, Bishop of Voronezh for some years and then a solitary for the rest of his life in the little monastery of Zadonsk (1727–1783), were both prolific, if not very original, writers. At a time when Russia was opening out more and more to the West, and when all that was mediocre or downright bad in a rapidly de-Christianized system of thought abounded there, they had the merit of recasting the religious education of their people, not in a narrow resistance to new influences, but by trying to make broad use of the best Western attempts at religious revival, whether Catholic or Protestant, that were able to reach them. Indeed they might even appear in the eyes of nineteenth-century Slavophiles as having contributed to the disintegration of the traditions of Russian Orthodoxy. But in fact they contributed much more to their rebirth. Beneath their veneer of Westernism, we can see some of the most precious spiritual values of old Russia brought back to life.

St Dmitri of Rostov[15] was of Ukrainian origin, the son of a Cossack officer. He was educated in the Kiev college founded by the Metropolitan Peter Moghila in a style closely inspired by Jesuit schools. The clerical formation was modelled on decadent scholasticism, with manuals in Latin. Preparation for the renewal of the clergy took place there none the less—a clergy endowed with a solid intellectual formation and remaining much more faithful than might be supposed to its own traditions. The incorporation of the Ukraine, at least the part bordering on Kiev, into the Muscovite Empire, and of her Church into that of Moscow, brought these methods with their strengths and weaknesses to the Russian clergy—the more so as Peter the Great drew on this *milieu* for churchmen to whom to entrust important responsibilities. It was thus that Dmitri was in turn Superior in a monastery and an

---

[15] See Kologrivof, *op. cit.*, pp. 291 *et seq.*

influential preacher before being appointed missionary bishop in Siberia. When he objected to this appointment, backed up by his friend and compatriot Stephen Javorsky, who was himself *locum tenens* of the patriarchal throne, the Emperor consented to give him the vacant metropolitan see of Rostov instead, and here he ended his days.

The major reason for his reluctance to take up the post assigned to him was his desire to finish an immense work on which he had embarked: a series of popular lives of all the saints in the calendar. This work, which was to take him many years to complete, was destined to become, with the Bible and liturgical texts, the main sustenance of modern Russian piety. But it was not admitted into the Russian Church without certain modifications necessitated by his Westernizing sympathies, including his adherence to the Western theology of Mary's immaculate conception.

But for the people Dmitri remained above all a living symbol of the good shepherd and an example of episcopal life that was typically Eastern—that is to say one in which the administrator gave place to the spiritual director and was first and foremost the animator of liturgical prayer as well as a model of evangelical charity.

St Tikhon's writings are more substantial, although G. Fedotov is no doubt right in suggesting that his personality was more arresting than anything he ever wrote.[16] The son of a village sexton in the governorship of Novgorod, Tikhon (Timothy in the world)[17] knew extreme poverty after his father's death and could hardly contrive to go on with his priestly studies. While professor in the seminary of Novgorod, he was drawn to solitude and received the monastic tonsure shortly before his ordination to the diaconate and then to the priesthood. But he was soon summoned by the Bishop of Tver (who intended to make him Superior of the monastery of Trinity-St Sergius) to teach in his own seminary and then to become its rector. Three years later he returned to Novgorod as auxiliary bishop. He was there for barely two years, for in 1763 he was appointed by Empress Catherine to the see of Voronezh.

His pedagogic and reforming activities, in particular with the clergy, were at once considerable. But in spite of this he had doubts about himself and was beset with worries, finally becoming so ill that he asked to be relieved of his post when he had barely arrived. The Holy Synod refused, recommending quite simply that he should get himself looked after. But in 1766 he implored the Empress to allow him to retire to a small monastery. He was granted his

---

[16] *A Treasury of Russian Spirituality*, p. 183.
[17] See Smolitsch, *op. cit.*, pp. 516 *et seq.*, and Kologrivof, *op. cit.*, pp. 329 *et seq.*

request in 1768 and left his bishopric so as to cloister himself at Zadonsk. There he stayed until his death, apart from brief departures to the neighbouring monastery of Tolche, where he would have preferred to establish himself had not its insalubriousness made this impossible.

But we must not see his retreat as idyllic. Though the surroundings of Zadonsk near the banks of the Don were very beautiful, and with a beauty admired by the Bishop who liked to walk along the river or through the woods in meditation, the minute house in which he lived was not so much poor as positively squalid. There was not even a bed to sleep on—just two cushions and a sheepskin to put over himself; no surface on which to put his books, but just an old leather bag. And, to cap all, neither the Superior—who was drunk and worldly and so discourteous towards his guest that he had to be sternly reminded by the Holy Synod of the respect due to a prelate—nor the majority of the monks had the slightest regard for him, but treated him as a hypocrite and a crackpot. Some of the more simple among them, however, understood him and became his friends. The most valuable accounts we have of him consist of the somewhat naïve notes kept by his servants and cell companions, the brothers Vassily Chebotarev and Ivan Efimov.[18]

We can easily see through the writings of these two men (as through his biographer and friend, the Metropolitan of Kiev, Eugenius Bolkhonitikov, who edited his works) that there was a morbid element in Tikhon's hypersensitive soul that had been grievously hurt by an unhappy and humiliated youth. His resignation from his bishopric, which was inexplicable to his contemporaries, can certainly be explained as much by straightforward agoraphobia as by physical illness. We know from his humble companions that during the first part of his life as a recluse he was of an irritability that he could only control by constant struggle with himself and voluntary humiliations. Scruples never ceased to torment him, first and foremost as to the lawfulness of his resignation, and there were periods of depression that bordered on anguish. We can find an echo of all this in his fear of death and judgment and the fascination that constant meditation on death nevertheless had for him.

He was strongly influenced by contemporary Western piety, both Counter-Reformation Catholic piety and Protestant piety with an emphasis on Pietism. Notable in this respect were his realistic meditations on the Passion (he had a series of detailed representations of it in his cell, unique in Orthodox history). Yet these

[18] These two texts have been translated in their entirety by Fedotov in his *Treasury*, pp. 186 *et seq.*, and pp. 205 *et seq.*

meditations were intermingled with the express aspiration of participating with the risen Christ. The imitation of Christ, which was a key term in his whole conception of the Christian life, culminated in a confident hope in the future transfiguration of the world of which, he said, each spring was a foreshadowing.

His life as a recluse was divided between long hours of reading the Bible and the lives of the saints, liturgical prayer, and whole nights passed in personal prayer. Every morning before attending the eucharistic liturgy, at which he communicated but which he never celebrated after his resignation, he worked at his spiritual writings. We find in them a direct echo of St Augustine and the *Imitation of Christ* as of Lutheran works such as Arndt's *True Christianity* (the title of which he appropriated for his principal work on the redemption), and Anglican ones such as the *Meditatiunculae subitaneae* by the Puritan Bishop Hull which inspired his own *Spiritual Treasury*. But what emerges more clearly than anything is the conviction, so characteristic of Eastern tradition, of the relationship between man (indeed the whole of creation) and the Creator, the redemption having no other end than to restore the image of God to his works. Hence the wonderfully enlarged sense of the imitation of the Saviour as he understood it. So in the end the supreme note of his meditation, often so sorrowful, not to say tragic, and coming from a wounded heart, was nevertheless God's glory, and this fills his spiritual testament.

But for all this to take on its full value we have to place it in its context of indefatigable charity—a charity that caused him to welcome every kind of misery for himself so that he could distribute the pension granted to him by the Empress to the poor who either visited him or of whom he heard tell. For them he deprived himself of everything that was given him, to the point of getting into debt. This tormented man who had fled his fellow men never tired of children, peasants and all the poor. They flocked to him, and when he could not welcome them in person a huge correspondence made him one of the first spiritual teachers of numberless Christians living in the world. He rediscovered the ministry he had abandoned, but vastly interiorized and humanized.

Finally we find the most diverse currents of ancient Russian spirituality deeply developed within this modern, westernized, introverted saint: the asceticism of death to the world of the recluses of Petchersk, the folly of a life incomprehensibly humiliated for Christ, the love of Christ based in the love of men—particularly the poor and the suffering—and above all the yearning for a world and a life transfigured in the risen Christ.

III

THE ORTHODOX RENAISSANCE IN GREECE AND RUSSIA

St Nicodemus the Hagiorite and the Orthodox Renaissance

A T about this time there was an undreamed-of renewal of the great spiritual tradition of the Byzantine East, and it occurred in the very place where that tradition had produced its classical synthesis (if we may call it so) with St Gregory Palamas shortly before the fall of Byzantium: namely, at Athos. The prime mover of the spiritual renewal, and hence of almost all the modern renaissance of Eastern Orthodoxy, was St Nicodemus the Hagiorite.[1]

It would be fair to say that, in canonizing Nicodemus recently,[2] the Patriarch of Constantinople consecrated this resurrection (for it can be called no less) at its source, though its potentialities are still far from being fully realized. It manifested itself on the decline of the Turkish Empire in a general reawakening of the Eastern Christian peoples whose development had been as if paralysed by their subjection to the *Sublime Porte*.[3] But owing to Nicodemus's true genius as much as to his holiness, the reawakening was able to escape the risk of phyletism from the beginning—the risk, that is, of an identification of Orthodoxy with the national consciousness of those Christian peoples who had been given their religious leaders as ethnarchs by their oppressors themselves. The separation of the two was due to the return to traditional sources achieved by Nicodemus and to the breadth of outlook, free from all national or cultural exclusiveness and provincialism, that characterized it. For we must underline this trait in Nicodemus: though he was still more widely open to the best of the modern West than the Russian

---

[1] See (in Greek), P. Theoklitos Dionysiatou, *The Life and Works of St Nico-demus the Hagiorite*, Athens, 1959, and P. Grumel's article in the *Dictionnaire de théologie catholique*.

[2] Canonized 31 May, 1955, at Constantinople, Nicodemus was introduced the following year into the calendar also of the patriarchal Russian Church.

[3] See M-J. Le Guillou, "Aux sources des mouvements spirituels de l'Eglise orthodoxe de Grèce, I. La Renaissance spirituelle du XVIIIe siècle", in *Istina*, 1960, No. 1, pp. 95 *et seq.*

saints we have just mentioned, he was no less eager for all that to bring back treasures specific to the Byzantine tradition—and this not through an interest in the past for the past's sake but in a creative restoration to life.

Born on the island of Naxos in 1748, Nicodemus (Nicolas was his baptismal name) entered the monastery of St Dionysiou on Athos at the age of twenty-seven. There he profited from the intellectual impetus given by the Athonite academy that had been founded towards the middle of the century; Eugenius Bulgaris, the best eighteenth-century Greek theologian, was for a while its rector. In some ways the academy resembled the Kiev college that we mentioned in connection with Peter Moghila, for it was open to Western influences, though in this case the influence was that of German philosophies rather than Catholic theology. Having received the Great Habit in 1783, Nicodemus thenceforth lived in a *skit* attached to the monastery of Pantokrator before withdrawing to the cell of St George, a dependency of the Lavra, where he died on 14 July 1809.

Despite his wide knowledge of, and broad sympathies for, contemporary Western Catholic spirituality, Nicodemus was ranked among the conservatives of Athos, primarily on account of the amazing theological, canonical and spiritual erudition that enabled him to give new life to Byzantine traditions. He produced at the Patriarch's request (and doubtless with many collaborators) the most important Byzantine canonical compilation, still in use to this day. This was the *Pedalion*, published in 1800.

But his real interests lay in the spiritual domain, and some years before he had produced a spiritual anthology whose influence was to go deeper still: this was the *Philokalia*, published in Venice in 1782. This work, in which his friend Macarius Notaras, Metropolitan of Corinth,[4] was a collaborator, though he himself was responsible for the introductions, consists of passages from the Greek Fathers—either entire or in part—chosen for their usefulness, together with a selection of the principal writings from the medieval hesychast tradition. The title—it means the love of, or search for, beauty—was taken from a similar compilation made by Basil and Gregory Nazianzen from extracts from Origen on the meditation of the Scriptures. The book is centred on the life of prayer, and more exactly on the "Jesus prayer" seen as the focus of Christian asceticism and the soul of its mysticism. Nicodemus could hardly have done more to revive the hesychast tradition than by thus showing that it was rooted in the most ancient tradition, while at the same time bringing out its essential content, going

---

[4] See Mgr Petit's article about him in the *Dict. Théol. Cath.*

beyond the secondary points of detail on which polemical argument had been concentrated.[5]

And while in this way perpetuating the quintessence of Byzantine spiritual tradition, Nicodemus applied himself to another work: a popularization and adaptation for the East of some of the most prized works and fruitful practices of the modern Catholic West. It is hard to know what to admire most in this achievement: the discrimination with which he selected his borrowings and adapted them without in any way betraying their content, or the breadth of mind of which his work gives such ample proof.[6] Though he was so intent on the specific rediscovery and renewal of Byzantine spirituality, he nevertheless appreciated the advantages that could simultaneously be drawn from methods of piety at the opposite pole from the tradition that was so rightly dear to him. If there is a work that by its very existence annihilates the systematic antitheses that have been raised between East and West (whether they be the outcome of uncomprehending Latins or of Easterners exasperated by this lack of comprehension), then it is Nicodemus's.

The two most remarkable examples of his work of assimilation are his *Spiritual Exercises* and his *Unseen Warfare*. The first is a shortened translation, with biblical notes and commentaries but no substantial alterations, of a series of meditations by the Italian Jesuit, Pinamonti, following the order and method of the Ignatian exercises. It is an obvious triumph to have distilled the essence of the methods of meditation and spiritual examination operative in the West for use in the East. But Nicodemus's success is perhaps more surprising in the case of *Unseen Warfare*, published in Venice in 1796.[7] Here again we have a translation (abridged in two places only, which are themselves repetitions), this time of Lorenzo Scupoli's *Spiritual Combat* and *Road to Paradise*, but

---

[5] Concerning the *Philokalia*, see J. Gouillard's introduction to his *Petite Philocalie de la prière du cœur*, Paris, 1953, and also the two volumes of translations by E. Kadloubovsky and G. E. H. Palmer, *Writings from the Philokalia* and *Early Fathers from the Philokalia*, London, 1951 and 1954, and also our previous volume.

[6] We can understand how rather naïve statements on the purely Orthodox character of Nicodemus's work should have given rise to L. Gillet's scathing reaction in his discussion of *Unseen Warfare* (published in *Sobornost*, 3rd Series, No. 12, pp. 584 *et seq*.). But though Nicodemus placed himself broadly within the Western school, he cannot be accused of plagiarism, for he himself stressed that he was only adapting the work of others. The deeply thought out nature of this adaptation (while it never distorts the original) cannot without injustice be denied. On the substance of his borrowings, see G. H. Viller, S.J., "Nicodème l'Hagiorite et ses emprunts à la littérature spirituelle occidentale", in *Revue d'ascétique et de mystique*, vol. V (1924), pp. 174 *et seq*. and 416 *et seq*. On all this matter see note 73 of P. Le Guillou, *op. cit.*, pp. 118–119.

[7] See H. A. Hodges' introduction to *Unseen Warfare*, translation of E. Kadloubovsky and G. E. H. Palmer, London, 1952, pp. 13 *et seq*.

with two short insertions of his own. The work is achieved with remarkable skill, and as if to establish a bridge between an outlook so representative of the Counter-Reformation and the tradition of the ancient East that he had brought to light in his *Philokalia.*

We can easily understand the delight with which Nicodemus applied himself to naturalizing Scupoli's two books within Orthodoxy, and with such success that there were Eastern monks who contrasted their spirituality with that of the West by basing their definition of the former on the pure expression of it as put forward in *Unseen Warfare!* Nicodemus was helped by the fact that the Neapolitan Barnabite, Scupoli, while dependent on the psychological and systematic spirituality of the post-Renaissance, developed it within a twofold theme taken from patristic spirituality and interlaced it with these two basic strands. These were, on the one hand, asceticism understood as a struggle against demoniac enslavement, and, on the other, its flowering into a spirituality not of suppression of the activities of the senses or of condemnation of creation, but of consecration of the world in a glorification of God by the whole of man, body as well as spirit.

Nicodemus's two insertions deserve our special attention. They are indicative first and foremost of the possible harmonization between modern Western tradition and the ancient Eastern tradition that he was helping to recover. But they are so rich in meaning that we can note the way in which, while always a synthesizer, he embraced the Orthodox tradition.

The first insertion comes after what Scupoli says about custody of the senses by means of constant reference of all their impressions to God and Christ. Nicodemus inserts here a new chapter which finds its inspiration in Evagrius. He proposes to the soul, after that positive asceticism, a going beyond the senses "in a contemplation of itself, or rather in the intuition of God through itself, and repose in him". This same chapter puts us on guard against visions and other imaginative impressions, so as to make us tend towards "pure prayer". However, having already spoken in this context of "recollection in the heart", he proposes, explicitly as an alternative to "pure prayer" defined in terms from Evagrius, the interior recitation of the "Jesus Prayer".[8]

Further on, when Scupoli, before speaking at length on meditation, recommends what he calls "mental prayer", meaning "the lifting up of the heart to God, accompanied by a request, actual or virtual, for something that we desire", or better still "the simple look by the spirit at God to beg his help", Nicodemus seizes the opportunity to develop what he has to say concerning the "Jesus

[8] Part One, chap. 25.

Prayer".[9] The prayer, as he so particularly recommends it, is "the prayer of the spirit and the heart (*noéra kaï kardiakè*)"—typical union of Evagrian and Macarian formulae—in which the invocation of Jesus, following the traditional formula of "Lord Jesus Christ, Son of God, have mercy on me", remains purely interior and silent although linked with the control of breathing. He adds that in this petition all other petitions are contained, although we can particularize them, and indeed even come back to the prayer formulated by the lips, if the effort of purely interior tension becomes too difficult.

So we see a very flexible synthesis at work between the purity of a transcendent mysticism and the humanity of a mysticism of Jesus, on the part of man as a whole.

The characteristics apparent in these insertions recur in the notes in which Nicodemus constantly corroborates and expands on the application of Scupoli's advice by quotations from the Greek patristics or the hesychast tradition. But, when occasion arises, he does not hesitate to invoke St Augustine and his words on interiority so as to justify, and at the same time enlarge upon, the Evagrian return of the soul (or more exactly the *noûs*) to itself. To what extent this is a matter not of simple eclecticism but of a meditated synthesis is best brought out in a note in which he tells of his own evolution of thought on the "Jesus Prayer". The three powers of the soul, he tells us, are required: intellect (*noûs*), discursive reason (*logos*) and will or spirit (*thelesis, pneuma*) work together in a single act in which the soul, by uniting itself with itself, is made disposed to unite itself with God. He thus explains immediately, without having to tell us more explicitly, how he reconciles Evagrius and Macarius at the heart of an Augustinian re-interpretation of modern Western methods.[10]

But these compilations and adaptations were not Nicodemus's only writings. Personal though these were, he wrote works of his own, among which the most important was his *Manual of advice on the Custody of the Five Senses and on the imagination of the Spirit (noûs) and the Heart*, published in 1801. It was an attempt at a popularization for the secular clergy and the laity of Hesychasm as rethought by him.

Parallel with these writings, the saint's activities were directed not only towards monastic renewal but towards the diffusion throughout the whole Church of the spirituality that would achieve it. He was one of the most effective propagators of the movement in favour of frequent communion, which met with most lively

[9] Chapter 45. See our study of this prayer in the previous volume.
[10] On all this see Hodges, *op. cit.*, pp. 47 *et seq.*

resistance from the monks on Athos. On this point again Nico-demus was undoubtedly inspired by the Counter-Reformation, and he was accused of Westernism precisely on this head, though his accusers saw him less as a crypto-Catholic than as a freemason—which betrays their ignorance of their abhorred West (it appears in addition that they confused freemasonry with Protestantism; and one of his letters was even falsified so as to foster the belief that he rejected the Real Presence).

His friend Macarius of Corinth had himself written a book in 1777 advocating frequent communion, and, having been denounced by an Athos monk, was condemned by Constantinople.[11] In *Unseen Warfare* Nicodemus added a note on this subject to what Scupoli had said about ill-advised directors who opposed this practice. They acted thus because of "bad and perverse custom", noted Nicodemus. Denounced in his turn, he was cleared of all blame by the *Synaxis* (the supreme authority of Athos) in 1807, two years after his death. This synthesis between frequent sacramental practice and the inspiration of hesychast prayer is by no means the least interesting of the syntheses we owe to him. Indeed we owe to him the reconciliation of the liturgical current and the wholly inner current of Byzantine spirituality within a spirituality of the eucharistic Christ.

Païssy Velitchkhovsky and the Spiritual Renewal in Russia and Rumania

The impact of Nicodemus's achievement came quickly and per-haps most surely to the Slav countries—notably Russia, but also Rumania—through the intermediary of another Athos monk, Païssy Velitchkhovsky (1722–1794).[12] He was at the root of the monastic revival in nineteenth-century Russia and also of an extension of the role and influence of the *startzy* that went far beyond the confines of the monastic world. An extremely original strain of religious thought, in which the laity played a preponderant part, was to find there one of the main factors in its development. Peter Velitchkhovsky, the son of the archpriest of the cathedral, was born at Poltava in the Ukraine. He fled the ecclesiastical career for which his family intended him, so as to find a monastic life of genuine poverty and zeal such as the Russian monasteries of the time could hardly provide. While at the ecclesiastical

---

[11] This book appeared anonymously, and, still anonymously, Nicodemus re-edited it and added to it in 1783. On all this see Le Guillou, *op. cit.*, pp. 121 *et seq.*

[12] See P. S. Tchetverikov, *Moldavskij Staretz Paissij Velitchkovskij*, Petseri, 1938, summarized by Kologrivof, *op. cit.*, pp. 379 *et seq.* Cf. Smolitsch, *op. cit.*, pp. 482 *et seq.*

academy of Kiev he was encouraged in his aspiration, however, by a monk of the Petcherskaia Lavra and a former hermit, Father Pachomius, whereupon he interrupted his studies and went to the monastery of Liubitch for a first attempt at monastic life. Here he made a discovery of passionate interest to him—the writings of John Climacus—but otherwise did not find the life that corresponded to his desires. With another novice he set off for Moldavia, and received the tonsure and the name of Plato at the monastery of St Nicolas on an island in the river Tiasmin. But he was disillusioned here too, so returned to Kiev and passed some time at the famous Lavra. Soon he was abroad again with another companion, still seeking the poor and solitary life, and they ended up at the monastery of Motronime. From there a Russian monk, Michael, who had taken the Great Habit, sent him back to Moldavia-Wallachia where he shortly joined him in the *skit* of St Nicolas of Trusteny. A little later, however, he went to yet another *skit*, that of Kiarnul, under the direction of the *staretz* and solitary, Onuphrius. Here he would probably have settled if there had not been a move to call him to the priesthood for which he did not feel ready. So he went to Athos where he established himself in 1746.

He found many Slav monks round about the Pantokrator monastery, but, having sought in vain among them for a spiritual teacher, he withdrew into solitude and dire poverty for four years, trying to make up for his lack of spiritual direction by copious reading of the Fathers. He received the Great Habit, with the name of Païssy, from a monk named Basil whom he had known in Wallachia, and shortly afterwards was co-founder with a Vlack monk, Bessarion, of a *skit* that rapidly developed—first with Rumanian, then Slav recruits—into a cenobitic community for the direction of which he finally accepted the priesthood in 1758. He settled his disciples round the old church of St Elias, depending on Pantokrator.

However, the growing influx of monks and laymen under spiritual direction, with the jealousy and conflicts to which his success as a *staretz* gave rise in spite of himself, soon sent him off on yet another migration. In 1763 he took his community of sixty-four monks to the monastery of the Holy Ghost near Dragomirna in Bukovin, which was put at his disposal by the Metropolitan. It was here, side by side with his regular spiritual lectures to a community still half Rumanian and half Slav, that he developed his considerable work of translating and popularizing the great books of the Greek spiritual tradition into Church Slavonic. His most important work was his abridged translation of the *Philokalia*, published a year before his death in 1793.

It has been said that Païssy was greatly influenced by the writings of St Nil. Not only does he seem to have been the first of the moderns to rediscover him (he had numerous transcriptions done of his works), but in the selection he made from the *Philokalia* he gave first place to authors familiar to St Nil and even to texts mentioned by him. However this may be, the form of cenobitism that he organized and advocated was the Basilian and Studite form, though always insisting on poverty, a full liturgical life, and far-flung good works. At the time of the Russo-Turkish war in 1768 the monastery doors were open to all refugees, men, women and children.

The war drove him and his community into yet another exile, first at Secoul in Rumanian territory and then at Neamtzu, though he did not abandon his direction of the former monastery. The development of his communities, with recruits from both the Slav and Rumanian worlds, became prodigious in this last period of his life. Secoul counted as many as three hundred monks, and Neamtzu seven hundred. His translating activities, into which he drew all his disciples who were capable of the work, continued right up to the end of his life, together with a vast spiritual correspondence. He popularized the hesychast spirituality which he had made most his own in an interpretation very close to the one we found in St Nicodemus. In this way he gave permanency to all that had caused his immediate influence to be so far-reaching—an unconditional welcome to anyone who came, and exhortation or spiritual direction that was never separated from active charity.

By means of his correspondence and his disciples Païssy had acted as the leaven of a monastic rebirth in the Russia he had left, even during his lifetime. But it was during the following century that his influence came to fullest fruition. This influence was, as it were, enshrined in the Optina monastery,[13] renewed in 1800 by the monk Theophanes who, after a period of soldiering, had served his novitiate under Païssy. But greater still was the part played at Optina shortly afterwards by Abraham, who had been formed by Macarius of Pechnocha, another disciple of the *staretz*. In 1821 the monastery was completed by a *skit* some distance away, dedicated to John the Baptist and destined for monks wishing to lead a more withdrawn life. Two other monks, the brothers Moses and Antony

---

[13] On Optina-Pustin and its *startzy* see Smolitsch, *op. cit.*, pp. 503 *et seq.* and Kologrivof, *op. cit.*, pp. 398 *et seq.* On the *staretz* type in general see Smolitsch, *op. cit.*, pp. 470 *et seq.*; S. Behr-Sigel, *op. cit.*, pp. 104 *et seq.*, and N. Arseniew, *La Piété russe*, pp. 115 *et seq.*

Pontilov, hitherto solitaries in the forests of Roslav, formed the basis of this new foundation; and they, too, were linked to the Païssy tradition. A few years later, in 1829, the arrival at Optina of the archmonk Leo (Nagolkin), from the monastery of Valaam on an island in Lake Ladoga, inaugurated the line of great *startzy* that continued uninterrupted until the beginning of the twentieth century. Father Leo (1768–1841) quickly attracted pilgrims from far and near. His influence was felt especially by humble people and religious. An exception to this was the noble and cultivated *staretz* Macarius (1788–1860) who was drawn to the monastery by Father Leo's influence and extended this influence to the intellectual world. The philosopher Ivan Kireevsky, who lived near the monastery, and his slavophile friends were the first to be won over. It was they who, under Macarius' direction, undertook an edition of the classics of Russian spirituality from St Nil to Païssy Velitchkhovsky, including, naturally, the latter's translations from the Greek, either with explanatory notes or in re-translations into modern Russian. These translations drew further visitors to the monastery in their turn: Gogol, Vladimir Soloviev, Constantin Leontiev, Dostoievsky (the monastery he describes in *The Brothers Karamazov* is drawn directly from Optina), Alexis and Leo Tolstoy. . . .

After Macarius's death, the last and perhaps the most famous of the Optina *startzy* was his disciple and collaborator, Alexander Grenkov, son of a village sexton in the Tambov region, who became Father Ambrose (1812–1891).

The *startzy* of Optina did not do original work except in so far as they pushed the diffusion of an essentially monastic spirituality into lay and secular circles. Within a monasticism regenerated by the rediscovery of its pure spiritual traditions, their great merit was to implement and popularize the synthesis prepared by Nicodemus and propagated by Païssy. Here we find the richest strands of the Eastern tradition: Basilian or Studite cenobitism, the Hesychasm of St Simeon and then of Athos, the poor and interiorized monasticism of St Nil, and the liturgical and social monasticism of St Joseph of Volokolamsk. It was by the intermediary of these *startzy* that the most original religious school of thought that the Orthodox East had hitherto known was impregnated with these riches. Never perhaps had a monasticism wholly faithful to its purely spiritual vocation been capable of thus fecundating the life of an entire people from the most humble levels to the most exacting intellectuals.

Theophanus the Recluse

Though the work of Optina was so representative of the nineteenth-century Orthodox renewal in Russia, it was far from being unique. We should compare it particularly with the work of Bishop Theophanus the Recluse (George Govorov in the world).[14] His life bears a striking resemblance to that of Tikhon of Zadonsk. He had intellectual ability and an intense priestly radiance, received his formation at the Kiev academy, exercised his episcopal functions for a short time only (first at Tambov, then at Vladimir) before withdrawing to the monastery of Vychinsky in 1866 to pass his last years in total seclusion, engaged in a vast correspondence, and, finally, wrote books—biblical commentaries (notably on St Paul) and spiritual works. Among these the most influential were a translation, not into Church Slavonic but Russian, of the *Philokalia* (with the collaboration of the Optina monks, in five volumes, from 1876 to 1890) and of *Unseen Warfare*. But he recast these two works. He altered the order of the first and added many texts, particularly from Syriac patrology. With the second he incorporated into the text the substance of Nicodemus's notes, and systematically eliminated typically Western expressions or developments, while enlarging on all that related to perpetual prayer in the sense of the constant presence of God in the soul, and all that related to spiritual warmth (carefully distinguished from sentient devotion).

And yet, more than any of the Russian spiritual masters we have mentioned, it was a simple and uninstructed monk who was to give supreme expression to Russia's religious genius; and a mystery man writing anonymously who was to leave us the most precious witness to this tradition in a few matchless pages. We are referring to St Seraphim of Sarov, and the *Stories of the Pilgrim*.

St Seraphim of Sarov

Perhaps we can best describe what St Seraphim stands for in Russian spirituality if we say that he was both its Francis of Assisi and its Curé d'Ars. More or less contemporary with the latter (1759–1833), he also drew amazing crowds of penitents of all sorts and conditions and from far and wide, and sent them away knowing more about themselves and comforted by his supernatural perception and boundless charity.

Like the *Poverello* of Assisi, he radiated joy and a heavenly friendship for all creatures; and there was the same heroic detach-

---

[14] See Hodges, *op. cit.*, pp. 59 *et seq.*, and Arseniew, *loc. cit.*

ment beneath the spiritual joy, and the same folly of the cross, while his power of easing souls and restoring them to serenity had been won by struggles no less severe than those of Jean-Marie Vianney. And yet he was in the pure line of Russian tradition by reason of his long and solitary asceticism recalling the *Paterikon* of Kiev, and by the light of transfiguration that haloed his mysticism.

He was the last Russian saint to be canonized under the Tsars, and though we have many first-hand accounts, an atmosphere of Golden Legend seems to invade them all só that it is difficult to make a critical assessment. But whatever imaginary amplifications took possession of those who came into contact with him, it seems unquestionable that he was a person in and around whom the supernatural took the place of the natural. We have some "sayings" of his that ring altogether true, and the account of conversations taken down by a neighbouring landowner, Motovilov, are too unlike anything else to have been substantially modified. But, as with the Curé d'Ars, his own *Instructions* are disappointing, and for the same reason: they are nothing but a rosary of quotations from his favourite reading and have come to us after being censored by the Metropolitan Philaretus.

In Fedotov's opinion the best synthesis that has emerged from these uncertain documents—behind which, however, we sense a totally exceptional presence—is an essay by A. F. Dobie-Bateman.[15] We can do no better than give a summary of it.

Prokor Moshnin was born at Kursk, the son of a builder who was soon to leave him fatherless, and at ten years old he was saved from a serious illness by a vision of the Virgin. Setting aside family concerns as soon as he could, he made friends with a *yurodyv* who predicted a great deal from his future. When he was eighteen he decided to become a monk, and a pilgrimage to the Petcherskaia Lavra, where he met the *staretz* Dositheus, strengthened him in this intention. He put it into practice by entering the monastery of Sarov in 1779.

He was subjected to the usual ordeals (he worked in turn in the bakery and in the carpenter's workshop) and he read avidly: Pseudo-Macarius, John Climacus, the *Philokalia*, and above all the New Testament. He practised the greatest austerity with regard to food and withdrew into the woods for days on end to devote himself to solitary prayer. Seriously ill again a year after his entry, he was again cured by a vision of the Virgin, this time with Peter and John to whom she uttered the enigmatic phrase, "This one belongs to our family." After that he devoted several years to collecting

[15] Fedotov has introduced it into his *Treasury*, pp. 246 *et seq.* See too his remarks on p. 242 of his Introduction. See too Smolitsch, *op. cit.*, pp. 497 *et seq.*

money for the monastery hospital and the building of the monastery chapel.

It seems that his illnesses, visions and taste for solitude caused him to be regarded as peculiar, for he was not given the monastic tonsure until 1786, with the name of Seraphim. Not long afterwards he was ordained deacon, and there is mention of his visions of angels in church, angels serving the celestial liturgy, and the Son of Man appearing in glory in the Holy Thursday liturgy to bless the faithful. Ordained priest in 1793, he exercised his sacred functions for a year (during which he either celebrated or communicated each day—another peculiarity) after which, his Superior, Pachomius, having died, he obtained leave of his successor to withdraw into the forest. There he spent ten years in a hut that he built for himself. He prayed and read or else cultivated the little garden that provided him with his food. We are told that he gave Gospel place-names to the places round about so that he might re-live the Saviour's life in his imagination. We are shown him intimate with wild beasts, including wolves and bears, who came and ate from his hands.

In 1804 he was "beaten up" by robbers. Despite his good physique he did not defend himself and refused to bring them to justice. They left him disabled and troubled in spirit. But after five months in bed the customary healing vision of the Virgin came again and he resumed his solitary life in the forest. For three years it took an extreme form that resembled the stylites: he spent nearly all his time in prayer on a high outcrop of rock, repeating the publican's phrase, "Lord, be merciful to me a sinner."

In 1807 there was a move to make him Superior of the community. Not only did he refuse, but for three more years buried himself in total silence, not even addressing a word to the brother who brought him his food.

In 1810, however, his legs could no longer support him and he was obliged to return to the monastery. For a further five years he remained in complete silence, never going out of his cell where he had neither bed nor fire, praying or reading the Gospel before the ikon of Our Lady of "Tenderness". He did not attend or celebrate the eucharistic liturgy, but communion was brought him every Sunday.

In 1815 he at last opened the door of his cell and started to speak, and from then until his death he was always surrounded by visitors coming from far and wide. Already during his silent seclusion miracles of healing had been attributed to him. These now became more numerous, together with words that revealed that he could see into men's hearts and was endowed with second sight or prophecy. But he won over those who flocked around him mainly by his affectionate gaiety from which there seemed to radiate the palpable presence of another world. He always greeted his flock with the Easter formula, "Christ is risen", and called them "my joy". To two monks who were exchanging discouraged comments in the wood he suddenly appeared and said, "None of these things should depress us, for Christ has brought everything under his sway, he has raised Adam, freed Eve and destroyed Death." Better still, he brought the supernatural universe in which he lived down to ground level. To Father Basil Sadovsky, chaplain to the Diveyevo nuns, he gave a handful of cakes, saying with a smile, "Look Batiushka, the queen was with me and this is what my guests left me." The good nuns naturally concluded that the cakes were a present from the Virgin Mary. On other occasions he handed over perhaps an apple, perhaps a leafy branch, as pledges of paradise. The words of a visionary, or simply his sense of humour? Who shall say? Better: on Annunciation Day, 1832, a year before his death, Sister Eupraxia affirmed that she had been present when Seraphim had a vision of Mary, the two SS John and twelve virgins, who talked of the father's coming death. This type of story long militated against Seraphim's canonization, and it is doubtful whether the Holy Synod would ever have gone through with it but for the intervention of the Empress Alexandra Feodorovna.

Seraphim, meanwhile, had made his coffin and kept it in his cell. The thought of his coming death seemed to reawaken his former struggles of which he had never spoken except in brief allusions to his years in the wilderness. He wept and said, "My life is drawing to a close. From the point of view of my spirit I feel that I have only just been born, but from the point of view of my body I am already dead." He bade farewell to the bishop and gave him candles for his forthcoming funeral. But on other occasions he said, "When I am no longer here, come to my grave. Come whenever you can and as often as possible. Bring all your difficulties, everything that weighs on you, everything that has happened to you, to my grave. Bow down to the earth, as if towards someone living, and say everything—I shall hear you. Then all your sorrow will fly away and disappear. Speak as if you were speaking to a living person. For you I live and shall always live."

On 2 January 1833 it was observed that a candle had set fire to his cell. People went in and found him on his knees in front of his favourite ikon. He was dead.

His asceticism and exhortations provide an accent not very familiar in Russia, a country excelling in penitent prayer: it was an accent on virginity as total and immediate consecration to God. But the counterpart of this absolute in consecration to God seems to have been the gift of the Spirit as the transfiguring experience of the whole of existence. Here we are in a direct line from Pseudo-Macarius and St Simeon. But the peaceful reaching out towards this experience, and its gratuitous and as it were unhoped for realization at the height of hope and expectation—these had never been better expressed than in Motovilov's story. Here again we have an example of the seemingly quite natural association of an ordinary man with the experience of a saint. But we are no longer in the legendary atmosphere of Sister Eupraxia's account. In Motovilov's story the familiarity of the real blends with the extraordinary in a way that eludes detailed analysis, and yet we feel we touch the essence of the saint's message. Motovilov met him in a snow-swept forest while he was cutting down a tree, and while the saint was lopping off the branches his companion, at the saint's invitation, sat down on the stump. Whereupon the saint revealed to this worthy landowner his (i.e. the landowner's) never-achieved search for the essential Christian experience. It was, he told him, life in the Holy Spirit; and while he was speaking his listener saw him as if transfigured, and the impression of a light and warmth that were not of this world communicated itself to him.

The Stories of the Pilgrim

St Seraphim's life can only be glimpsed across the golden mist of other people's testimony, and it is difficult to grasp his personality with any precision over and above the impression that it made on others, though we cannot have any doubt as to its vigour. The *Stories of the Pilgrim*,[16] on the other hand, is a piece of writing that gives us the delightful illusion of hearing the very voice of the person confiding in us, though, if we look closer, we may feel this to be an illusion. Admirable in their naïve simplicity at first glance, and an untarnished reflection of popular Christianity, the *Stories* seem a much more conscious piece of work when really examined, the work of an artist who cannot conceal his culture however hard he tries. May it not be a pious piece of fiction disguised as fact? There are, however, too many loose ends and too many unaffected reflections for this to be possible. The most likely conjecture is that it is a series of recollections let fall by the mysterious "pilgrim" and collected either by his spiritual father in Irkutsk or by some monk on Athos in whom he confided.

[16] Cf. Fedotov's introduction to his own translation in his *Treasury*, pp. 280 *et seq.*

However this may be, the pilgrim was a sick man and an untimely widower who could not bear to stay in the place where his happiness had come to an end, so set off on endless wanderings that had no earthly goal—though he seems to have spent some time on Athos and perhaps in the Holy Land. From the very first page he becomes our friend and we are drawn into his peregrinations—first across Russia where we find all the characters with which Russian novels have familiarized us, from the drunken soldier won over by the Gospel, to pious aristocrats; from peasants who at first seem like brutes but in whom we later discover secret mystical leanings, to semi-intellectuals whose frantic rationalism masks (rather unsatisfactorily) an unsatisfied romanticism. But it was above all a *spiritual* quest that our wanderer was engaged on, one of constant prayer by means of the Bible and the *Philokalia* (in a battered copy of the old Church Slavonic translation by the *staretz* Païssy) carried by the pilgrim in his scrip with the crusts of bread that formed the provisions for his journeys.

Unexpected encounters, either with learned monks or with those solely instructed by the Holy Spirit, came to guide and corroborate his own groping experience and gave birth to the treasures contained in these stories. On a deeper level they illustrate in an untheoretical and vital way the *xeniteia* taken up again from Abraham's—in which we recognized one of the oldest themes of Christian asceticism. The spirituality of the "Jesus Prayer" no doubt here produced its sweetest fruit, of an altogether Gospel-like humanity.

Fedotov is no doubt right to warn us against the chimerical supposition that this apparently popular but in fact so refined Hesychasm was representative of a Christianity really common among the humble people of Russia. But we may certainly see it as having been the supreme expression of the Russian spiritual experience, exemplifying the very best in Orthodoxy: folly for Christ; the kingdom to come anticipated by death to the world; and a transfiguration of all things—making them all the more human for us for having been rediscovered in the hands of the Risen Christ. These characteristics show yet again, and better than ever, that this Christianity, though so monastic in inspiration, was in the last analysis no more than lay evangelism, that is to say evangelism of the "people of God", in the purity of a new-found source.

PART TWO

Protestant and Anglican Spirituality

INTRODUCTION

NOTHING is more difficult to discuss than Protestant spirituality. If we set aside the few modern Protestant theologians bold enough to claim kinship with Pietism or
Revivalism, we cannot help noting that it is only the more or less
Catholicizing Protestants who have unhesitatingly admitted Protestant spirituality at all; while, if there is a point on which Barthians,
Bultmannians and neo-Lutherans seem to have agreed, it is in
viewing all this kind of reality as suspect. When mysticism is under
discussion, the theologians of these schools—while unable to deny
that there have been mystics throughout the whole history of
Protestantism, and different as their respective positions are—have
been completely united in their insistence that where true Protestantism is concerned, mysticism is the most unacceptable reality of
all.[1] Barth, Ebeling, Nygren, Brunner himself[2]—despite his avowed
sympathies for certain Pietistic and Revivalist tendencies—are
unanimous on this point. For all of them, mysticism in Christianity
is an essentially Catholic fact, and they would be ready to affirm
that it was the element in Catholicism that justified Protestant
opposition more than any other.

The reason they give is always the same: mysticism is an essentially pagan element in religion, foreign to the Bible and irreconcil-
able with the Gospel. A large part of what follows will be devoted
to discussing this thesis, which can hardly fail at first sight to seem
totally absurd to anyone with first-hand knowledge of the mystics of
Catholic tradition. We hope to show by facts and texts that it rests
solely on *a priori* judgments, and cannot find even apparent justification except as the outcome of confusions and misunderstandings.

[1] On this question of the interpretation of mysticism on the part of Protestant
theologians, see Hasso Jaeger, *La Mystique protestante* in the collective work *La
Mystique et les Mystiques* soon to be published by Desclée de Brouwer. We would
like to express our debt to Fr Jaeger, who has allowed us to make wide use of his
researches.
[2] Cf. Karl Barth, *Kirchliche Dogmatik*, t. IV/2, pp. 567 *et seq.* and *Die pro-
testantische Theologie im 19. Jahrhundert*, Zollikon-Zurich, 1947; G. Ebeling,
Wort und Glaube, Tübingen, 1960; A. Nygren, *Eros et Agape*; E. Brunner, *Die
Mystik und das Wort*, 2nd ed., Tübingen, 1928.

It is interesting to note how this erroneous and bizarre (to say the least) idea should have recently achieved the status of a positive article of faith—one of the few on which the majority of modern Protestant theologians agree. The explanation is to be found in the evolution towards the Pietistic movement and more especially in Romantic religious thought. It is undeniable that Pietism—at the heart of which the most striking Protestant mystical figures emerged—seemed to certain Protestants (as Schleiermacher's work shows),[3] a step towards a spirituality without dogma, and ultimately towards a religious syncretism in which everything specifically Christian seemed to have disappeared. It is also undeniable that Schleiermacher and his followers were effective collaborators in the rise of the Romantic movement which, especially in Germany, brought not only a wave of conversions to Catholicism but a new and altogether unexpected justification of Catholic spirituality to the contemporary mind. But even before this Pietistic currents of thought, while paving the way for Schleiermacher's liberalism, had developed avowed sympathies with Catholic spirituality and come into harmony with it. This was why Protestant theorists who sought regeneration by a return to sources condemned all Protestant mysticism, for they saw it as tending either to Catholicism or to some form of neo-paganism; which testified in its turn, or so they thought, to the underlying paganism in Catholic piety.

We cannot hope in our Introduction to discuss all the data of this problem, but we must at least try to unravel the confusions they have caused, as these seem to us to be at the root of all the (at least theoretical) anti-mysticism of modern Protestantism.

The explanation lies in the complex and vague nature of what is called Pietism—a complexity and vagueness that merely take the contradictions inherent in original Protestantism, beginning with Luther, a step further.

Pietism wished to react against the negative rationalism of the first forms of radical Protestant thought within which all positive faith had vapourised, and also against the conservatism—often hardly less rationalistic in its way—of a scholastic Protestant orthodoxy within which all religious life seemed to have been stifled. But although Pietism was at first nourished on the great traditional doctrinal affirmations of the Christian faith, and more precisely on the undoubted renewal brought to these by the first positive Protestant affirmations, it was unable or unwilling to give

[3] See *Reden über die Religion*, critical edition of the 1779 text by R. Otto, 1889, and of the 1821 text by F. M. Schiele, 1902; Fr. tr., *Discours sur la Religion*, with an important preface by I-J. Rouge, Paris, 1944. On Schleiermacher and mysticism see R. Otto, *Mystique d'Orient et Mystique d'Occident*, Fr. tr., Paris, 1951, pp. 228 *et seq.*

itself theological reinforcement—and this not so much through weakness as through weariness with conflicts that had become sterile. When it did so, however, Pietism, whether consciously or not, certainly rejoined the Catholic tradition, following the logic of the religious intuitions that inspired it. When it refused to do so it drew attention solely to the subjective aspect of religious experience; this was inevitable, and in accordance with a trend that had started with Luther. Hence there arose a perversion of religious experience culminating in a religiosity without anything specifically Christian about it—of which Schleiermacher's liberalism is the best exponent.

Schleiermacher and his group, however, who are at the root of both liberal Protestantism and religious Romanticism, brought to light another complexity that defies simple judgments. Whatever the ambiguities of the exaltation of "religious feeling" defined by Schleiermacher as the "feeling of dependence", its legacy has not been purely negative from the point of view of authentic Christianity—far from it. In the first place it had the merit of promoting a rediscovery of the social character of religion as contrasted with the rationalizing individualism of the time. More precisely still it prepared the way for the distinction that Troeltsch was to make between organic societies (*Gemeinschaft*) which are true communions, and more or less artificial institutional societies which are no more than organizations (*Gesellschaft*).[4]

In a more general way it prepared for the fruitful distinction between the supra-rational and the merely irrational with which the eighteenth century had been so prone to confuse it.

The ambiguities occur when this line of thought is unable to admit the presence of a transcendent religious object, through being the child of Pietism's omissions as much as of its riches; a transcendent religious object revealing itself in a Word that imposes itself objectively on man instead of limiting itself to interpreting his subjective experience. In other words it is not their concentration on the symbol that is the basic error of Schleiermacher and his followers (down to Tillich), but their incapacity to admit any symbol as being more than a projection of the human mind. From this there inevitably results a factitious equivalence between all religious experiences, and ultimately the reduction of religious experience to the highest awareness that man can have of himself. In this line of thought the substitution of an almost deified State for the Church—with Hegel and his followers, includ-

---

[4] E. Troeltsch, *Soziallehren des Christentums*, 3rd ed., Tübingen, 1932. See also F. Tönnies, *Gemeinschaft und Gesellschaft*, 2nd ed., Berlin, 1912.

ing the Marxists—becomes inevitable, together with the vapouriza-
tion of the "religious" into a vaguely pantheistic experience.

But when religious Romanticism does not accept this immanent-
ism and the agnosticism that necessarily goes with it, it can lead
(and did so, especially in Germany) to a genuine rediscovery of the
Church and the revelation that gives her her principle of unity—a
rediscovery of the Church not in some nondescript communal
experience, but in a communal adherence to God revealing himself
in his Word, expressed in human words and finally made flesh of
our flesh.

These important distinctions, however, have often been obscured
even among sincere Catholics, for they themselves have shared in
the ambiguities so apparent in Schleiermacher and lying at the
root of both religious liberalism and religious romanticism. And
here lies the sole justification, tenuous though it may be, for the
tendency of modern Protestants to identify Catholicism and natural-
ism (or paganism) under the heading of "mystical". But we must ask
ourselves whether such Catholics were not victims of these confusions through the influence either of Protestantism, or of the
survival within Catholicism of those medieval tendencies that
prepared for the advent of Protestantism under a form vowed to
schism and heresy. We mean those tendencies towards immanentist
subjectivism already apparent in the fourteenth and fifteenth
centuries, which made the break-up of the Reformation inevitable,
and also the final bogging down of Modernism (in the line of
Tyrrell).

And here we must mention yet another aberrant factor whose
side-effects both on the internal contradictions congenital to
Protestantism and on the more recent crises in Catholicism have
not always been sufficiently brought out. We are thinking of that
current of Gnosticism, whether dualistic or monistic, that underlay
most of the medieval heresies, which the Renaissance then encouraged by its neo-Platonist strands, hermetic and cabbalistic,
and which then passed into the Protestant sects before invading
the more academic forms of Protestantism with Jakob Boehme; it
also penetrated certain sections of Catholic thought in the line of
Baader and Schelling (second period). This current certainly reinforced the tendency to confuse genuine Christian mysticism, based
on the Word and the incarnation of the transcendent God, with a
merely pantheistic mysticism in which the Christian dogmas are
vapourized in an altogether immanentist symbolism of interpretation. It is here that we are at the apex, or rather the root, of the
confusions that have won its bad name for mysticism in contemporary Protestant thought.

But here again we must be discriminating in our judgments, for even this current cannot be dismissed out of hand as a disturbing factor in Christian spirituality. We must remember that in spite of its turbid, even Satanic, implications, the gnostic current has more than once played the part of a beneficial leaven in the rediscovery of corporateness, of presence in the world, without which the religious man loses himself in an abstract piety that is neither truly Christian nor truly biblical.

Yet the historian of Catholic piety should recognize that a one-sided emphasis on the subjective and psychological aspect of religious experience, or on a more abstract and metaphysical rather than a dogmatic approach, has sometimes led to an equivocal syncretism that still lingers on in many minds. We see traces of it in the over-facile acceptance of a "natural mysticism" seen as an introduction to a truly Christian supernatural mysticism. How, too, about the supposition—based on superficial comparisons and an often fanciful theology of the "salvation of the infidel"—that the mysticism of grace underlies all sorts of non-Christian experience just as much as it underlies the experience of the saints? Such deviations, let us repeat, far from being typical products of Catholicism, derive from strands of thought that are foreign to true Catholic tradition and paved the way in the late Middle Ages for Protestant "novelties": first and foremost, individual experience as opposed to ecclesiastical dogma; faith in one's own faith instead of faith that clings to a transcendent Word, and yet is able to create true communication, definable (if not exhaustively) in human words.

All this we shall clarify in our essay by reference to facts and texts, but it serves to forewarn us of the delicacy of the problems to be considered, and should forearm us against the temptation to put forward facile and prefabricated solutions. With the Catholic theologian who cannot accept the factitious simplifications that seem to have become axiomatic among a number of Protestant theologians, such solutions would be a patent sign not of true orthodoxy but of mere verbiage. When discussing spirituality and mysticism as they appear among our Protestant brothers, we should be guided towards careful discrimination in our judgments, not by any easing up of Catholic truth but by a total respect for it.

The unfolding of Anglican spirituality is very closely linked to the unfolding of Protestant spirituality. But when Anglicanism goes beyond its permanent temptation to be only a compromise or a *complexus oppositorum*, and tries to recuperate at least part of the tradition of the ancient Church, then it is the point where the positive elements of both Protestantism and modern humanism are reconciled with Catholicism. In Anglicanism we find what the most anti-Catholic Protestants note with distaste and tend to explain mistakenly, namely the deep Catholicity of all that Protestantism has produced in the way of true spirituality, and this not by abandoning its principles but by sifting and renewing all that was most positive in their origins.

I

THE SPIRITUAL PRINCIPLES OF THE REFORMERS

Luther: his Basic Intuition and how he expressed it

THERE is no doubt that the problem that presented itself to Luther,[1] first as a personal one, then as one whose solution would inspire all his public activity, was directly spiritual. It was the problem stated by the rich young man in the Gospel when he said, "What must I do to be saved?" It presented itself so acutely to the young monk, not because he had any particular propensity to sin but simply because he had a very sensitive conscience; a conscience quickened by a life overburdened with occupations, within an exacting spiritual environment where it was tempting to believe that holiness was pre-eminently an affair of rigorous ascetic practices (we must remember that he belonged to the reforming trend of the Augustinian Hermits). The famous "Tower experience" was probably less the discovery of an idea— an idea in fact traditional and one that he must often have come across in reading St Paul or the spiritual writers he favoured in the Augustinian school—than the discovery of the total reversal of his habitual behaviour that the idea involved if taken really seriously. We are saved by faith in Christ, or more precisely by his salvific death; not by any works that we may accomplish of ourselves. This notion, or rather the vivid intuition of it that suddenly struck him, released him from the feeling of stagnation and despair into which he had been plunged by a spiritual effort centred on the human effort itself, one that crushed him under observance and a whole conception of Christian holiness bound up with legalism.

[1] We can find all Luther's works in *Lutherswerke, Kritische Gesamtausgabe*, Weimar, 1883, *et seq.* We cannot give a bibliography of Luther here. There is a good outline in vol. I, *Histoire générale du Protestantisme* by G. Léonard, Paris, 1961. Our interpretation of his thought and of the way he developed it owes much to the remarkable study, *Die Reformation in Deutschland*, by Joseph Lortz, 3rd ed., Freiburg im Breisgau, 1948, and to innumerable conversations we have been able to have with this master of Lutheran studies in the Catholic Church. But it goes without saying that the conclusions we have drawn from them are entirely our own.

As a result of discovering that grace was a gratuitous gift of divine generosity alone in the crucified Christ, he discovered, or re-discovered, that the Word of God was God's personal intervention in the believer's life, and that vital faith in the Word was the most personal act the believer could make.

This double intuition, which was the direct result of his funda-mental experience (that of gratuitous salvation), was the starting-point of all his reform. On the plane of religious institutions this took the form of a revitalization of all those institutions which seemed to him capable of becoming, or re-becoming, the transparent expression of the Word thus understood. On the plane of the interior life, it unified all spiritual life within the experience of faith as a welcome to that same Word—a welcome created by the Word itself. Thus faith could no longer be conceived except as an inten-sely personal relationship between the believer and the Word, in which God not only revealed himself but communicated himself in the most vital way.

There are two factors involved in the drama which very soon became the drama of the Reformation that he wished to bring about, and that would finish up with a schism in Christendom and doctrinal affirmations that could only be condemned as heretical. At a deeper level the drama resulted from Luther's being im-prisoned more than he realized by a corruption of Christianity inherited from the medieval Church and by which he was at the same time confronted; with the result that, in answering objections raised by his preaching, he never managed to grasp what really impugned his first intuition or intuitions, simply because he carried it within himself. Consequently he attacked not so much what in fact went against his intuitions as what could often have nourished and enlightened them. And as the ineluctable development of even the strictly Lutheran Reformation proved, his work itself showed not a hoped-for blossoming but a rapid paralysis of the original spiritual impetus.

How can we define the negative element which seemed from the beginning, and then more and more, to hang like a parasite on the spiritual movement of which Luther was the great initiator? We can see it at work in a whole series of surely related manifestations, but its source remains obscure and difficult to pin down. It seems certain that the intellectual framework within which Luther was formed, and especially the attitudes of Nominalist philosophy and closely associated late Augustinian theology, played a considerable part here.[2] But these factors were the first fruits rather than the

---

[2] On this question see Paul Vignaux, *Luther commentateur des sentences*, Paris, 1935, and Bengt Hagglund, *Theologie und Philosophie bei Luther und in der*

causes of the corruption against which the Lutheran Reformation, and the Protestant one in general, acknowledged itself to be ineffective. In any case, far from escaping this major corruption, and far even from criticizing it, the "Reformation" installed itself within it and from there defined itself and defended itself.

It could be said that there were tendencies in the intellectual and spiritual evolution of the late Middle Ages which, far from being arrested by the Renaissance and the Reformation, spread quickly, as if the last obstacles that had put a brake on them had suddenly been removed. The true notion of divine transcendence as it had been gradually, painstakingly and lucidly defined by the Fathers of the Church—in contradistinction to the concepts of ancient thought—seemed to have evaporated. People no longer conceived of absolute transcendence going hand in hand with the most intimate immanence, so characteristic of the God of the Bible. Either God became merged with the highest experience that we could have of ourselves and of him (as in all the pantheistic deviations that abounded on the fringe of the mysticism of the Low Countries well before the Reformation), or else he remained the Sovereign and the All only by becoming a stranger to man and unable to enter his life except by annihilating it—with the result that man on his side could not assert himself except by thrusting God away towards some inaccessible horizon.

Let us note that the two corruptions—monism and the most radical dualism—usually go hand in hand. They are as it were the two poles of a world where the infinite has once more become that *apeiron* or simple negation of the human order that it was in pre-Christian Greek thought.

Was this collapse of theist metaphysics, so painstakingly built up by early Christian thinkers, the cause or the effect of specifically Nominalist theses, reducing being to act, vapourizing all idea of distinct and stable substances? It is hard to say. Or rather we should have to answer, yes and no: the two seem to have engendered each other. But above all the two were a natural product of a new orientation of the human mind—indeed of the whole of man— tending to be absorbed in itself. Knowledge was already taking itself for its own object, to such a point that it could not concern itself with any other object, indeed doubted if there could be another object. But even before this had happened human activity,

occamitischen Tradition: Luthers Stellung zu der Theorie der doppelten Wahrheit, Lund, 1955. Heiko Augustinus Oberman, author of the most important contemporary work on late Nominalism (The Harvest of Medieval Theology, Harvard University, 1963), has promised us a comprehensive study on Nominalism and the beginnings of the Reformation which is still lacking.

like human sensibility, had taken itself for the predominant (and soon to be the exclusive) end.

Hence, on the religious plane, we get both the active Pelagianism towards which much late medieval spirituality had inclined, and also the exclusion of "works" as implied in the formulae to which Luther himself inclined when he wanted to express his liberating intuition theologically. Justification by faith alone in the grace of God alone became a forensic justification wherein Christ's merits made good our lack of merits, but without our being, or having to be, in any way changed thereby.

In other words no possibility seems to have been envisaged in the polemics aroused by Luther (either on his or his opponents' side) other than the alternative between a salvation that man must achieve by himself, with grace as a mere excitant or adjuvant of his will (when it was not, as with Pelagius, the crowning of the human effort brought by God in an external way), and a salvation where everything was from God, but in the sense that man could have no part in it; that his will did not have to be changed thereby. We get the inevitable impression, as we follow these polemics (including the one that brought Luther up against the most intelligent of his adversaries, Erasmus), that the way was as if blocked to all minds by an action of God that transforms and regenerates us, which is indeed *his* action—that of the Creator and the Saviour—but which recreates *us* and thus truly saves us. The controversy seems to have been between those who believed man to be effectively corrupted by his own fault, but concluded as inevitable consequence that God, in order to save him, did not heal the corruption but palliated it as if from outside; and those who believed that God could not save man except in so far as man had never really been corrupted, and that all he thus needed was an encouragement—no less external— to produce the fruit of good works in which his salvation lay.[3]

The tragedy of the situation arose from the fact that both sides seem to have been in tacit agreement in envisaging either an action of God that was for that reason necessarily external to man's action, or an action of man that was for that reason necessarily external to God's action. The very idea of God's action in man creating or re-creating a living relationship between God and man seemed equally inconceivable to both camps. Those who wanted to bring them together, like Seripando or Melanchthon,[4] envisaged a makeshift justification in which man really must do something, but something necessarily insufficient, while God in Christ did the

---

[3] On the opposition between *De libero arbitrio* by Erasmus, and *De servo arbitrio* by Luther, see our work, *Du Protestantisme à l'Eglise*, pp. 167 et seq.

[4] On Seripando and Melanchthon see H. Jedin, *Girolamo Seripando*, 2 vols., Würzburg, 1937.

essential, but an essential paradoxically insufficient in its turn, since it neither produced, nor dispensed with, man's participation—a solution, despite its good intentions, worse than the two extremes, since it lost sight of the absolute grace proclaimed on the one hand, and the nonsense felt on the other of a salvation that would save us from outside without having to change us even in the measure that it saved us.

However, that this vicious circle was not initiated by Luther or his disciples is proved by the fact that Nominalist theologians, who had such an influence on Luther, had been thinking along these lines already. For Ockham and Biel grace of itself had nothing to do with our will. God either absolved us or condemned us according to whether he decided to consider our actions good or bad, without there being any necessary and intrinsic connection between the actions and his judgment. If, however (so they said), we had to co-operate in our salvation by good deeds, this was because God in fact desired it, according to the tradition of the Church. But this in itself had no essential bearing on his grace; it was no more its effect than its cause, the two realities being on two planes of existence that had no relationship with each other.[5]

The tragedy appears at its height when we see Luther's radical inability (an inability shared by most of his contemporaries, opponents as well as followers) to conceive of a creative and salvific relationship of God with man, joined to a wonderfully vivid sense of the whole of the spiritual life as a living relationship with God in Christ. So we arrive at this paradox that, for want of an adequate expression, he pushed to the furthest extreme the one most inadequate for affirming this personalism: namely, forensic justification. Going against all idea of man possessing merits of his own outside the living relationship with Christ, he proclaimed that Christ saves us by faith, but without having to change us in any way, therefore without faith having to be "informed" (as the schoolmen said) by love, and he did this precisely so as to maintain that we cannot be saved except in the relationship wherein Christ establishes us with him.[6] The misfortune was that he did not seem to see that at the very moment when he was so vitally concerned to express the necessity and unique value of this relationship, the formulae he used emptied it of all real content.

[5] On Ockham see P. Vignaux, *Justification et prédestination au XVIe siècle*, Paris, 1934, pp. 119–122. Concerning Biel see the texts published by Feckes, *Gabrielis Biel quaestiones de justificatione*, Münster, 1929, and chaps. 2 and 6 of *op. cit.* of Oberman.

[6] We are indebted here to the analyses quoted by Hasso Jaeger. See too A. Nygren, *Eros et Agape*, vol. 3, pp. 288 *et seq.*

3*

But why did this happen? Because he wanted to oppose the affirmation of merits which seemed to him (and not without excuse in the expressions and even the concepts of his contradictors) to constitute a holiness that had its own consistency and left aside the living and permanent relationship of saved with Saviour. His rejection of sanctifying grace inhering in the soul, of which the medieval authors had spoken, is extremely revealing in this respect.[7] As this was a substantial holiness, sanctifying nature as such, it excluded (as he saw it) or minimized actual grace, of which God was at all times the sole master and author; whereas sanctifying grace for St Thomas (though his successors lost sight of it), far from rendering actual grace useless or superfluous, had no meaning and no purpose but to hand us over to it while disposing us towards it by an adaptation of the depth of our being—an adaptation that could only be the work, in us, of the Creator himself. In other words this substantial grace as understood by St Thomas was precisely that by which God took hold of us, not only at the surface where our actions emerge, so to speak, but in the depths of our personality, and not at all so that we might thus act independently of him and his actual graces, but so that we might live solely in dependence on them.

Here we touch the heart of the misunderstanding between a concept of nature as a true creation of God, that is to say as possessing an authentic reality but wholly bound to God, or the permanent basis of relationship with God, and a concept of nature as being foreign to God inasmuch as it had its own existence and was thus opaque to all divine action—although it was still called created. For want of this opacity man's nature (as we are now considering it) could not do otherwise than melt into God if God were to touch it, or, if this did not happen, it would be that God had as it were melted into man's nature.

In fact this double possibility appeared as a perpetual threat hanging over all mystical statements towards the end of the Middle Ages, and when Protestantism in its turn underwent mystical invasions this double threat never ceased to be confirmed. Either the person of man would be annihilated in God, or God, as transcendent person, would volatilize in man (though this "or" gave place to "and" in many cases).

And this brings us to one of the most delicate historical problems that initial Lutheranism posed: that of the relationship between Lutheran spirituality and traditional mysticism.

---

[7] Cf. A. Nygren, *op. cit.*, pp. 307 *et seq.*

Luther and Mysticism

Let us repeat yet again that modern Protestant theorists agree in praising Luther for having reintroduced strictly biblical "faith" and thrust to one side typically Catholic "mysticism". For all that we should not underestimate Luther's unquestionable dependence on mysticism, and especially medieval mysticism, not only where his formulations were concerned but at the very heart of his spirituality.[8]

However, though he made use of this mysticism it is true that he criticized it, and his criticism gave rise to the radical criticism of all mysticism that Protestantism later put forward. But more important than the dependence of the criticism is the interpretation that Luther gave to mystical formulae whether he accepted or rejected them, for this interpretation lies at the root of the inadmissible distortions of mysticism which in the end justified his rejection, and the rejection as such. Yet it is here that we find the supremely paradoxical and hence dangerously ambiguous expression of all that was most original and authentic in Luther's experience.

Luther leaned heavily on what modern historians have called mysticism of essence linked to the Pseudo-Areopagite tradition as he found it among the mystics of the Low Countries, and particularly in Tauler and the *Theologia Germanica* (which he re-edited); and also on the "mystic marriage" doctrine such as he found it in St Bernard's commentary on the *Song of Songs*. But the way in which he combined these two sources reveals both his originality and his ambiguity at their height. In Areopagite mysticism he valued the affirmation of the hidden God remaining hidden even in his revelation; but he reproached it with its seeming underestimation of Christ, the incarnation and the cross. In Bernardine mysticism he valued its Christic character and its absorption in the cross of the Saviour, but he reproached it for absorbing the cross into the glory, for proposing as an attainable summit in this life the consummated union wherein the cross is as it were surpassed (if only in the *excessus*, the transitory ecstasy) by a blessed union anticipating the resurrection.[9]

So he combined them ingeniously by identifying, on the one

---

[8] On all that we imply in this paragraph we are especially indebted to H. Jaeger, *op. cit.* Rufus Jones has given a succinct but striking account of all that Luther owed to the medieval mystics, *Some Exponents of Mystical Religion*, London, 1930, pp. 114 *et seq.* See too O. Scheel, "Taulers Mystik und Luthers reformatorische Entdeckung", in *Festgabe D. J. Kaftan*, Tübingen, 1920, pp. 298–318, and also H. Strohl, *Luther jusqu'en 1520*, Paris, new edition, 1962, pp. 193 *et seq.*

[9] On this point see W. von Loewenich, *Luthers Theologia Crucis*, 2nd ed., Munich, 1954.

hand, the hidden God with his sole revelation on the cross, and, on the other, union with him with faith, in which the believing soul was united to Christ not by being thereby raised beyond its sinning and mortal condition, but by being closely bound to him who died once and lives for ever, though the soul itself, in itself, paradoxically remained in sin and death. This was, for Luther, the Christian's cross in which he consummated his union with the Saviour; he consummated the union not beyond the cross, in some *theologia gloriae*, but in the cross itself.

How are we to understand these words? First, and more than ever, we must distinguish between the primary vision and the theological terms in which it was expressed.

His basic vision was authentically Christian—that is undeniable —and perhaps shows Luther's originality at its best, in a blinding renewal of the most traditional truths. But its expression remained tied more narrowly than ever to the fatal alternative we have described.

His basic vision was man's personal relationship—on the sole basis of faith in Christ, God made man and crucified for man— with the God who reveals himself in the essential act of his transcendent love engraved for ever at the heart of our history.

But the formulation, if we take it literally, amounts to saying that this relationship excludes, on the one hand, the radical incomprehensibility of God which will subsist until the union consummated with him in eternal glory. The relationship, indeed, not only manifests itself to us directly and positively only in the cross, only in Christ in as much as he wanted to be crucified—which is true—but seems no longer to exist at all save in the mystery of the cross, and not in a mystery inherent to God of which the cross would be but the manifestation to our sinful world. On the other hand, from the believer's side, the relationship excludes all effective participation in the resurrection and the glorification, in any effective holiness (imperfect as it may be on earth) and in any real insight (mixed with darkness as it still is): and this is excluded not only in this life. It is hard to see how even in eternity man could become holy or participate in the vision of God—without for that purpose becoming God, not through participation but essentially.

So we come up against the alternative more rigorously than ever: either total agnosticism, total alienation between God and man, or else mere fusion of man in God, if not of God in man. This personalization of the relationship with the God of love coming to raise man to him thus presents the absolute obstacle to all possibly effective realization of it at the very moment when it reaches the height of its affirmation.

The Bible, the Catechism and the Liturgy in Lutheranism

Though the preaching of Luther's basic spiritual doctrines, with their strengths and their weaknesses, was very important for the future of Protestantism, his influence did not stop there. In all the countries through which Lutheranism and Protestantism spread—in forms very different, perhaps, from the one he had originally created—he was a religious teacher whose activity went far beyond his personal theses.

To begin with he brought back a piety directly inspired by the Bible, and diffused it among the common people who, we suspect, had never seen anything like it since patristic times. The quality of his translation of the Bible, and the efforts he made to bring out its full effect not only by a renewal of preaching and catechetic teaching but by a translation and re-ordering of the traditional liturgy, must be reckoned as even more important, taken by themselves, than his doctrine on the Word of God. This shows the same weaknesses from the point of view of Catholic faith as his doctrine on salvation; and, as in his doctrine on salvation, these are less weaknesses of his own than an aggravation of weaknesses already apparent in medieval piety: for instance the notion of inspiration which exalts the divine authority of Holy Scripture in a dangerously ambiguous way and at the expense of its human element; and the affirmation of this authority in opposition to that of the Church and her tradition, whence its subjection to all the hazards of individual interpretation. Real and grave as these weaknesses were to show themselves to be, and to the detriment of a restoration of the Word of God to its true place in the spiritual life, it is probable that the positive element in his vivid sense of the Word as God's creative and salvific action—one with the revelation and communication of Christ's grace—had beneficial results outweighing the baleful influence of the errors accompanying it. But his work in bringing the divine Word to the faithful, and in conditions in which they could draw the maximum from it, surely represented the most positive aspect of his achievement. By this alone he brought within the reach of innumerable souls the means of compensating, more or less consciously, for the negative side of his personal influence. It is here that we must look for the primary source of the renewals of Protestantism, renewals that allowed people to separate the positive from the negative elements in Luther's doctrine, allowed them, quite simply, to tap at the source a Christianity which completely transcended his particular influence.

In spite of some slight warpings of the truth—much less serious in fact than an obtuse polemic has for long maintained—Luther's Bible shows substantial fidelity to the original texts, enhanced by an astonishing sense of the biblical idiom and the biblical world, and served by magnificent language in terms of both popular vitality and spiritual elevation. For the first time, Luther's Bible gave a Christian people the possibility of speaking a language that reached its maturity in the act of giving expression to the fundamental Christian message.[10]

Luther's Bible was widely diffused and became the basis of a popular culture both human and religious. It was helped in its work of moulding popular spirituality by the two catechisms in which Luther summarized his spiritual teaching as he saw it. These obviously bear the stamp of his teaching on justification by faith in God's grace alone. Yet in his catechisms he set aside his polemical preoccupations almost entirely—with the equivocal theological constructions they produced—and gave an interpretation of his doctrine that could best be reconciled with traditional faith. Indeed it is hard to find in these manuals—and their influence has been prodigious right up to our own time—more than omissions or inadequacies in their exposition of the Catholic faith. Moreover, the positive elements of the Catholic faith that we find there are among the most central ones, and are frequently expounded with a felicity of wording hard to equal.

His particular charisma lay in the direct and compelling way in which he picked out the spirituality of the dogma, and transmitted the savour of the Bible in terms easily assimilable and marvellously suited to engrave themselves on the popular mind. His commentaries on the Creed, in particular on the doctrines of the Trinity and the redemptive Incarnation, are justly famous for their spiritual beauty and their strength of conviction. Catholic teachers lost no time in realizing this and trying to emulate these commentaries. But we have to admit that they trailed far behind him in the art of expressing the great truths of the faith for simple minds.

Here, for example, is his commentary on the second article of the Apostles' Creed:

> I believe that Jesus Christ the true God, begotten of the Father before all worlds, and also true man born of the virgin Mary, is my Lord, who hath redeemed me a lost and condemned man and hath delivered me from all sins, from death and the power of Satan; not with gold and silver, but with his holy and precious blood, and by his innocent sufferings and death, that I might be wholly his and might live under him in everlasting righteousness, innocency and happiness, in like manner as he himself rose

[10] On Luther and the Bible see H. Bornkamm, *Das Wort Gottes bei Luther*, 1933, and M. Rieu, *Luther and the Scriptures*, Colombus, 1944.

from the dead and liveth and reigneth for ever and ever. This is most assuredly true.[11]

But if we want to understand typically Lutheran piety we must also recognize the place held, or won, by a liturgy that became really popular in Germanic lands for the first time, while remaining astonishingly close to traditional forms.

The Lutheran churches retained more or less entire the externals of Catholic worship: altars, crucifixes, statues, vestments, liturgical chants, lights, incense, etc. And essentially sacramental worship was maintained with a large proportion of the prayers consecrated by tradition. For a long time Luther seems not to have dreamed of introducing modifications other than the reading (or chanting) of the lessons in the vulgar tongue, with a homily on the text of the day. He consented only with regret to an extension of the vulgar tongue, and above all in order to counter sectarian innovations by a number of his disciples in their own territory.

The only really basic modification he initiated, after the progressive disappearance of private Masses, was the reduction of the Canon of the Mass to the words of the consecration, the Preface and the *Sanctus*. He was led to this by his growing opposition to the sacrificial formulae applied to the Eucharist which he tended to interpret as a "work", in opposition to the reception of the salvific Word in faith as an efficacious sign of divine grace. But it is remarkable that here, too, and perhaps more than ever, the modifications he brought to the legacy of the medieval Church, far from going against tendencies that had made their appearance long before him, merely brought them to a head. There is no need to underline that this exclusive concentration on the words of consecration was merely the culmination of a trend already only too evident in medieval theology. In Luther's *Formula Missae* of 1523, the celebrant passes directly from the Preface to the *verba Christi*, the *Sanctus* itself greeting the elevation and making the whole of Mass culminate in the consecration of the species, removed from its traditional context, then comes at once to the Communion. This was but the canonization of a process initiated by medieval piety, where the Presence overshadows the sacrifice, and the Communion itself is seen only from the angle of the individual reception of the Presence.

Again, religious individualism in the Lutheran liturgy, centred on sin and forgiveness and emphasized by the development of formulae of confession, whether just before the Communion or at the beginning of Mass, was not a reform going back to early ideas and

[11] From *The Shorter Catechism.*

practices but a final stage in a disintegrating evolution of the liturgy that had started well before Luther. The reduction of the eucharistic sacrifice to a mere "thanksgiving", in the sense of individual thanks for the gift received from Christ—the only meaning accepted by Luther for the sacrificial words retained in the Eucharist—has the same origin and shows a deviational tendency initiated long before Luther which he merely brought to its culmination.

If many of the Churches that went over to the Reformation were more radical still in jettisoning elements already undervalued in the Middle Ages, we must remember that there were others, both in Germany and Scandinavia, that never consented to the total elimination of the prayers omitted by Luther, and he himself was to show curious regrets in this respect.

However this may be, Lutheran piety deviated from truly traditional Catholic piety by giving the Real Presence and its reception in adoration the pre-eminent place that it had won in the course of the Middle Ages at the expense of the mystery of our communion with both the sacrifice and the Sacrificed. But it is only fair that we should recognize the positive factor contained in a reintegration of the collective celebration to its true place and of the communion of the faithful as well as of the priest, as a possible counterpart to the otherwise catastrophic acceleration of medieval religious individualism, and the no less catastrophic emphasis on the sacramental Presence at the expense of the sacrificial mystery.

But if we are to appreciate the real significance of the transformation wrought on the people's piety, we must realize that the substitution of the *Formula missae* for the ancient Canon involved no change that they would notice: for a long time the secret words recited low by the priest during the singing of the *Sanctus* or the *Benedictus* had hardly been known or followed by the people. Thus the Lutheran Mass gave them a piety in which nearly all the positive elements of medieval popular piety were not only retained but enriched—as much by the meditated hearing of God's Word as by Communion (and frequent at that) as a normal and integral part of the celebration.

To this must be added the enrichment brought by the daily chanting or recitation of the office of Mattins and Vespers in the vulgar tongue (the former comprising the main elements not only of the vigil but of Lauds and Prime), with plentiful lessons from the Bible replacing the medieval choral office. And we must also mention the litany which was restored to its three most venerable elements: a recall to the mysteries of the redemptive incarnation, an invocation for deliverance from all ills, and an intercession for all the Church's needs and for those of sinful and suffering mankind.

The liturgical year was wholly retained, the feasts of the Virgin and the saints not being suppressed but relegated to a secondary place in relation to the proper of the day, and within this framework the restitution of ancient public prayer to the piety of at least the best of the faithful was undoubtedly one of the most positive elements of the Lutheran Reformation, narrowly linked with the popularization of biblical teaching and piety. Luther stabilized the most Catholic possibilities in a way we find it hard to imagine, and this right up to the Thirty Years War, or even the Enlightenment.[12]

But we must not forget the most innovating aspect of all of Luther's Reformation—choral song. This was composed of the content of traditional hymns, sequences and anthems, strongly personalized (though individualism was avoided) and vigorously rhymed, and surely remains a liturgical creation whose effects have never been anything but beneficial. Here again it was the aspects of the reformer's religious themes most in accord with Catholic orthodoxy that were put forward—in virile and largely popular language and music. What these songs were able to achieve in the diffusion of a surely evangelical piety cannot be over-estimated.[13]

Christian Freedom and the Individual Vocation

But we would have a very inadequate picture of Luther's spirituality if we confined our study to his doctrinal principles and their realization in the context of the human soul or the liturgical gathering. For he also revived the primitive doctrine of the universal priesthood of the faithful—though sometimes in words so extravagant that they ended in depreciating the ecclesiastical ministry—and he associated it with striking success with the doctrine of lay action marked with the Christian imprint. If we want to understand the basic significance he gave to each of these strands, we must look at his short treatise on *Christian Freedom*.

Here the distinction between faith and works is again discussed, but it becomes the distinction between the Christian life considered in its source and the Christian life considered in its effects, that is to say between the interior life—the direct contact with Christ in the living faith that should be its soul—and the external activity into which it should overflow and show itself, above all in brotherly

[12] The most comprehensive work on the Lutheran liturgy is *The Lutheran Liturgy* by Luther D. Reed, 2nd ed., Philadelphia, 1959.

[13] On Lutheran chorals see P. H. Lang, *Music in Western Civilization*, New York, 1941, pp. 207 *et seq.*, and W. Nelle, *Geschichte des deutschen evangelischen Kirchenliedes*, Hamburg, 1909.

love. The inner man is king and priest through his direct bond with Christ, with the Word of God received in faith. That is why he is free from all external needs and obligations (since, with Christ and the faith that binds him to Him, he has all that is needful and the one thing needful). However, as this does not prevent the outer man from being subjected here and now to bodily needs, he is also concerned with the bodily needs of others. And it is in effective charity that our faith in Christ will show itself, together with the trustful and exultant gratitude that should inspire all our life of grace, as it should also be the witness of our faith before men.

The priesthood common to all Christ's members thus operates in all the faithful, as much by the glorification of God in the prayer of faith as by service to our brothers, whatever be the form in which we are called to serve them, according to the condition in which God has placed us and the aptitudes he has given us. Thus it is no longer only the life of the priest or the religious that is priestly or religious, but the life of every lay Christian, provided it is illumined by faith and animated by love.

This picture of things lends itself to two possible deviations: either (as we have said) Luther's views might lead to a depreciation of clerical life or of the life consecrated by vows, and an underestimation of the apostolic mission given by Christ to certain people; or they might lead (as inevitable consequence) to a confusion between the body of the Church and Christian society in general, and hence to attributing to secular authority what should by rights belong to apostolic authority. Another typical example, let us say, of so-called reformation in fact deriving from a corruption that had been threatening throughout the Middle Ages and especially since the fourteenth century.

But it is none the less true that Luther was the first, at least since patristic times, to proclaim the priesthood of the faithful so clearly and to propose so concretely a genuinely lay spirituality such as would sanctify life in the world with all its domestic or professional responsibilities. However, an excessive pessimism about the world tended to weaken the force of this initial statement on more than one occasion—a pessimism deriving from an exaggerated distinction between the outer and the inner man which was only medieval Augustinianism with its neo-Platonic and pessimistic vein pushed to an extreme. But, more important, Luther's teaching on the authority of princes could well stifle all individual or collective effort towards the effective Christianization of social and political life, while his exaggerations in defining each person's vocation in terms of the place that birth alone had given him ran the risk of leading to mere passive acquiescence towards given situations. The fact remains, however, that Luther was the first to restore all their vigour to the apostolic affirmations concerning the total consecration of the Christian's life.

And faced with spiritual systems centred more and more on "religious" whose lives were ceasing to represent a perfect lay life but a clericalized life outside the laity, Luther was equally the first to expound the possibility of, and the practical way for, a consecration of the ordinary lay life.

Reformed Protestantism and Zwingli

Notwithstanding Lutheranism's ambiguous formulations and unjustifiable polemical systematizations which tended from the start to distort its rich spiritual affirmations and hence to create schism through heresy, we must recognize that the Lutheran Church (at least in the measure in which it fulfilled its founder's aims) never appeared and never presented itself as other than a Catholic Church superficially modified or altered. But while Lutheranism was developing along these lines, other forms of what was to be called Protestantism came into being, and these proposed to replace the Catholic Church from top to bottom with another Church, or rather with other Churches.

Even in Germany Luther soon found himself faced with disciples demanding that he should preach total anarchy not only in the Church but in the State, by reviving the apocalyptic evangelism that had been rampant ever since the twelfth century. He was so alarmed by this sectarian evangelism—which was nothing more, in fact, than a continuation of medieval sects but now no longer stemming from Catholicism but from Protestantism (because it encouraged individualism and called authority into question)—that he instigated violent and bloody repression against it. As this anarchical sectarianism had never more than a relatively marginal existence within Protestantism, and only half belonged to it, we shall discuss it later.

At about the same time, however, other "reformers" rose against Luther of whom he could not so easily get rid, as they were given a certain intellectual and social respectability by the support of local authorities (without which, in fact, he himself could not have kept going). Moreover, he was astute enough to see that they represented a greater menace than the sects from the point of view of the reform he wished to promote.

Among those "reformers" who had no desire to be Lutherans, Luther himself singled out Ulrich Zwingli as being the most representative. He came from Zurich and was canon and preacher of the *Grossmünster*, and this remained his setting to the end, for his activities were much more limited geographically than Luther's. Unlike Luther, he was less the creator or inspirer of the reformed Churches more or less similar to his own which developed throughout the Rhine Valley, than a strikingly typical example of the collective state of mind of which they were the product. It is important that we should study this state of mind, as it contributed to forming average Protestantism much more than did Lutheranism.[14]

This reformed Protestantism, supported especially in Germany by a number of secular authorities such as the Hohenzollerns of Prussia, tried by all possible means to take the place of Lutheranism, notably by insistent propaganda which included measures of constraint and spoliation, though it usually stopped short of open persecution, as this would compromise people whose favourite theme was freedom of conscience and simple rational fidelity to the Gospel. It was because these Churches were later to adopt the practical organization put into effect by Calvin that they are persistently and misleadingly called "Calvinist" by Catholics, though they have always called themselves simply "reformed". This is misleading because the "reformed" Churches as a whole, and leaving aside the Presbyterian synodal organization and some minority groups of Scottish and Dutch theologians, have always felt the greatest repugnance for the theological theses that properly belong to Calvinism. It was Zwingli who so excellently expressed the basic mentality of the "reformed" churchmen (even more than their doctrine, which was always fluid) even if we cannot strictly call them his disciples.

We can describe their mentality historically by saying that it was a radical, and above all a rationalizing, form of those "evangelical" tendencies to be found among the intellectual bourgeoisie on the eve of Luther's Reformation and influenced to a greater or lesser degree by Erasmus.

It would go beyond the scope of our study to make a detailed analysis of the pre-Reformation scene, for it was extremely complex and lent itself to the most divergent developments and orientations. But it would, for instance, be a great error to imagine that the Protestant Reformation was the only possible outcome, or the only logical issue, of biblical and evangelical humanism, widespread as this belief is. This is made amply plain by Anagnine's and Toffanin's works[15] and also by M. Bataillon's admirable

---

[14] Zwingli's literary output may be found in M. Schuler and J. Schulthess, *Huldreich Zwinglis Werke* (Zurich, 1828–1842, 8 vols., completed by G. Schulthess and K. Marthaler, 1861).
[15] Cf. E. Anagnine, *Giovanni Pico della Mirandola*, Bari, 1937, and G. Toffanin,

Erasmus and Spain[16]—works that show that the most direct and natural outcome of Christian humanism of which Erasmus remains the major exponent (with his application of critical philology to the Christian texts and his discovery of history as human development) was a "return to the sources" of a kind to favour a reform of Catholicism in conformity with its deepest nature. This is what we find in the Spanish Erasmian Catholics such as Gimenez de Cisneros or Sancho Carranza; or the Italian ones with the group of cardinals round Paul III such as Morone, Sadoleto, Seripando and Contarini; or the English ones with Thomas More, John Colet and Pole (though the last named was more directly linked with Italy); or the Dutch ones with Adrian Florenz (the future Adrian VI). All that was positive and not narrowly conservative in the Catholic Reformation inaugurated by the Council of Trent was an outcome—and much more besides.

On the other hand the type of sociological Catholicism which was conservative as to forms but little concerned with the spirit, the Catholicism of the Curia and well-provided churchmen and a largely negative Counter-reformation, found its main cultural support in a paganizing humanism, decorative, even sensual.

Another form of the pagan tendency in humanism—more philosophical, rationalizing, neo-Aristotelian or neo-Stoical—paved the way for modern unbelief and an ideal of the State freed from all spiritual tutelage, which would lead in its turn to the absolutist, then totalitarian, forms of contemporary society.

Protestantism itself, and especially "reformed" Protestantism, proceeded from a Christian humanism still steeped in the platonizing Augustinianism and rationalizing Nominalist scholasticism that had developed at the end of the Middle Ages, and was thus constantly threatened with being overwhelmed by the preceding tendency, that of purely secularizing rationalism, though we must not confuse the one with the other.

It was of this humanism and this Protestantism that Zwingli was so characteristic. Luther had placed himself firmly within the reformist humanism of the first type, that of Erasmus and his disciples, and was not to be drawn away from Catholic tradition save by what could mix (in him, as in Erasmus and others) in half-conscious connivance with that current. But polemics hardened this secondary element in him, whereas more searching reflection in Erasmians who had remained Catholics gradually managed to

---

La Religione degli Umanisti, Bologna, 1950, and *Storia del Umanesimo*, Bologna, 1952 (3 vols.).

[16] See if possible the Spanish edition, revised and augmented by the author, Mexico, 1950 (*Erasmo y España*).

eliminate it. Calvin in many respects went the opposite way. Setting out from the Christian humanism that had broken away from ancient tradition, to be dominated more and more by the Augustinianism and semi-rationalism of the later Middle Ages, he gradually weaned himself from this tendency so as to come ever closer to fundamentally Catholic humanism. And that was precisely where the "reformed" churchmen refused to follow him.

While taking advantage of the convenient structure he gave to their churches, they accepted little or nothing of the religion he had set up, which they viewed as reactionary. They preferred the spirituality to which Zwingli gave the first coherent expression, a spirituality freed in practice from traditional dogma even when it kept something of it through atavism or, quite simply, so as to avoid going against the conservatism of the authorities or the simple faithful.

The "reformed" religion in fact had no dogmatic system despite sporadic efforts, from Calvin to Barth, to provide itself with one. Its simplified religious humanism, which superimposed the moralism, spiritualism and somewhat limited rationalism of the preceding intellectual generations on its historical criticism (to the point of confusing them), produced a religion which was but the *Devotio moderna* stripped of the Catholic supernatural—which it was anyway dragging after it rather than being nourished by. The Gospel became the whole of religion, but a Gospel from which the pure psychologism of a religion centred on man had in practice emptied out the supernatural. The supernatural was already redundant before being formally ousted in the second Protestant generation by more daring thinkers such as Socinus, Castellion and Servetus, precursors of all the theologians who were to call themselves in turn "Unitarian", "rationalist", "radical", "liberal" and "Bultmannian".

In the various confessions of faith that he produced, Zwingli certainly starts off with the dogmas of the Trinity, the Incarnation and the Redemption by the cross, and even the Marian dogmas of perpetual virginity and the immaculate conception. But there is no sign that these doctrines played any real part either in his own spiritual life or in that which he preached to others, for they are referred to only in passing and as if as a reminder.

He then goes on to expound justification by faith, having made it plain that he discovered it himself in the New Testament and owes nothing to Luther. This is justification by means of a wholly interior piety towards Christ, replacing any form of religion where religious institutions (such as the sacraments or the practice of traditional asceticism) have any intrinsic value. Such institutions are not tolerated except as a pedagogic means to back up the word and sustain a wholly interior religiosity; they are acceptable only as concessions to the weak and the less intelligent. The sacraments enshrine no mystery; Christ is not present in the Eucharist in any way that we would understand. They are no more than vivid images that speak to the simple and remind us of what we know already by means of the word: the love that God has shown us in Jesus Christ.

Moreover, Christ himself is understood not as God made man—though he is always qualified as the Son of God and the Redeemer and there are references to his salvific death and indeed to his resurrection—but as a man exceptionally aware of the presence of God within him. The Christology is radically Nestorian, and the soteriology tends to explain expiation and substitution in terms of a supreme example of obedience as reparation for sin. Original sin is reduced to a sort of moral sickness as opposed to a condition of guilt, so that the Redeemer becomes a sort of doctor of souls, a religious psychiatrist before his time. He saves souls by turning them towards the true life of children of God by means of the communicative virtue of his example.

There is nothing supernatural here. Indeed we could say that Zwingli achieved the realization of a perfect natural religion or morality—where the Gospel is reduced to an interiorization of the Old Testament precepts, and the beatitudes and the announcement of the Kingdom of God are no more than a picturesque way of describing the advent of a wholly inner religion and a religious moralism instead of ceremonial religion. The folly of the cross, the ecstasy of the soul, have no place in this bourgeois and rational piety, where the parables are seen as no more than a poetic and popular expression of a religion of commonsense.

But Zwingli resembled Calvin on one point, and this was in his strong social sense—though for a long time it did not receive much response in this type of Protestantism. Like all the reformers, he held to the medieval ideal of Christendom as fused with the social body. This led him to an early attempt at a democratico-Christian constitution and a justification of the sacraments of Baptism and the Lord's Supper as holidays on which the body social could affirm its evangelical inspiration. It is hard to say whether he had any more success than Calvin in this part of his programme. Though the free cities and small bourgeois states greeted Protestantism as a liberation from the Church and her authority, they showed no great willingness to let the reformed preachers impose a social and political ideal on them, any more than the bishops or the religious orders before them. And the majority of the faithful won over to this type of Protestantism only retained the sacraments because they did not see how they could give them up without riding roughshod over the letter of the New Testament. Before long, however, they were retained only as an embarrassing survival with hardly any religious significance apart from the somewhat childish imagery that people were still happy to see in them.

This was the reformed spirituality which became as it were the basis of common Protestant spirituality wherever powerful Lutheran or Calvinist influences were not at work (or, later, Pietistic or Catholicizing ones). It presented itself as a purification of religion, a rational simplification aimed at bringing it back to the Gospel. This theme recurs constantly in Zwingli's writings and formed the basis of Protestant apologetics with regard to Catholicism. In fact reformed "evangelism" threw in a whole lot of pseudo-evidences together with the Gospel and seemed hardly able to distinguish the one from the other—pseudo-evidences that had nothing biblical about them and were no more than the residue left by the *Devotio moderna*, medieval Augustinianism and Nominalist scholasticism.

The first of them was the opposition between the inner and the outer (which had played a big part with Luther but had never gone as far as this). The outer, whether it meant Church-as-institution, the sacraments, or ascetic practices, was automatically reduced to the role of being no more than an expression (always suspect and dangerous at that) of the inner, or else was condemned outright as materialistic and idolatrous. This was plainly a direct result of Platonism as absorbed into medieval Augustinianism, according to which man is spirit, that is to say a soul foreign to matter and receiving from matter nothing but corruption. The purpose of this was to achieve the "worship in spirit and in truth" of St John's Gospel, and flee the "hypocrisy of the Pharisees" denounced in the Sermon on the Mount. But they overlooked the fact that the Sermon on the Mount did not condemn external practices as such but only their lack of concord with the inner man, and especially an exaggerated use of them with a view to covering up inner deficiencies. They were mistaken, too, in interpreting "worship in spirit and in truth" as "spiritual and sincere worship" (using "spiritual" in the sense of "what goes on in the soul"), whereas the Johannine phrase means worship in which the divine Spirit (not man's) is the principle, and where God's "truth" (that is to say the divine reality of the Incarnation) is the corner-stone.

In a more general way, despite a whole series of tendentious interpretations in the use of biblical phrases which has become so customary in Protestantism of this type that we hardly notice it any more, this aspect of their religion in fact derived from an intellectualistic dualism that had nothing particularly biblical or evangelical about it, and was indeed at the opposite pole to the Bible.

The same could be said of their conviction that evangelical religion was one and the same as the "religion within the limits of reason" of which Kant was to speak, merely putting into words what had already been taken for granted by Zwingli and all those whose inclinations he so admirably expressed. This conviction ignored the apocalyptic element in the Gospel of the Kingdom, the transcendence of the Spirit in the New Testament, and the "mystery" lying at the heart of the synoptic parables and St Paul's Gospel—the "mystery" that makes St John's "signs" not a mere expression of a world wholly within man but an irruption "into the world" of what is "not of the world".

And finally this religion of conscience, in which conscience was less the voice of the Spirit than the Spirit merely the exaltation of conscience, completely ignored Christian heroism: the folly of the cross, the boundless generosity of "the love of God spread in our hearts by the Holy Spirit" (which is not to say that it did not have a nobility of its own). It was a religion so reasonable that it was latent rationalism—in spite of seeing itself as a child of the Gospel —and was in fact no more than the last fruit of a scholasticism that had become impenetrable to the Christian mystery, before eliminating religion itself in a free-thought faintly tinged by mystical moralism.

Sincere and moving as piety towards Christ may have been in these Christians who were so biblical in desire but so platonizing and rationalizing in fact, it was a piety that did no more than colour with religious emotion and tenderness what otherwise would have been a mere intellectualist ethic. But when it was coupled with a dogma from which it did not really proceed and of which it would rid itself without much pain or effort, we may well wonder whether it retained of the Gospel much more than "the perfume of an empty vase". Though Jesus was still proclaimed divine and called the Saviour, he was no more than the ideal image of the religious man, but in the context of a religion whose God had become so interior to man that we may wonder whether he was anything more than a symbolic expression of our highest aspirations. A contemporary Protestant theologian such as Tillich might have delighted Zwingli by his affirmation that the Protestant principle is the rejection of all mediation between man and God, but he would have shocked him by adding that this God was nothing but the symbol of his best and deepest "me". Though, in saying that, was he not merely extracting the integral logic from the ambiguous "evangelism" of reformed Protestantism? It is at least tenable.

The Calvinist Reaction

Historians of Protestantism, whether Protestant, Catholic or agnostic, have inclined to interpret Luther's intransigent opposition to Zwingli on the question of the eucharistic presence as no more than indicating his basic conservatism and his "medieval" biblical literalism. But a careful study of the controversy points to the sure instinct by which Luther felt a purely symbolic interpretation of *Hoc est corpus meum* to be a striking example of the tendency to volatilize the biblical revelation on the pretext of spiritualizing it. Yet he himself had become too involved with the platonizing dialectics about the inner and the outer, and with rationalizing individualism (much more medieval in fact than his supposed literalism), to be able successfully to oppose the growing ascendancy of both these strains within the reforming movement. This was the task that fell to Calvin, and it constituted his greatness. But he had a weakness of his own, and this lay in his lack of understanding of Catholic tradition—which made him put forward a sort of neo-Catholicism or substitute Catholicism rather than extract the essential from the Catholic tradition and leave the caricatures alone. The product of his inventive genius was artificially justified by an appeal to primitive Christianity. The Catholic Church purified of its corruptions, such as he attempted, or thought he attempted, to re-establish within a Protestantism in sociological and doctrinal decomposition, was entirely his brainchild. And if most of the reformed Churches took over the firmly organized framework that the Calvinist Church offered them, they would never (a small number of theologians apart) accept the Calvinist system that gave it its point and tried to infuse it with a soul.[17]

Calvin's work, however, positive as it was from many points of view, remained enclosed within the intellectual limits that Luther, too, had been unable to sunder. The same inadequate notion of divine transcendence, inherited from Nominalism, was never called in question, and Calvin's rigorous logic drew inexorable conclusions from it which contributed in the long run to the slim success of his doctrine. The same applied to Augustinian Platonism which prevented him from providing a notion of the sacraments that

[17] There is a Calvin bibliography in G. Léonard, *Histoire générale du Protestantisme*, vol. 1, pp. 352 *et seq.* We can find the whole of Calvin's works from vol. 29 to vol. 87 of *Corpus Reformatorum*, edited in Brunswick beginning in 1863 by G. Baum, E. Cunitz and E. Reuss.

really joined up with primitive tradition, anxious as he was to reinstate them as more than mere images.

Calvin was a legal man and a humanist and had been reared (so it seems) in a profound contempt for all things clerical. His theological culture was self-taught, and he never (unlike Luther) had any sympathetic understanding of Catholic tradition either as regards its worship or its theology. In his desire to make *tabula rasa* so as to rebuild the Church exclusively on what was given in the New Testament (he was wholly medieval in his lack of a sense of history), he took from it only extracts here and there which, isolated from their context and interpreted in terms of a foreign frame of thought, he then built into a system. It was doubtless an admirably coherent system, but in building it he does not seem to have realized how much he depended on *a prioris* that were all the less criticized the more they were tacitly received from the "corrupt" Church which he proudly claimed to be replacing at all points. Thus in the greatest as much as in the mediocre Reformation thinkers—all of whom were logicians rather than historians— we find the same illusion: the "primitive" that they wanted to reestablish to the detriment of the evolved (judged to be irremediably decadent) was in fact very often only the most recent; a recent too near for them to be able to criticize it, and operating as a screen against all genuine rediscovery of the essential.[18]

The Calvinist Doctrine of Sanctification

From the point of view of our spirituality, the most important complement brought by Calvin to Lutheranism was his doctrine of sanctification. The most decisive correction which he imprinted on reformed piety—in great danger of turning towards a humanism that was only superficially Christian—was the way in which he linked up this sanctification with Lutheran justification.

He was a firm supporter of Luther's doctrine on purely gratuitous justification received through faith alone. And in one sense, though he made many explicit declarations on the necessarily dogmatic and objective content of faith, he abandoned none of Luther's personalism either, for he saw faith and the certainty of personal predestination as one and the same thing. But he obviated the danger of subjectivism inherent in this position by removing saving faith from the perilous isolation in which it had been placed by the relegation

---

[18] The best study on Calvinist doctrine is vol. IV of *Origines de la Réforme*, by P. Imbart de la Tour, *Calvin et l'Institution chrétienne*, Paris, 1935, though an inadequate knowledge of Catholic theology prevents him from placing Calvin's personal attitudes in their exact context. J.-D. Benoit has also published a good critical edition of *L'Institution chrétienne*, Paris, 1960.

of "works" outside salvation, together with the inner transformation of the believer. Faith, he said, was authentic and saving only
if it showed itself in a sanctification of the whole being.

Whenever Luther was cornered on this point by his adversaries,
he, too, answered that he did not eliminate works but made them
an inevitable by-product of faith. But his repeated statements
about their lack of necessary connection with salvation, together
with his description of the "saved" as *simul peccator et justus*—
seeming to exclude not only all possibility of spiritual progress, but
also any change in the "justified" man in relation to the condemned
man that he had been the moment before—are hardly reconcilable
with his statements in the opposite sense.

Calvin, on the other hand, while also maintaining that justification precedes, and is hence independent of, any possible works that
man may do, added that a faith that did not produce both external
works and the progressive sanctification of our whole being was but
an appearance of faith and therefore would not have justified us.

As with others of Calvin's exegetical expositions, we may question this clear-cut distinction, given that he retained the close connection between "justification" and "sanctification". Modern
exegetes, indeed, are more or less agreed that it is an interpolation.
On the other hand, it certainly does not link up with any of the
theories of grace that had become classic in the Middle Ages,
though it certainly links up in a roundabout way with the essential
of the traditional Catholic position and the doctrine of the New
Testament. The pure gratuity of salvation and of man's whole life
under grace is maintained there, at the same time as the necessary
transformation of his whole life without which "grace" and "salvation" are reduced to a *flatus vocis*.

Calvin linked up again with traditional doctrine when he
described this new life as death to self. But he departed from it not
so much when he criticized monastic asceticism (which he seemed
only able to envisage under Pelagian or dolorist distortions) as
when he attempted to outline the positive aspect of the new life. It
was a life that the Holy Spirit created within us, yes, but the only
gift of the Spirit that Calvin seemed willing to enlarge upon was the
gift of understanding the Scriptures. And in his rigid rejection of
all history as development, he went so far as to identify the content
of the Old and New Testaments to such a point that his vision of
Christ's law was reduced to a thorough understanding of the ten
commandments. On this point we cannot see that he went any
further than Zwingli's down-to-earth notion of the "evangelical"
life as a thoroughly bourgeois humanism. The generous impulses
of *agape*, together with any meaning of the cross other than as

representing stoical support in adversity, were as closed to him as forms of traditional asceticism that went beyond strict moral discipline. In this respect he fell very short of the best in Luther.

But the most serious defect in his doctrine went deeper. It lay in a persistent incapacity to insert the effects of grace within our humanity while effectively conceiving of its radically supernatural character.

Again we come up against the inadequate grasp of divine transscendence that marks Calvin, too, as a child of his time; not because of any innovation his time produced, but because of its inheritance from the late Middle Ages.

Certainly Calvin extolled the theme of God's glory more than any of his contemporaries—more, even, that St Ignatius himself. But, as Imbart de la Tour has rightly pointed out, God, for Calvin, could only be great in so far as man was small. His greatness was not the greatness of the infinite but the greatness of a humanly jealous God, jealous because he was only comparatively great.

All this showed itself in Calvin's rejection of, or wilful ignorance of, the idea of grace inhering in man, in whatever way this is understood. God certainly acted in man for his sanctification, yet for that very reason the resultant sanctified action could not be man's. After justification, just as before justification, the Council of Orange's verdict on the not-yet-justified man remained wholly true: of our own, we have only sins and lies. So not only could we not be proud of our good actions (everyone is agreed on that), but they were good only in as much as they remained foreign to us—actions wrought in us by God but not becoming our own for that.

It might appear that this was merely a paradoxical way of putting things, such as we find in all mystics and many preachers when they try to show the impossibility of separating off the part in a good action that might be exclusively our own, or of conceiving of our possible autonomous participation in it in relation to the grace in which we share.

But there was worse to come. Calvin as much as Luther, and much more than Zwingli, feared and wanted to exclude from the authentic Reformation all those whom he called "*phantastiques*", or sectarian illuminati. It followed that he refused to recognize any light of the Holy Spirit within us other than as manifested in an understanding of the true meaning of the Scriptures. Even this can have a perfectly acceptable meaning if only we admit that the true meaning is ultimately "mystery", in the Pauline sense of the word. But it does not seem that this was Calvin's meaning. For him, *fides ex auditu* had to be taken in its most literal sense. Contrary to what many of his followers would understand by what he called "the interior witness of the Holy Spirit", the Holy Spirit (according to him) does not give us any sort of personal, intuitive or supernatural interpretation of an obscure text. For Calvin as for Zwingli, and much more than for Luther, there was no obscurity whatsoever in the Bible. It was within the reach of every intelligence prepared to do some elementary work and not already too perverted to discover the obvious meaning. The *testimonium internum Spiritus Sancti*, far from being an inspiration that would give us immediate, experimental knowledge—however obscure—of what the Scriptures are about, signified an adherence to the letter of the Scriptures (judged to be transparently clear) that God made possible by the entirely natural play of our intelligence; and there was even no need for this to be uplifted by grace (in whatever way this be understood). Once again: in Calvin there was nothing remotely equivalent to, for instance, the Thomist doctrine on elevating and sanctifying grace.

This was brought into sharp relief by a third consideration. Calvin made double predestination the corner-stone of his entire system. In other words he rejected absolutely the distinction between what God wills and what God permits. In his view God willed, and in consequence produced, in exactly the same way, the obduracy of some and the salvation of others. There, in the last analysis, lay the only mystery that he admitted: that of God's will. But God's will operated no differently in men whether it was leading them to, or refusing them, salvation. It merely opened its eyes to some while it closed them to others. But there was nothing substantially different in them themselves in the one case as in the other. The obduracy of some was God's action in them, no more or less positive than the salvation of others. In the one case as in the other it was by a providential disposition of circumstances that God led them to their salvation or to their perdition, and nowhere does it appear that it was by any special communication of himself to the most intimate part of their being that he saved those who were saved.

This finds supplementary corroboration in the fact that Calvin regarded sanctification as something that could and should be obtained from outside by an efficacious organization of Christian society. Calvinist Geneva has often been described, with its progressive constriction in a corset of infinitely detailed rules, and its organization of a system of espionage and punishments, with hardly any place left for a private life, let alone a personal one. But we must not forget that in Calvin's own opinion (we have only to read his letters, sermons and admonitions to the town councils) there was no such thing as a genuinely Calvinist Geneva. The realization of his ideal to which the *"Magistrats"* never resigned themselves (and can we blame them!) would have been something along the lines of the Jesuit state of Paraguay, with all the population led to church, to work, or to the wholesome recreations permitted by authority, category by category, in rows and in uniform.

We can understand how this ideal appealed to the sovereigns of Prussia, and before long they were converted from a vague Lutheranism to the reformed religion. But we can also understand how the worthy burghers of the free cities of Switzerland and the Rhine Valley never really submitted to it, still less the French Huguenots and the good and studious Dutch. And it was only the uplift of Puritanism that made this yoke tolerable in Scotland, England and New England. But Puritanism, as we shall see, had itself been possible only through a subtle metamorphosis of Calvinism. Meanwhile we can easily understand the reaction of Luther's disciple, Melanchthon, always ready for diplomatic compromises: Had this doctrine anything to do with Christianity, he asked, or was it not a superficially Christianized form of Stoicism?

The rejection of all substantial sanctification of human doing and being in grace, carried right to the heart of the Calvinist doctrine of sanctification itself, cannot but lead to the following conclusions —paradoxical, but in the logic of the system: the desire to uphold the transcendence of grace by avoiding admixing it in any way with human action, added to the desire none the less to sanctify human action in the justified, necessarily culminates, if not in a salvation that is but a *flatus vocis* (as in forensic justification), then in what is to all intents and purposes Pelagianism. In other words it culminates in an activism in which we are forced to find, first in suggestions and then in external constraints, the driving power that we refuse to find any more in inner grace. Thus not only do we come back willy-nilly from grace to law, but from law to legalism, and finally to a fatalistic voluntarism which, as Melanchthon rightly noted, can hardly be distinguished from ancient Stoicism.[19]

The Calvinist Sacraments

Calvin's doctrine on the sacraments and in particular on the Eucharist represents another effort to recover an essential element of Christianity that had been imperilled or simply ignored by the reformed Churches. Here in particular we have to admire his attempt to restore depth and mystery to Christianity, though once again we shall have to note the ultimately deceptive nature of the undertaking.

[19] On all this see Imbart de la Tour, *op. cit.*, pp. 85 *et seq.*, and J. Boisset, *Sagesse et Sainteté d'après Calvin*, Paris, 1957.

Unlike Zwingli, Calvin held that the sacraments were more than mere symbolic gestures with no real content of their own. They were more than just signs that we give of our faith, but seals or pledges by which God ratifies the promises of his Word. They had an effective content, and faith alone could grasp it. The Lord's Supper entailed the real presence of the body and blood of the Lord (rejected completely by Zwingli and the other Swiss and Alsatian reformers). On the other hand Calvin rejected the Lutheran statement of a presence *in, cum, sub pane* as well as the Catholic doctrine of transubstantiation, because for Calvin Christ's body could not be anywhere but in heaven, and there could be no question of bringing it down to the level of the species. But the Word of God, by offering us Christ's body and blood by means of the species, raised us up to the heaven where he dwelt, so that we were truly nourished by his flesh and blood, though spiritually.

There can be no doubt that Calvin wanted this to be understood in just as real a sense as the Catholic or Lutheran sense of presence. It was the corner-stone of his mystical doctrine of the union of the Christian with Christ and of his incorporation with his risen being, and formed the basis of his doctrine of the Church. All this is very Pauline and seems to bring us very near to Catholic doctrine. Moreover, Calvin drew the logical conclusion and insisted on frequent communion—without very much success, be it said, even in Geneva. He would have liked to restore the Eucharistic Supper to its normal place after the service of readings and prayers, at least every Sunday.

But to return to his theory of presence—and once again we are up against his prejudiced repudiation of any genuine conjunction of the Creator with his creature. But if this was denied in the eucharistic species, it seems at least to be admitted in the faithful. But in what sense? How are we to understand this presence that does not really come down to us but to which we ascend? Calvin tells us that it operates through faith in the word attached to the sacrament. His intention is obviously to confer the maximum of reality on the divine Word and to assure us that faith possesses itself effectively of the reality offered. But his explicit refusal to admit that the presence is objective, that it is offered to the unbelieving communicant just as much as to the believer (though his lack of faith would prevent him from perceiving it), creates the same ambiguity that we saw in the matter of the presence of the Spirit in the work of sanctification. The believer's ascent to heaven so as to unite himself with Christ by faith, which faith is released by the word accompanying bread that remains bread and in which the gift from on high is in no way present—surely this is no more than the thought or feeling created in him by the word accepted in faith?

Once again we are up against the two alternatives: either there is no sacred reality effectively communicated to man, or else the communication is reduced to a mere psychological process in which the sign and the word intervene in the form of substantially unchanged species of this world, just as other species or elements of the visible world influence us in one way or another. In the Calvinist sacrament, either faith does not truly join up with its object (the spiritual manducation of Christ's body) or else faith joins up with it only in this ambiguous sense of the word faith— that is as maintaining itself by the sight of the sign and the sound of the word. Whatever Calvin may say, we have surely come back to the Zwinglian sacrament—that is, a purely mental evocation of the object of faith, in which faith expresses itself; and not an efficacious sign given by God which really communicates the object to man.[20]

The Calvinist Church and our Incorporation with Christ

The same praiseworthy endeavour to rediscover the reality and mystery of Christianity is apparent in Calvinist ecclesiology, but it always ends up in the same deception.

Nothing is more revealing of Calvin's consciously neo-Catholic reaction than the space he allotted to the Church in the successive editions of his *Institutes*—from a few pages to a quarter of the work. But still more important is the formal reappearance of a Church that is the mother of believers because the mother of their faith, a Church that is neither the invisible ultra-Augustinian Church of Luther in his first phase, nor the merely religious organisation handed over to the supposedly Christian State and depending on its authority alone, such as Luther set up later to combat sectarian anarchy.

Contrary to what Melanchthon said in the Augsburg Confession, the Calvinist Church was not just the Word faithfully preached and sacraments celebrated in conformity with their institution. The Calvinist Church had a structure of its own independent of the State whether Christian or not, and on Calvin's express word it proceeded from the divine will as affirmed in the New Testament. However, though he thought he was establishing a Church based

---

[20] On Calvin's eucharistic doctrine, see two articles by J. Cadier, "La présence réelle dans le Calvinisme" and "La Doctrine calviniste de la Sainte-Cène", in *Etudes théologiques et religieuses*, Montpellier, 1938 and 1951. Cf. R. S. Wallace, *Calvin's Doctrine of the Word and the Sacrament*, Edinburgh, 1953, and chap. 1 of Howard G. Hageman, *Pulpit and Table*, London, 1962.

institutionally on Christ and the apostles—he wanted to build it through the hierarchy of the councils of "elders" holding together and maintaining the pastoral ministry by their authority—his Church was in fact his own reconstruction of a model supposedly provided by Scripture. It was in no way whatsoever the product of continuous and organic growth, starting with Christ and his apostles and proceeding through the regular succession of bishops receiving from the apostles, then transmitting in their turn, a personal mission from the Saviour. Nothing of this kind was implicit in the rite of ordination by the laying on of hands as he hoped to restore it. This expressed no more than the commission by the contemporary community of a function exercised in its name. In other words we have the same story with the Church and its ministry as we had with the sacraments: they transmitted nothing, strictly speaking, and they contained nothing. They summoned up a heavenly Church which made one with the body of the risen Christ. They did not bring the mysterious presence down into our midst. They merely raised up our thoughts to it through the witness of the word and the signs that accompanied it, while conforming our wills to it by authoritarian methods.

In a Church such as this we do not see how the Christian's incorporation in Christ would have been anything else but his eucharistic communion. Once again we come up against the ineluctable alternatives: either no union at all, or this deceptive union—deceptive because ultimately wholly human and purely psychological—melting away into the inculcation of a teaching, and imposed conformity from without to the legalistic norms this teaching prescribed.

In fact the very idea of the living continuity of a tradition—the natural accompaniment of an enduring presence—was so foreign to Calvin that in his efforts at reconstruction it seems never to have crossed his mind to borrow from the liturgical tradition in which the Church had traced her continuity. He certainly imposed, or tried to impose, obligatory formulae for the prayers accompanying biblical reading, the Lord's Supper and baptism, but these were all his own inventions, like the Church whose expression they were intended to be. They were not the product of the true Church of the New Testament continuing right down to our own time, but of a theology based *in abstracto* on New Testament texts interpreted in terms of *a prioris* deeply foreign to it.[21]

---

[21] Imbart de la Tour was the first to point out the importance of Calvin's evolution on the doctrine of the Church (*op. cit.*, pp. 98 *et seq.*). See too Auguste Lecerf's studies on Calvin's ecclesiology in his *Etudes calviennes*, Paris, 1949.

The Glory of God

Calvin's most important contribution to Protestant spirituality was his conception of God's glory, or, to put it better, God's glorification, as the final end of Christianity.

When Luther reduced all Christianity to the dialogue between the Word and faith, the dialogue itself being reduced to the acceptance of saving grace in man's justification, he unknowingly brought to a head the ever-growing anthropocentric orientation of medieval piety. He had reacted strongly, however, against Zwingli's deeply secularised Christianity. But this instinctive reaction would have lacked the effective means of asserting itself in a genuine restoration of theocentrism had it not been for Calvin and his *Soli Deo gloria* superimposed on *Sola gratia*.

We might say that Calvin understood and expressed with unequalled power how the salvation of man by grace—far from reducing God to being viewed by man as nothing but the source of his good—brought man back to viewing himself (even in as much as saved) as nothing but the docile instrument of God's glory. In God's glory lay the final significance of man's sanctification and the reason for its crucial importance in the Calvinist perspective. Man is not saved merely because punishment for his fault has been removed from him, nor even because blessedness has been promised him, but because he is dedicated to the only life that has significance —a life wholly given over to the glorification of God, in action as in prayer.

God's glory, as Calvin understood it, lay first and foremost in his action, his power acknowledged as the only one that counts, the only one that is good, the only one that is real: there lay the first object of justifying faith. With the result that all man's doing and all man's being could be devoted to nothing but blessed obedience to the divine will alone.

The grandeur of this vision of divine glory, or rather of divine glory *alone*, explains Calvinist iconoclasm. No picture, statue or intermediary of any kind could be placed between God and man without thereby becoming an idol in which the notion of the true God foundered. But also no other goal could be proposed to man except that of serving the Almighty by conforming all his thoughts and all his wishes to his design alone.

And here we come up against the basic weakness of this grandiose aim and vision: namely, that the Creator's transcendence was real only in so far as the creature tended towards nothingness. The fact that the damned glorified God just as much as the elect— though damned for whatever reason, and by the same will that saved others—singularly devalues this glory. And when we see all genuine union between God and his creatures slipping away at each stage of the Calvinist system, as if God's glory would somehow be diminished if he communicated himself effectively, what positive element of his glory remains? A God who remains glorious only by distancing himself from men and being as it were indifferent to their lot, is a God conceived—whatever anyone may say—within a pre-Christian and even a pre-biblical framework.[22]

Calvinism thus remains the most lucid and courageous attempt, within original Protestantism, to break out of the vicious circle in which the Reformation found itself through its acceptance and building up of the de-Christianized image of the world inherited from the late Middle Ages. But, as the subsequent history of Protestantism shows, the circle could only really be broken by a return to the truly Catholic tradition.

Sectarian Protestantism: the Apocalyptical Visionaries

On the fringes of Lutheranism, meanwhile, a type of Protestantism had made its appearance that was altogether different from what Luther himself, or the Churches calling themselves "reformed", desired. This was the Protestantism of the sects which from the first appealed to the example of the reformers but was rejected by them as much as by the Catholics. The sectaries became all the more the bogey of respectable Protestants by reason of the somewhat complacent Catholic assertion that they differed from the reformers only by a yet more rigorous application of the reforming principles.

This argument, however, was far from being justified. It is true that the sects had something in common with the Protestants of the Lutheran and reformed Churches, Calvinist or otherwise. But what they had in common was mainly errors received from medieval thought and piety and not yet jettisoned by the reformers: subjective individualism (whence all the illuminations), and a defective notion of divine transcendence and divine immanence (whence all the pantheistic and dualistic errors).

The first eruption of sectarianism in the reformed Churches had certainly been encouraged, if not directly provoked, by Luther's revolt against ecclesiastical authority, his first formulations on Christian freedom and the priesthood of the faithful, and his exaggerated pessimism with regard to the world. But his and others' shocked reaction was caused by the radicalism with which these ideas were applied—first by Carlstadt in the liturgical domain

---

[22] Cf. Imbart de la Tour, *op. cit.*, pp. 206 *et seq.*, and W. Krusch, *Das Wirken des Heiligen Geistes nach Calvin*, Göttingen, 1957.

(reducing the Eucharist to a mere brotherly banquet), then by Thomas Müntzer and his group who tried to form a community of pure Christians, removed from the world, rejecting both its civil and religious authority, re-baptizing adults, and proclaiming the imminence of the last judgment.[23] Faced with the growing excesses of these first Anabaptists who established communism and preached that to true believers all was pure (the resultant disorders were the inevitable and customary outcome of such statements), Luther not only encouraged but instigated merciless repression.

At about the same time other Anabaptists appeared in Switzerland and along the Rhine Valley under the influence of Menno Simons (whence the name of Mennonite that they still have today), though these soon separated their cause from that of the others. Practising a Lord's Supper of the Zwinglian kind and baptizing converted adults only, they formed communities leading an austere life cut off from the world and claiming to reproduce primitive Christendom; and they unquestionably pursued a peaceful and pure existence despite a certain apocalyptic illuminism.

Persecuted indiscriminately with the formidable sectaries from whom they had so soon separated themselves, they sought refuge in Holland where they welcomed and influenced similar sectaries from England. Then they, like the English ones, emigrated to America where they organized rural societies that exist to this day.

Rembrandt was drawn to them though he did not formally belong to their sect, and he certainly reproduced the best of their piety in his work: a recollected piety, mildly exalted, and, despite its narrownesses and simplifications, estimable for its evangelical fervour and its desire for a social life impregnated with faith but without any of Calvin's dictatorialism.

These different kinds of Anabaptists revealed the basic characteristics of the Protestant sects, with the deviations that remained their constant threat: characteristics that showed themselves in a Church that was a true community of prayer, and where everyone was determined to permeate their whole existence with the Gospel and thus cut themselves off from the conformist and indifferent masses. So these sects played a role within Protestantism not unlike that of monasticism in Catholic Christianity. They were also alike in their desire to return to the model of life of the early Church. But their idea of this was a popular simplification and a fanciful archaism of the kind cherished by so many of the reformist humanists and epitomized in Zwingli. They laboured under the delusion

---

[23] On the first Anabaptists, see L. G. Walter, *Thomas Müntzer (1489–1525) et les luttes sociales à l'époque de la Réforme*, Paris, 1927, and J. Lecler, S.J., *Histoire de la Tolérance au siècle de la Réforme*, vol. 1, Paris, 1955, pp. 202 *et seq.*

that the curtailing of ecclesiastical and liturgical forms to a sort of family life tinged by an evangelism inherited from the *Devotio moderna* was the Church of the apostles.

However, the sects contrasted strongly with the religious but rationalizing humanism of the bourgeois Churches, first by their fervour, then by the generosity of their effort to lead, if not a poor, at least a simplified life dominated by religion, and lastly and most of all by their avid desire for extraordinary religious experiences. They were obsessed by the description of the Spirit's manifestations in the *Acts*, and notably by the gift of prophecy, and they tended to live in a state of exaltation.

The danger of Müntzer's disciples was that they saw the Spirit in no matter what form of collective hysteria, whether spontaneous or induced, and they confused prophecy with apocalyptic-type dreamings. But these deviations (if not always present, at least always threatening) did not prevent the sects from maintaining an evangelical ferment within Protestantism that was often very pure precisely in as much as it was naïve. Despite the aberrations to which their undirected and not very enlightened faith was prone, their search for the life of the Spirit kept alive a desire or an expectation that unquestionably belonged to the most authentic Christianity.[24]

Gnostic Mysticism

At the same period similar mystical longings in intellectual or semi-intellectual circles found an outlet not so much in visions and unusual experiences as in fantastic speculations. And the two currents constantly overlapped. It is here that we see most clearly the continuity between the Protestant conventicles and those explosions of gnostic mysticism which the Middle Ages had known and which had flourished particularly along the Rhine as a popular and warped fringe of Rheno-Flemish mysticism. That same area saw the rise of—or anyway was pre-eminently influenced by—the first inspirers within Protestantism of that religious esotericism that developed and spread through the seventeenth and eighteenth centuries and well before the Romantic movement.

Caspar Schwenkfeld (1490–1561) was born at Ossig in Silesia, a member of the decayed nobility enamoured of theology and, at first, one of Luther's most ardent disciples. But he soon became

---

[24] On Menno Simons and moderate forms of Anabaptism, cf. Lecler, *op. cit.*, pp. 215 *et seq.*, and John Horsch, *Menno Simons, his Life, Labors and Teaching*, Scottdale, Pennsylvania, 1916. We should also study the very curious and much more "illuminated" personality of David Joris, another Dutchman (cf. Lecler, *op. cit.*, pp. 221 *et seq.*).

worried by the Lutheran Reformation's failure to produce a genuine reform in Christian life, and, having vainly besought Luther to excommunicate disciples who did not pursue a zealous way of life, he became the soul of the conventicles within the Lutheran or reformed Churches—at Wittenberg, Augsburg, Ulm, Tübingen and Strassburg. These conventicles were a sort of first sketch of the *collegia pietatis* that Spener was to create a century later.

To these pious groups Schwenkfeld preached a mystical doctrine which interpreted Luther in terms of Rhenish mysticism, but he soon deviated into a form of pantheism peculiar to himself which earned him from Luther the epithet of Eutychist.

He taught that natural man was impervious to the influences of grace, but that Christ was a new man, not only because he was God made man, but because mankind, in him, had itself been engendered of God, hence was preparing itself to be integrally divinized to the point of becoming divine. It was the same for the believer nourished on Christ, the Eucharist being but an image of this absorption in Christ, and through Christ in God. He was denounced by the Lutherans, and for a time the Schwenkfeldians formed a sect of their own.[25]

Valentin Weigel (1533–1588) proposed another mystical and pantheizing interpretation of Lutheranism in his turn, and under the same influences. He insisted particularly on the idea of an inner light given to the genuine believer which made him independent of all external teaching as of all external authority. But over and above Schwenkfeld's medieval mystical sources, we find here for the first time the speculations of Renaissance naturalist mysticism drawn directly from Paracelsus; and thence an assimilation of the work of grace in the soul to the work of a divine immanence in nature conceived pantheistically, and an assimilation of the process of the soul's divinization to the processes of alchemy.[26]

These first sketches of a pantheistic mysticism within Protestantism, drawn from mixed Renaissance sources and paving the way for theosophy, prepare us for Jakob Boehme's strange and grandiose work in the following century. This was to spread the influence of these currents of ideas far beyond the small conventicles.

---

[25] See A. Koyré, *Mystiques, spirituels, alchimistes du XVIe siècle allemand*, Paris, 1955, pp. 1 *et seq.* Cf. W. Nigg's study on Schwenkfeld in his *Heimliche Weisheit*, Zurich, 1959, pp. 54 *et seq.*

[26] Cf. Koyré, *op. cit.*, pp. 81 *et seq.*, and W. Nigg, *op. cit.*, pp. 96 *et seq.* We do not mention Sebastien Franck, frequently criticized by these two, for, as Koyré well points out (*op. cit.*, pp. 21 *et seq.*), his ultra-spiritualism puts him right outside Protestantism strictly speaking.

Conclusion of the Origins of Protestantism

So we see the emergence of divergent orientations which were to be the basis of a permanent crisis in subsequent Protestantism and affect its whole spiritual development. The reformers' great intuitions which could have proved so fruitful—the sovereignty of grace in salvation, faith in the Word of God as sole source of all Christian spirituality, God's glory to be recognized and promoted as this spirituality's essential goal—together with the new developments offered by a realization of the positive significance of the lay vocation to the idea of the priesthood of the faithful—all these positive intuitions emerge as unhappily intermingled with the errors underlying the warped evolution of late medieval thought and piety. These errors, far from being uprooted by the Protestant Reformation, reached their culmination in it.

The result was a spirituality that avoided a quietism indifferent to the world and the life that a Christian should live in it, only to fall into practical Pelagianism, and which wrested itself from Pelagianism only by an apocalyptic prophetism totally cut off from the world and always threatened with illuminism or a mystical esotericism, the snare of all dualistic or pantheistic gnoses. The way out of this destruction of the Reformation by its own uncriticized *a prioris* could only lie in an instinctive dissociation—or, better still, a decisive separation—of its positive religious principles, renewed by the highest tradition, from its negative elements, merely inherited from an exhausted Christian piety and culture. But a distinction of this kind could only result in an at least implicit rediscovery of the true Catholic tradition. And this was what the second Protestant generation was soon to prove.

II

PROTESTANTISM AFTER THE
REFORMERS AND THE BEGINNINGS
OF ANGLICANISM

Johann Arndt (1555–1621) and his True Christianity

THE Lutheranism of the end of the sixteenth century evolved in due course into a scholasticism in which different parties disputed the heritage of Luther's complex thought. But an orthodoxy soon emerged which was accused of crypto-Catholicism and bitterly attacked as such by the reformed Churches and all those who wanted a fusion with them as sponsored by a number of cities and influential princes. And it is certainly undeniable that the Lutherans could only effectively combat the Protestant drift towards the reformed Churches of the Swiss and Rhenish type by emphasizing the basic elements of Catholic tradition retained by Luther and interpreting his doctrine of justification along these lines.

This was naturally the case with theologians who were concerned to foster spiritual renewal, for Luther himself, as we have seen, certainly presented his doctrine along these lines in his more pastoral writings.

A work of unparalleled importance from this point of view was Johann Arndt's *True Christianity*.[1] Born in the duchy of Anhalt, Arndt was outstanding for his fidelity to Lutheran liturgical traditions (that is to say, in practice, Catholic ones), and he refused, when pastor of Badeborn, to give in to the reformist tendencies of Duke Johann-Georg whose desire it was to banish images from the churches and the exorcisms from the rite of baptism. Obliged, like many orthodox Lutherans after him, to renounce either his benefice or his convictions, he renounced the former and became pastor successively at Quetlimberg, Brunswick and Eisleben. It was in Brunswick that he published in 1606 the first volume of his *True*

---

[1] J. Arndt (often spelt Arnd), *Vom wahren Christentum*, Braunschweig, 1609. Concerning Arndt, see W. Koepp, *Johann Arndt*, Berlin, 1912.

Christianity, to which three further volumes had been added by 1609. A fifth and sixth were published posthumously. This work brought down the most violent accusations on his head—first and foremost that he was leading the way back to Catholicism. This did not prevent *True Christianity* from enjoying a prodigious success over a long period. It has been estimated that no spiritual work apart from the *Imitation* has been so widely read.

Arndt explained the book's purpose in a letter to the Duke of Brunswick of January 1621. His primary aim, he said, had been to lead theological students away from a mainly polemical and scholastic theology and towards a doctrine of the spiritual life. Thus they would be able to foster a living faith in the faithful, a faith—as he put it—that would form the inner man in us by union with Christ, and produce its fruit in a transformed life. To this end Arndt did no more than develop a positive interpretation of salvation by faith. He had already done this in his sermons, notably those on the *Shorter Catechism.* His method was to expound Luther in terms of his sources, and especially Staupitz, the General of the Augustinian Hermits, who at a decisive moment of Luther's spiritual evolution had told him to turn away from looking at his sins and absorb himself in Christ the Saviour. With Staupitz, Arndt linked the authors of the *Devotio moderna,* Tauler and Saint Bernard. The soul of his doctrine lay in the believer's union with Christ penetrating his whole life, and we can find the key to the transformation that he was so fond of describing, in the phrase: "It is faith that fashions the love of Christ in the faithful heart."

So it comes as no surprise that *True Christianity* (which was translated into Latin in 1687 without its author's name) could be read with edification as much by Catholics as by Protestants (and even, as we saw earlier, by the Orthodox such as Saint Tikhon of Zadonsk). But it must be emphasized that Arndt remained no less faithful for that to Luther's inspiration at its deepest and most original. If he interpreted its formulations in a particular sense, this was assuredly the sense most in keeping with the New Testament whence, Luther affirmed, all his doctrine came; and, let us repeat, this was also the sense that Luther himself had never ceased to develop in his pastoral writings.

Arndt also produced new editions of classics translated into German, such as the *Imitation* and the *Theologia Germanica*; and he published a collection of prayers, the *Paradies-gärtlein* (the little garden of paradise, 1612) in which he distilled in the words of private prayer the whole tradition by which he had been fed.

We must underline an important point before leaving Arndt. In contradistinction to many Pietists who were to claim kinship with him in succeeding generations, his insistence on a doctrine that would nourish the interior life rather than on polemical and scholastic theology did not imply that he underestimated theology, nor, *a fortiori*, that he was indifferent to doctrine. Quite the contrary; for although his work may not be a treatise on dogmatic theology, he makes it amply plain that piety could never be separated from traditional dogma in his mind.

Johann Gerhard and Paul Gerhardt

Arndt had never aimed at writing a theologian's book but a pastor's. His most famous disciple, however, Johann Gerhard (1582–1637), was an eminent theologian, the father and the greatest mind of all Lutheran orthodoxy in the seventeenth century.[2] Professor of theology at the University of Jena, he laid down the essence of his teaching in the nine volumes of his *Loci communes theologiae* published between 1610 and 1621. They make up a veritable theological *summa* of Lutheranism. But all their doctrinal exposition is directed to the life of grace within us and constitutes, as it were, the theological justification for Johann Arndt's spiritual work.

One of the most striking features of Gerhard's work is his return to the Greek Fathers and notably St Athanasius (whom he often compares with the Latin St Hilary), St Cyril of Jerusalem and the Pseudo-Macarius. His grasp of these authors' spiritual and intellectual universe was quite amazing. Like Erasmus, but with more depth, he was—with his French contemporary Huet—one of the first to rediscover the fruitful principle of the "spiritual meaning" in patristic exegesis: that is, the interpretation of the whole history of salvation in relation to Christ, and its application to the Christian in the Church. At the same time Gerhard went beyond Luther's facile and superficial criticism of the Pseudo-Areopagite for substituting a philosophical idea of the hidden God for God who reveals himself in the obscurity of the cross, and returned to a just interpretation of the mystery inherent in all possible knowledge of the biblical God, of which the obscurity of the cross is the perfect manifestation. Again, following in the footsteps of the Greek Fathers and of Pseudo-Dionysius himself, Gerhard—especially in his theology of the Eucharist—developed and justified the mystical doctrine of union with God, and with God in Christ,

---

[2] On J. Gerhard, see B. Hägglund, *Die heilige Schrift und ihre Deutung in der Theologie Johann Gerhards*, Lund, 1951. Gerhard, be it noted, left us some rich works of piety besides his theological works: *Schola Pietatis*, Jena, 1612; *Quinquaginta Meditationes sacrae*, Jena, 1616, etc.

that Arndt had already put forward as the ultimate meaning of justification through well-understood faith.

Thereafter, and in spite of the fact that Gerhard's successors hardened orthodox Lutheran theology and more or less brought it back to the polemical scholasticism from which he himself had managed to wrest it, the theme of the *unio mystica* never ceased to be deepened.[3] We come across it in König,[4] Hollaz,[5] Calov[6] and Quenstedt.[7] Moreover, there can be no mistaking the sense in which they used the expression. *Unio mystica* did not mean a particular psychological experience, but the reality of the presence of Christ in the Christian which was the fruit of eucharistic communion received with justifying faith: the "Christ in us" as inevitable consequence of what has been done by "Christ for us". By this definition they were doing no more than holding to the original meaning of the expression in the Fathers of the Church. But it is certain that for them *unio mystica*, in a life illumined and penetrated by living faith, had to become the object of a personal experience, or, to put it better, had to impregnate the experience more and more.

Orthodox Lutheran spirituality was to find both poetic and popular expression in the hymns of Paul Gerhardt (1607–1676). Their poetry was homely and intimate, yet full of such religious richness and pure and direct emotion that they certainly represent one of the highest peaks ever attained by Protestant spirituality.[8] Their influence spread quickly. Right down to our own time the singing and meditation of Gerhardt's hymns in all Lutheran countries, and even beyond, have contributed to forming a piety in which we find the best of the *Devotio moderna*, a love of God, Christ and man in the spirit of St Bernard, and a mystical aspiration both ardent and serene—and all intermingled with the most evangelical interpretation of the Lutheran faith and a certain honest candour, sweet and strong, which seems to be a specifically German gift.

John-Sebastian Bach was nourished by these hymns and he fre-

[3] See O. Ritschl, "Das Theologoumenon von der Unio mystica in der späteren lutherischen Theologie", in *Harnack Ehrung*, Leipzig, 1921, pp. 335–352. In a general way the best studies on the orthodox Lutheran theologians are H. E. Weber, *Glaube und Mystik*, Gütersloh, 1927; "Das innere Leben der altprotestantischen Orthodoxie", in *Rechtglaubigkeit und Frömmigkeit* (ed. H. Asmussen), vol. 2, Berlin, 1938; *Reformation, Orthodoxie und Rationalismus*, vol. 2 (*Der Geist der Orthodoxie*), Gütersloh, 1951.

[4] F. König, *Theologia positiva acroamatica*, Rostock, 1665.

[5] D. Hollaz, *Theologia positiva*, Wittenberg, 1682, pp. 495 *et seq.*

[6] A. Calov, *Theologia didactico-polemica*, Wittenberg, 1685.

[7] J. A. Quenstedt, *Examen theologicum acroamaticum*, Leipzig, 1707, pp. 927 *et seq.*

[8] See P. Gerhardt, *Dichtungen und Schriften Gesamtausgabe*, ed. H. von Cranach-Sicart, Munich, 1957.

quently introduced them into his compositions—so that we may say that in Bach's music and Gerhardt's poetry all the grandeur and homely humanity to which Lutheran piety lent itself came together and as it were embraced. Bach and Gerhardt together gave a universal popularity to the hymn *O Haupt voll Blut und Wunden* which was directly inspired by *Salve caput cruentatum* (for long attributed to St Bernard) and marks the climax of the Matthew Passion.

> O sacred head, sore wounded,
>   Defiled and put to scorn;
> O kingly head, surrounded
>   With mocking crown of thorn:
> What sorrow mars thy grandeur?
> Can death thy bloom deflower?
> O countenance whose splendour
> The hosts of heaven adore.

But it was in *Befiel du deine Wege*, so rightly dear to all German Protestants, that we find the perfect expression of Lutheran faith as the ardent orthodoxy of the seventeenth century understood and lived it.

The circumstances of its composition enhance its significance. Born in Saxony like Luther, Paul Gerhardt had been driven out of his parish of St Nicholas in Berlin for having, like Arndt, opposed the "Prussian Union", that is to say the compulsory absorption and assimilation of Lutherans within the reformed Church under the Hohenzollerns. With no resources, and not knowing where to go for shelter, Gerhardt put up at an inn after a day's walking. His wife, who accompanied him into exile, gave way to exhaustion and despair, and the unhappy pastor did not know how to comfort her except by repeating the words of Psalm 36, "Commit thy life to the Lord, and trust in him; he will prosper thee." Then, when he had consoled her, he went out into the garden and composed the following verses:

> Commit thou all thy griefs
>   And ways into his hands,
> To his sure truth and tender care
>   Who earth and heaven commands.
>   Who points the clouds their course,
>   Whom winds and seas obey,
> He shall direct thy wandering feet,
>   He shall prepare thy way ...
>
> Leave to his sovran sway
>   To choose and to command

> So shalt thou, wondering, own his way,
> How wise, how strong his hand.
> Far, far above thy thought
> His counsel shall appear,
> When fully he the work hath wrought
> That caused thy needless fear.

The story concludes like one of those pastoral idylls so beloved by eighteenth-century Germans, which reached their tender, arch perfection in Jean-Paul's *Quintus Fixlein*. It is said that envoys from the Duke of Merseburg arrived just as he had finished the second verse to offer him the small parish of Luebben where he ended his days in peace.

Cranmer, the Prayer Book, *and the Origins of Anglican Spirituality*

While these developments were occurring in Germanic Lutheranism, a new type of Church was being worked out in England. Its initial inspiration had affinities with the continental reformed type of Church, and especially with the strictest Zwinglianism,[9] but within half a century a paradoxical play of circumstances was to guide it to a spirituality from many points of view very close to Lutheran neo-Catholicism. We are naturally speaking of Anglicanism. It is important to note, however, that this term was not forged until the nineteenth century (in F. D. Maurice's circle, it appears), to denote a Church and a spirituality (rather than any particular doctrine) which had up till then been known as Protestant. A number of Catholicism's institutional elements had always been preserved to a greater or lesser degree within this Church, but it was not until the Oxford Movement that an effective Catholic soul was breathed into it—except briefly and sporadically.

It is well known that right up to his death Henry VIII did not want to hear of any religion other than the medieval Catholicism, more or less tinged with religious humanism, that he had defended with his pen against Luther. This performance had won him the title of Defender of the Faith from the Holy See, shortly before a combination of domestic troubles and personal passion was to involve him in schism. The accommodating prelate whom he needed for his ecclesiastical policy, Thomas Cranmer, was so very accommodating only because of an irregular situation of his own (he had married, very discreetly, in Germany, the daughter of the reformer Osiander, and had brought her back with him more discreetly still: to be precise, in a trunk). It is difficult to say—with

---

[9] For the history of the Anglican schism the crucial work is Philip Hughes, *Reformation in England*, 3 vols., London, New York, 1951–1954.

Cranmer as with Zwingli—whether and to what degree this situation was the cause or the effect of the religion that this singular archbishop developed for his own use. Like Zwingli, he was extremely cautious in promoting it. He proclaimed it openly only when a change of monarch (with the accession of the sickly minor, Edward VI) allowed him to do so in safety. But Cranmer, who had been formed in Cambridge in the early years of the sixteenth century—when Erasmian humanism rubbed shoulders with Wycliffian survivals and echoes from the Swiss, French and German reformed Churches—always retained a literary and historical sense and taste for the tradition enlightened by humanism that was totally lacking in Zwingli and his disciples. It was this side of his baffling and complex personality that produced the two successive *Prayer Books* of which he was the author. The first *Prayer Book*, together with the ecclesiastical hierarchy retained through royal conservatism, formed the institutional basis of the Catholicizing tendencies destined to reappear many times in Anglicanism.[10]

Cranmer's first *Prayer Book* is without doubt his masterpiece from the point of view of the composition of services and the style of the formularies—a style at least as admirable as that of Luther's Bible. But recent research has established that it was the second *Prayer Book*—contrary to what has often been said about its being the product of continental reforming pressures so prevalent in England for a time after Henry VIII's death—that truly corresponded with Cranmer's personal theology.[11] This, where the Eucharist was concerned, was Zwinglianism at its most extreme. It rejects all idea of a real presence, even a totally spiritualized one, and does not see in the Eucharist—apart from a purely symbolic evocation of Christ's death—any other sacrifice than an act of faith in saving grace of which this death assures us, and an act of consecration of the faithful to the service of God: the "reasonable sacrifice" of which St Paul spoke, but shorn of its rootedness in the eucharistic mystery.

As the first *Prayer Book* was drawn up when Henry's conservatism and the unchanged faith of the bulk of the faithful still acted as a restraint, Cranmer couched his theology in a paraphrased and slightly simplified translation of the canon of the Roman mass: ambiguous phrases could still enshrine traditional beliefs while

[10] The best general study on Cranmer is T. Maynard, *The Life of Thomas Cranmer*, London, 1956.
[11] See E. C. Radcliff's study, "The Liturgical Work of Archbishop Cranmer", in the *Journal of Ecclesiastical History*, 1956, pp. 478 *et seq.*, and Gregory Dix, *The Shape of the Liturgy*, London, 1945, pp. 640 *et seq.*, also W. Jardine Grisbrooke's preface to his book *Anglican Liturgies of the XVI and XVII Centuries*, London, 1958.

preparing the way for their disappearance. In the second *Prayer Book* he no longer resorted to camouflage but expressed what had in fact been his deepest thought from the start. Here the eucharistic preface is no more than an introduction to the consecration, and sacrificial formulae have all been transferred to a "prayer of offering" intended to follow the communion, and clearly signify nothing but a commitment on the part of the communicant to a life enlightened by the Gospel. Still less did he retain many of the formulae that had for long signified something quite different in the Christian language. The outcome was that—at any rate in England and even after the seventeenth-century restorations—the Anglican liturgy containing Cranmer's second eucharistic system was much less adapted, even than the Lutheran liturgy in its altered forms, to transmit anything whatsoever of Catholic tradition, though something of it could conceivably have been recovered under this cover. Other Churches influenced by Anglicanism, such as the Episcopalian Church of Scotland and, later, of the United States, used the eucharistic liturgy as presented in Cranmer's first (not second) system, which lent itself better to recuperations of this kind though under cover of equivocations.

The irony of the situation was that the main reason for the jettisoning of this liturgy under Charles I and Archbishop Laud, in a Scotland penetrated by Calvinism, was not so much because the faithful were able to detect "popery" in its appearances, as because the Zwinglian discarding of the real presence had been scented out by the Calvinist theologians.[12]

But if the influence of the eucharistic liturgy was, and continued to be, weak in average Anglican piety as in other non-Lutheran Protestant Churches (where its celebration soon became altogther exceptional apart from two or three times a year), the influence of the divine office as reformed by Cranmer was immense. And this influence could only be beneficial from the point of view of Catholic tradition, for it was in the services of Mattins and Evensong— of which he was the creator—that his genius appeared in its most positive light.

Cranmer showed himself very dependent on the Catholic breviary as reformed by the Franciscan Cardinal Quiñones, and applied most of its principles to the letter, even copying out word for word its explanatory rubrics. But Cranmer showed a much keener sense of tradition than Quiñones, who, aiming only at the edification of the clergy, had retained all the monastic hours while discarding the ancient characteristics of the different hours, and notably of the two great services of Mattins and Vespers. Cranmer, on the

---

[12] Cf. Jardine Grisbrooke, *op. cit.*, first chapter.

other hand, in his desire to restore a genuinely public prayer in which the faithful could again be associated as they had been up to the end of the patristic era, had deliberately retained these two hours alone, essential ones in the old parochial and cathedral services. But he managed skilfully to combine them with the most precious elements of the tradition of monastic prayer which he adapted for the purpose; these were the recitation of the whole of the psalter, spread out over a month, and the reading each year of the whole of the Bible—two lessons at each service, the first from the Old Testament, the next from the New. At the same time, by the chanting of the *Te Deum* and the *Benedictus* every morning, and the *Magnificat* and the *Nunc Dimittis* at night, added to the finest prayers of Prime and Compline, he managed to preserve the appropriate atmosphere for each of these major hours while safe-guarding the most precious treasures of western Catholic piety. Finally, by adding both a penitential introduction that retained the best of medieval piety, and a conclusion composed of verses and responses adapted from the ancient *preces* and followed by prayers admirably put together from ancient elements, to the basic aspect of praise and scriptural meditation of the former service, he made of these morning and evening prayers a liturgy corresponding to the pastoral needs of the whole Christian community. The splendid language of religious majesty and the melodious style in which these formulas were expressed made them a means of education by worship of which no Church, Catholic or Protestant, has the equivalent today.[13]

After the first extravagances of Protestant iconoclasm under Edward VI had set aside these formularies, and Mary Tudor's Catholic reaction had seemingly abolished them entirely, the catastrophic policy of Paul IV and St Pius V with regard to England aggravated the harm already done to the Catholic cause by the violence and tactlessness of Mary and her ministers. But Cranmer's seemingly buried liturgy saw light again first under Elizabeth and then under James I. It contributed greatly to forming a Church that kept a sufficiently Catholic façade to satisfy (more or less) the people whose religion was still hardly encroached on, and a sufficiently Protestant one to satisfy a clergy influenced by continental evangelism; while the crown and the government saw themselves more than ever in conflict with "popery".

That this compromise succeeded in providing a religion that was more than a mere cover for politics has often caused surprise.

---

[13] The original texts of the two *Prayer Books*, of 1549 and 1552, were re-edited in 1949 by E. C. Ratcliff, with a bibliography: *The First and Second Prayer Books of Edward VI*, Everyman Library, No. 448.

But this is because two factors are always underestimated: first, that there were cultivated minds in England, and particularly among the university clergy, deeply impregnated with the ideal of reformist Christian humanism represented by Erasmian influences, but already embodied in such great men as John Colet and Thomas More; and secondly, the total ineptitude of the Roman Curia at this time as it made common cause with the narrowest elements of the Counter-Reformation in a policy centred on Spain and against Elizabethan England—for this rendered middle- and upper-class loyalty to Catholicism morally impossible in England, short of outstanding courage and vision. These circumstances favoured an effort to bring forth—within the framework of Henry's schism renewed by Elizabeth—a sort of reformist Catholicism which could have triumphed over Protestantism by taking over its best arguments, had it not been for the political blunders of the Stuarts.

But for this to happen there had to be a group of pre-eminent men capable of infusing the Elizabethan compromise with a soul. The first and certainly the greatest of these was Richard Hooker. His immense learning and deep piety seized and exploited to perfection the possibilities provided by a situation at first glance so confused. There followed preachers like Bishop Jeremy Taylor or the poet John Donne, thinkers (usually moralists rather than theologians) like the Caroline Divines, spiritual writers like Bishops Andrewes and Cosin, village parsons (but products of the same refined culture) like Herbert, and devout and learned laymen like Sir Thomas Browne, Nicholas Ferrar, Vaughan and the unforgettable Izaak Walton. They all either set out spontaneously along similar paths, or deliberately followed the one opened up by Hooker.

The publication of King James's Bible (the Authorized Version) and the restoration of the churches and the liturgical life pursued by Laud and other bishops under Charles I helped and encouraged them in their genuinely spiritual creation. This had become so substantial by the time of Charles I's defeat that, after the interlude of Cromwell's Commonwealth, it could resume a life openly that had maintained itself in exile, for instance in favoured retreats such as Golden Grove where Jeremy Taylor sought refuge.

The fatal combination of Catholic sympathies, total personal amorality and political absolutism, which was the hallmark of the post-Restoration Stuarts, seemed to strike a mortal blow at this royalist religion in which the English kings no longer believed and which, moreover, they would not have wanted to practise any more than the one they believed in afresh. But despite the progressive suppression of the group of Non-jurors, who were to push this first Anglo-Catholicism to its limit, indeed into an impasse, it survived in the High Church tendency right up until the Oxford Movement.

The secret of this astonishing vitality in what would seem at first glance to be no more than the island religion of a handful of erudite people practising an aristocratic piety, lay in the succession of admirable personalities we have just mentioned, and in the quality of their Christian culture.

Richard Hooker (1554–1600)

Richard Hooker, the true father of Anglicanism much more than Cranmer or Henry VIII, was a humble country parson whose vast erudition earned him the appointment of Master of the Temple. He finished his life, however, back in a rural parish where he had gone to escape the controversies forced upon him in the city and to meditate over them and put down his conclusions in a massive and deeply integrated work.[14] Did he have a great mind? No, if we understand by this a mind of striking originality. But if we take it to mean a mind capable of vast critical learning combined with wide and, above all, deep human and spiritual experience, together with an imperturbably serene judgment, then undoubtedly his was one of the greatest in religious history. His major work, *The Laws of Ecclesiastical Polity*, is perhaps the only theologico-philosophical work that could sustain comparison with St Thomas's *Summa* —with this difference (which the British would find it hard to acknowledge as a shortcoming), that it is the work of a moralist rather than a metaphysician. In the Englishman's book—so typical of his time as he was—even more than in Aquinas's, there are whole sections, and even whole layers essential to the structure, that strike us as definitely outdated, and yet its substantial humanity and sustained quality of reflection give it a perennial actuality.

When Hooker arrived to take up his appointment at the Temple, he found an outstandingly eloquent Puritan theologian, Walter

[14] The first edition of Hooker's treatise, *Of the Lawes of Ecclesiastical Politie*, dates from 1593. This consisted of the first four volumes. The fifth came out in 1597. *The Sixth and Eighth Books according to the most Authentic Copies* came out in 1648. Gauden's edition (1662) of the complete works added a seventh. Keble brought out a new edition of the 8 books in 5 vols. (1836) and this was revised and re-edited by R. W. Church and F. Paget in 1898. Paget published an *Introduction to the Fifth Book* in 1899 (re-issued in 1907). New editions of the first 5 books by R. Bayne (1907) and C. Morris (1958). For an extensive bibliography cf. C. S. Lewis, *English Literature in the XVIth Century excluding Drama*, Oxford, 1954, p. 654. On the life of Hooker see C. J. Sisson, *The Judicious Marriage of Mr. Hooker*, 1940, which corrects Walton's errors. On his thought, see L. S. Thornton, *Richard Hooker, A Study of his Theology*, 1924, and J. S. Marshall, *Richard Hooker and the Anglican Tradition*, 1964.

Travers, already installed there as preacher at the evening service. Travers had built up a congregation that Hooker's matchless genius, but much less brilliant talent, found it difficult to reach. But the long and patient thought prompted by his colleague's opposition was to produce an analysis and synthesis whose balance and consistency were in sharp contrast with the simplifications and paradoxes of even the best Puritan theology. In Hooker's work the permanent features of Anglican spirituality were all prefigured.

As the title of his book indicates, Hooker's guiding idea united the resources of late sixteenth-century humanism with one of the most highly elaborated ideas in what could be called Thomist humanism: the idea of law. It was not by chance that his thought fastened on this theme and made it the thread of the whole work. His starting-point in the defence of what was most traditional in Anglicanism (and which aroused Puritan irritation) was a discussion of the opposition, taken up again by the Lutherans, between grace and law. In what sense was it true that grace fulfilled the law, just as much as, and more than, it seemed to dispense with it? That was the fundamentally evangelical question that he put to those who wanted to set the Gospel up against tradition.

Hooker placed himself in the purest line of humanism when he reminded them that the arguments concerning Scripture and tradition must necessarily take account of a third term: reason. By reason he did not mean an abstract dialectic but a lucid analysis of reality, and reality in its entirety, natural and supernatural, and first and foremost the historical reality in which grace was revealed to us by itself penetrating concrete human reality.

Hence the position to which all the well-known defenders of Anglicanism would follow him: Protestants in general hoped to bring the Church back to her primitive purity as against the corrupting innovations of medieval Catholicism; on this point the Anglican Church was as Protestant as any. But a dispassionate analysis of Protestantism as imported from the Continent, and of the primitive Church, showed that Protestantism, under the sign of returning to the primitive Church, had in fact introduced innovations no more justifiable than those with which it reproached the Roman Church. In other words, in the name of the principle of the Reformation, the primitive Church had to be re-investigated, and that was what the Anglican Church could and should do.

We can raise the objection that the idea of the primitive Church put forward by Hooker did not in fact correspond to it any more than the Protestant reconstructions that he was fighting. This is true up to a point of the primitive Church strictly speaking. It is much less true of the Church of the Fathers to which he attached himself in preference. Nowadays we talk a lot about Constantinian Christianity, and usually with condescension. But no Christian theologian was ever so deliberately Constantinian as Hooker, with his idea of the Christian city, or—as he put it—the body politic, achieving identification with the mystical body of Christ in as much as the members of the one were also members of the other, and the visible head of the one exercised his authority only as trustee of divine authority, submitting his empire to that of Christ. But this did not mean for Hooker, any more than for the fourth- or fifth-century Fathers who were his inspiration (such as Eusebius of Caesarea or Cyril of Alexandria), that there should be a permanent inquisition or a Calvinist dictatorship, Prussian-style.

For Hooker, Christianity did not reveal the arbitrary will of a God who, faced with perverted nature, either saved or damned. Without being Thomist in all things, he was the first of the great Reformation theologians to discard the conception of *potentia absoluta*, which derived from Scotus or, more, from Ockham, and was the more or less explicit basis of all the Lutheran and Calvinist theologies of grace. With him, as with St Thomas, all law found its origin in God, in the identification of the infinite will with infinite reason. And as for man, however weakened his free will might be through sin and the darkening of the intellect that was its inevitable consequence, his deepest being could not but aspire to knowledge and realization of the divine law. The redemptive incarnation came to answer this latent desire.

Hooker accepted the imputed, extrinsic justification that Christ brought to faith alone, as the principle of our salvation. But it was so, he said, precisely by being the principle of a "secret grace" which should transform our life into Christ's life. Hence, according to him, an inherent justice; never perfect here below but always tending towards perfection; not a quality or a new essence that we might possess, but a constant disposition to abandon ourselves to God's grace, a disposition whose source, at every moment, lies in grace itself.

This, it will be noted, comes back to the Thomist notion of the relationship between sanctifying grace and actual grace, while carefully avoiding repeating Thomist formulae—doubtless so as to forestall misunderstandings and endless arguments with Puritans. He went further and, precisely in the name of the justified sinner's total and unremitting dependence on him who justifies, expressly rejected justifying faith of that type because it ceased to be faith in the Saviour so as to become faith in our salvation as in a fact already established.[15]

[15] *The Laws, etc.*, ed. Morris, vol. I, pp. 6 and 16; vol. II, pp. 146 and 232.

But, and it is here that Hooker's Constantinian Christianity was at its best, just as the life of those justified in Christ should unfold in and through human society into which Christ wished to insert himself so as to regenerate it through the individual, so this life could not be revealed and communicated to the individual except in and through this society. Thus the Church was not merely a free association of believers, as Zwingli held, nor a society that could be refashioned from scratch according to some revealed model picked out of the New Testament by individual exegesis, as Calvin thought. The Church was essentially a historical body, growing organically.

Thus, far from everything not explicitly mentioned in the New Testament having to be jettisoned (as the Puritans wished), everything established by constant and universal tradition had to be retained—provided it was not in flagrant contradiction with the teaching of Christ and his apostles. In other words the usual position of the reformers was reversed. Modern man, having cut himself off from his roots without realizing that he had thereby become a prisoner of his more recent past, could not confront revelation alone and without intermediary, nor be a sovereign judge of what revelation did or did not impose. It was tradition that judged this and imposed itself on his interpretation of Scripture, so long as it did not show itself to have deviated into a formal denial of Scripture.

What interests us here is the spirituality enshrined in this conception which Hooker further developed in the fifth book of *Ecclesiastical Polity*, in the commentary justifying the Anglican retention of Catholic institutions such as the liturgy and the sacraments. Not only did he reintegrate the sensible and the social within the spiritual life, but also the rational, grace not at all replacing nature but healing it and raising it up. This raising up (following the Greek Fathers) was seen as the image's participation in the life of its divine model: transfiguring illumination, purification and union, in which the cross is never absent, no, but everything is absorbed not in its heart-rending paradox, but in the peaceful serenity of an anticipated resurrection, as with St John.

The Sermons and Poems of John Donne

But we must not imagine that Anglican spirituality was confined to a distinctive form of platonizing patristic humanism in which the drama of the condemned sin and the sinner justified in the cross (felt so powerfully by Luther and later by the Puritans) faded away into a neo-Alexandrine wisdom. For another Anglican ecclesiastic who was a contemporary of Hooker—but, unlike him, late in taking orders, and indeed late in coming to a fervent Christian life—

was expressing just that dramatic aspect of Christianity in sermons and impassioned poems at the same time as the massive *Ecclesiastical Polity* was being slowly but surely put together in the silence of a country parsonage.

Ironically enough, John Donne (1572?–1631) was a renegade from Catholicism, having been formed in the school of St Ignatius, and though, like many others, he rebelled against it and derided it, he none the less retained it in his bones.

Donne's religious sincerity has been called into question more than once by Catholics, and for two reasons—first, because he appears as the same passionately sensual man in the pious writings of his later days as in the profane works of his early life; and secondly because he allegedly moved over from Catholicism to Anglicanism because he could not resist the gilded security offered him by the deanery of St Paul's after his late ordination. But objective study has forced us to the conclusion that both these accusations are groundless. Donne as a writer, and especially as a poet, expressed with a power seldom equalled the drama of those sensual men whose sensuality is exacerbated because never appeased, and this because it is a deviation from, or a misunderstanding of, longings that in fact go far beyond the senses. These men throw themselves so violently into the search for sensual satisfaction only because they expect from it what it cannot give. They only appear to be seeking pleasure; and their conversion is their acknowledgement of their former mistake—a mistake coming from a temperament that they obviously cannot cast off merely because of their conversion, however sincere this may be.[16]

This is shown up in Donne by the fact that his passionate love for *one* woman, involving him in a marriage that destroyed all his hopes of social success, led him away from sheer sensuality and into genuine love, love made up of fidelity and the gift of self. This love led him to an awakening of true piety, deepened by a life of sickness and poverty shared with the loved one, and consummated in her death and the expectation of his own which would reunite him with her.

And now, what can be said of his abandonment of the Catholic Church in which he had been brought up, and of his tardy adherence to the Anglican Church in which he was ordained and provided with an ample benefice? Not only did he himself seem to

[16] On John Donne see C. S. Lewis's excellent studies, *op. cit.*, pp. 469–470 and 546 *et seq.* His complete poems and a good selection of his prose works (notably his sermons) have been produced by John Hayward, *John Donne, Complete Poetry and Selected Prose*, London, 1946. There is also an excellent edition of *The Divine Poems* with introduction and commentary by Helen Gardner, Oxford, 1952. See too Louis Martz's chapter on him in *The Poetry of Meditation*, Yale University Press, New Haven, 1954, pp. 211 *et seq.*

have no illusions as to the interpretation that would inevitably be given to his move, but he appears to have resigned himself to it only after long hesitation and as if to an act which, after his marriage, would consummate his loss of rank in public opinion. The piety that then awoke in him was basically Catholic, very close to the Middle Ages, and wholly dominated by the methods of systematic meditation in which the Jesuits were past masters. This being so, why did he join the Anglican Church? First, as an English patriot penetrated, like Hooker, with the idea of the Christian city, he saw Catholicism (identified as it was with the current policy of the Curia) as bogged down in temporal matters and Machiavellian manœuvres. And secondly, the spirit of humanistic reform, fostered by his culture and embodied in Hooker and Andrewes, seemed to him to be stifled in Catholicism. We may regret that he was insufficiently clear-sighted, or that he did not display a more courageous independence of mind, but there are absolutely no grounds on which to place suspicions of insincerity. His religious poems at any rate are a cry of the deepest sincerity.

They are the outpouring of a soul driven to trust in God alone because it knows so well that it still connives with sin. Faith in the dying Christ inspires it, and it awaits both Christ's undeserved forgiveness and the inaccessible victory over self.

> Batter my heart, three person'd God ...
> ... for I
> Except you'enthrall mee, never shall be free,
> Nor ever chast, except you ravish mee.[17]

The theme of sin alternates with the theme of death: either hated death, death that reveals the nothingness of desire and also the nothingness of love which is stronger than desire itself; or else longed-for, awaited death, death that lifts the believer beyond the war he wages with himself, lifts him to where all tragedy and disillusion are surmounted in the love that is stronger than death:

> I joy, that in these straits, I see my West;
> For, though theire currants yeeld return to none,
> What shall my West hurt me? As West and East
> In all flatt Maps (and I am one) are one,
> So death doth touch the Resurrection.

> ... We thinke that Paradise and Calvarie
> Christs Crosse, and Adams tree, stood in one place;
> Looke Lord, and finde both Adams met in me;
> As the first Adams sweat surrounds my face,
> May the last Adams blood my soule embrace.

---

[17] Helen Gardner, *op. cit.*, p. 11.

So, in his purple wrapp'd receive mee Lord,
  By these his thrones give me his other Crowne;
And as to others soules I preach'd thy word,
  Be this my Text, my Sermon to mine owne,
  Therefore that he may raise the Lord throws down.[18]

These themes also inspired his sermons and his spiritual life.

Despite all the Jacobean baroque of their culture, their overload of profane quotation only brings out more clearly the realism of a man fully of this world, who has come to find his brothers there so as to help them get out of it with him.

Baroque Donne undoubtedly was to the highest degree, both in his piety and his art, by reason of a paroxysm of conflict in which sensuality seems forced by the reflective intelligence itself to be burned to ashes so that the will, liberated, can spread its wings to the invisible sun of grace. Not only did this renegade from Catholicism reaccommodate all the emotional side of medieval piety within Anglicanism, but—more and more and right to the end—he galvanized his faith by a systematic discipline of the life of the senses worn out by attrition against will and conscience. It was like a holocaust of the senses in which they themselves ignited the fire that would consume them.

Louis Martz has made a detailed analysis of what this endeavour owed to the technique of Ignatian meditation, and also the part played in it by transfigured passion. But we must not imagine that he has done more than deduce from his final position his point of departure. We observe the same influence at work not only in many other Anglicans but even more in the Puritans. If doctrinal conflicts and perhaps still more invincible prejudices set Christians against each other in those years, religious psychology—consciously manipulated as never before by the clear-cut methods of a spiritual technique—knew no confessional frontiers. Donne's use of this technique did not prevent him from feeling and expressing at least as strongly as Luther the paradox of *semper peccator semper justus*.

Izaak Walton's life of Donne ends up with the haunting, not to say grotesque, picture of Donne posing on his deathbed in his winding-sheet for the sculptor of his tomb, then recovering again so as to give a final sermon on the subject, before dying for good and all. The picture is surely characteristic of a preoccupation that became an obsession in most minds at the end of the Renaissance; minds governed by exalted faith just as much as by the gnawing despair of the least gay libertines that ever existed. In Jeremy Taylor's masterpiece, *Holy Dying*, the theme achieves its most

[18] Helen Gardner, *op. cit.*, p. 30.

elaborate orchestration, so elaborate indeed that we might be tempted to see nothing in it but macabre virtuosity, but here we would doubtless be mistaken.

Jeremy Taylor (1613–1667)

In Jeremy Taylor there was a contrast not unlike the one we find so disconcerting in Bossuet. Both of them had incomparably great religious imaginations and both wrote a prose suggestive of Bach's organ music, or perhaps Handel's (though Taylor's registration was more varied, the idyll-like recitatives alternating with fugues at full blast). But, unlike Bossuet's, Taylor's splendid poetry was not in conflict with the meannesses of an upstart bourgeois. During the Commonwealth he did not waver in loyalty to his Church and his king, thus shattering what seemed all hope of a brilliant future. He buried himself in the semi-clandestine chaplaincy of Golden Grove in Wales which belonged to his friend and protector Lord Carbery, and, like the Gentlemen of Port-Royal, did not think the job of teacher in the village school beneath him. A sacred lyricism no less Pindaric than Bossuet's expressed a humanistic religion that might have seemed a bit tame but for his constant sense of the precariousness of this world, the charms of which he nevertheless felt keenly. This feeling was totally unlike Donne's passion: it showed itself in a tender friendship for children, for nature, a tenderness for friendship itself, and especially with sensitive women such as Lady Carbery, the memory of whom calls up the deepest emotion in his writings. As Douglas Bush has rightly pointed out, we should not judge him by modern anthologies largely governed by the tastes of the Romantic critics (Coleridge in particular) which contain only his virtuoso pieces. Taylor was before anything the first in a series of great Anglican casuists whom Pascal, had he known them, would have unhesitatingly placed next to the Jesuits in their understanding of human nature. But in his more subdued conception of original sin, the author of the somewhat heavy *Ductor dubitantium* joined up rather with the optimism of Zwingli—in total contrast to the confused depths of Luther or the cold rigour of Calvin.[19]

Taylor's manual on the Christian life, *Holy Living*, is so balanced as to seem almost dull; and if his funeral oration for Lady Carbery

---

[19] Complete works in 15 volumes ed. R. Heber (1822); revised ed. in 10 vols. by C. P. Eden (1847–1854). L. P. Smith has produced an anthology from a strictly literary point of view, *The Golden Grove*, Oxford, 1930, containing a bibliography corrected and completed by R. Gathorne-Hardy in 4 articles in the *Times Literary Supplement* (25 September, 2 and 9 October, 1930 and 15 September, 1932). There is a biography by Edmund Gosse in the *English Men of Letters* series. The best study of his thought is W. J. Brown, *Jeremy Taylor*, 1925. Numerous editions of *Holy Living* and *Holy Dying*.

touches us perhaps more humanly than Bossuet's unforgettable elegy inspired by the death of Henrietta of England, the macabre splendour that dazzles us in his *Holy Dying* enchants us more readily than it edifies us—as with the thunderings of the *Traité de la Concupiscence*, and still more so. Taylor's pastoral intentions cannot be doubted, however, though his talent as poet and writer went far beyond the substance of his wisdom which was, when all is said and done, fairly limited; a wisdom drawn from all the ancient sources but to which the Bible and experience brought the richest contribution. For all that he was characteristic of an average, if not a mediocre, Anglicanism in which a deeply poetic culture gave fullness to the commonplaces which otherwise would have bordered on platitude.

Religiously speaking, he was undoubtedly at his best in his prayers. At a time when the use of the *Prayer Book* was forbidden by Puritan authority, he excelled in reproducing its spirituality in his own way and informing all its detail with the realities of human life, thus fostering family piety as a model of popular religion, in which the most humble felt thoroughly at home, yet where there is not a suspicion of vulgarity.

Lancelot Andrewes (1555–1626)

If Hooker was the religious thinker who first conceived what we call Anglicanism, Andrewes may be viewed as the first pastor who tried with some success to get it adopted by the English Church, mainly because he lived it with such rare intensity. The son of lower-middle class London parents, he was a fellow-student of Spenser at Cambridge, then chaplain in turn to Archbishop Whitgift and Queen Elizabeth before returning to his old college, Pembroke Hall, as Master; thereafter he was chaplain penitentiary, then dean, of Westminster Abbey, and bishop successively of Chichester, Ely and Winchester, before he was finally laid to rest in a baroque tomb in Southwark Cathedral. On the evidence of this career we might well suspect that he was one of the court prelates so contemptuously stigmatized by Milton and other Puritans, but in fact he was the most perfect embodiment of the accomplished scholar that the Anglican Church has ever produced. Stupefyingly erudite, but even more cultivated than erudite, he was none the less a pastor unreservedly devoted to his flock, and, to cap all, practised a spirituality of inner contemplation that approached mysticism.[20]

[20] Lancelot Andrewes's *XCVI Sermons* was published by Laud at the request of the king in 1629. His whole work was re-edited in 11 vols. by the *Library of Anglo-Catholic Theology* from 1841 to 1854. F. E. Brightman, in his introduction to the translation of *Private Devotions*, London, 1903 (reprinted New York 1961),

Andrewes was one of the principal authors of King James's Bible, whose success was perhaps even more surprising than that of Luther's, for it was the work not of one man but of a fair-sized group working on multiple previous versions. The beauty of its style, more polyphonic but no less melodious for that than that of Cranmer's *Prayer Book*, henceforth always accompanied both the liturgy and the family piety of Anglicanism, and indeed of all English Protestantism, whether popular or cultured.

Andrewes's sermons and doctrinal writings show a staggering erudition both patristic and theological, yet he must have enlivened the forbidding number of their pages with simple and vivid language, for we know that he was highly esteemed by his contemporaries, which speaks well for their seriousness at least. But he only really revealed himself in his *Preces privatae*, a collection of personal devotions compiled over a long period for his own personal use, and communicated shortly before his death to a few friends such as Archbishop Laud. These prayers immediately became popular and were translated into English.

They are the work of a scholar every bit as much as his sermons, a scholar possessing intimate knowledge of all the Fathers, Greek as well as Latin, and of most of the ancient liturgies (here he was a pioneer), as well as of medieval authors both spiritual and scholastic, not forgetting Sophocles, Euripides, Virgil and, of course, Erasmus. His prayers are composed like prose-poems, in broken lines so as to suggest the rhythms and pauses of contemplative meditation, and are usually in Greek or Hebrew, but sometimes Latin, depending on the sources. But we must not conclude from this that they are sophisticated and unsuitable for the ignorant, even if it is only the learned who can fully appreciate the complexity and richness of their composition. All the ingredients mentioned above are so well knit together (unlike the sermons which suggest flowing expression rather than careful construction) and so intimately welded into the serene fervour of personal prayer, that we hardly notice them, or anyway we forget the diversity of their origins. And better still, the simplest Christian can get nourishment from these richly knowledgeable prayers. Never has the image of the bee going from flower to flower to gather a honey of fragrant simplicity been so apt.

These devotions fall into four categories: prayers of penance,

has given a full study of the critical problems presented by the text. The English translation by Newman and Neale was reprinted by the S.P.C.K. in 1920. One of the best studies on him is that of R. W. Church in *Masters of English Theology*, London, 1877. See too the pages devoted to him by D. Bush in *English Literature in the earlier XVIIth Century*, Oxford, 1945, pp. 300 *et seq.*, and P. A. Welsby, *Lancelot Andrewes*, London, 1958.

meditations on the mysteries of the faith, contemplative praise of the divine work of creation and redemption in the world, and finally prayers of intercession in which concern is shown for all the most homely details of life: the whole assembled within a constant vision of Catholic unity. All the expressions conducive to piety put forward by the Bible along these four lines are collected here, illuminated by ancient liturgical tradition, and in constant contact with a humanist pastor's own experience. The only things that date in his prayers are, obviously, intercessions such as this one:

Do well, O Lord
  visit with thy mercies
    thy whole creation   world
    all our race   inhabited earth
    the commonwealth of the world:
    the Church at large   Christendom
      the churches ⎫
      the commonwealths ⎬ severally:
      the church   ⎫
      the commonwealth ⎬ among us   fatherland
        the orders in either
        the persons in the order   sacerdotal
          the king's
          the prince's
        the succession
    the city
    the parish   All Hallows Barking
    the two schools
    the university
    the college: the parish of St Giles
                          Pembroke Hall
                          the churches
                            of Southwell
                            St Paul's
                            Westminster
                        the dioceses
                            of Chichester
                            Ely
                            Winchester

  house
  kinsfolk
  those that have mercy
  those that serve
    neighbours
    friends
    commended.[21]

[21] Ed. Brightman, p. 272.

But the very precision of this prayer suggests to us an equivalent that we could make our own. And all the rest—the prayers of contrition, confession of faith, and praise—are so essential, so near to the sources in inspiration, that this prayer, intimate though it is, receives from them some equivalent of the timeless liturgical prayer that formed them, though brought down to the personal context:

> Into thy hands, O Lord, I commend myself
>   my spirit, soul, body:
> Thou hast created and redeemed them,
>   O Lord, Thou God of truth:
> and with me, mine and all things mine:
>   Thou hast granted me them, O Lord,
>   in thy goodness.
> Preserve Thou by lying down and mine uprising
>   from this time forth for evermore:
>   to remember Thee in my bed,
>   to search out my spirits;
>   to wake up and be present with Thee.
> I will lay me down in peace
>   and take my rest:
>   for it is Thou, Lord, only
> that makest me dwell in safety.[22]

Bremond, reading the zigzag of what he called these "gilded prayers", declared that he found nothing mystical in them, any more than in Newman who, up to the end of his life, kept Andrewes's collection on the prie-dieu where he made his thanksgiving after Mass. Indeed familiarity with these two men can reveal as nothing else the orientation and mystical feeling lying in the type of meditative life that does not look for unusual experiences but just for absorption in the word of God, with the harmony of Catholic tradition as commentary.

There is an excellent portrait of Andrewes in Jesus College, Cambridge. It shows that he had the lean but very human face of a scholar, a pastor, but above all of a man of great spirituality. The white vellum volume in his hand could be the copy of his *Preces* that he sent, unfinished, to Laud on the eve of his death (or so Brightman conjectures). Judging by this book, which he intended for a few friends at most, we may say that he was undoubtedly the spiritual master of Anglicanism, a master who could not only hold Anglicans like Newman, who had returned to Catholic unity, but win over loyal sons of Puritanism such as Dr Alexander Whyte, the Scottish free-churchman who re-edited him and sang his praises.

[22] Ed. Brightman, p. 273.

Three Anglican laymen: Izaak Walton, Sir Thomas Browne, Nicholas Ferrar

If we wish to test the spirituality of Hooker and Andrewes in terms of its influence and capacity to penetrate the lives of others, we should look not to the most brilliant sermon-writers but to the type of layman whom it formed. And the period immediately following Hooker and Andrewes, the period when Donne and Taylor were preaching, provides us with three laymen who showed up its diverse possibilities and deep unity to perfection.

Izaak Walton (1593–1683) was such a perfect model of the Anglican layman after his pastor's heart that it would need very little for the picture to become a caricature.[23] Biographer of the first great men of the Anglican Church, and friend of innumerable dignitaries, he was the very incarnation of good nature, and no one could have been more serenely contented with his lot, his world and, above all, his Church. But we must be prepared for the prosperous churchwarden's unruffled candour to conceal a humour that was all the more devastating in that it was so unobtrusive. And in a troubled epoch torn with fanatical strife, Walton's persistent serenity and unchanging loyalty to his Church and his king showed a strength of soul that was all the more impressive for being so discreet.

The friend and parishioner of John Donne, he painted an edifying portrait of him while not concealing that the ardent faith of his last years was built on the ashes of plentiful wild oats. He saluted the "judicious" Hooker (whom he could obviously only describe at second hand) as the unquestionable master, but owing to his humility (not entirely without malice) which led him to use erroneous information that he did not dare call into question, he passed the master off as a defenceless old boy harried by a shrew.[24] Concerning Sanderson, that other great Anglican moralist besides Taylor, he made it equally clear that he only knew his mind and heart through his books. In his life of Henry Wotton, a cosmopolitan and a courtier before ending up with orders in the provostship of Eton, he showed how simplicity of faith neither eliminated nor transcended human curiosity and worldly ambition. It was in the idyllic picture of the perfect country parson, George Herbert, that

[23] The *Lives* were first published separately (that of Donne appearing first in 1640 prefacing an edition of his *Sermons*). Re-publication of them all in the original text with an introduction by G. Saintsbury in *The World's Classics*, Oxford, 1927, and often reprinted. The first edition of *The Compleat Angler* dates from 1655. Numerous editions since, and particularly by J. Buchan in the same series, 1935. On Walton and his circle see Stapleton Martin, *Izaak Walton and his Friends*, 2nd ed., London, 1904.

[24] Cf. Sisson's study mentioned in note 14.

he really brought humility and devotion into relief, by the fact of the aristocratic pride that both had to overcome, and only succeeded in doing so with great difficulty.

But it was in a work that had no apologetic or edifying purpose that Walton best depicted his religion as it threaded its way through his life—not all the days of his life, but his days of leisure. His *Compleat Angler*, as has been rightly noted, has so much charm because it offers us (though without consciously seeking to do so) the portrait of the author after the portraits of his various models. This most English and Anglican of all books, the first and most successful of those "nature" books that fill whole libraries in England, is in fact the most human of books and depicts a man who could only be a Christian in the inimitable manner of the Church of England. These gentlemen on the fringes of the aristocracy had certainly nothing of the "bourgeois gentilhomme" about them. They were friends of silence and solitude, beguiled by the most peaceful of sports, but where rivers and meadows and woods of the most favoured part of England (that of the southern counties) lent themselves easily yet discreetly to contemplative reflection. They did not have to hold forth on theology for us to know where their allegiance lay. Their piety was perhaps untroubled by great mystical flights (and yet how do we know? They were much too well-bred to mention them), and yet the presence of God behind the iridescent veil of this world in which they moved so peaceably was never forgotten, and it hovered over the playfulness of their friendly conversations like a perfume of subdued charity.

This rural England, where the very inns were held from the manor and the parsonage, is well sketched in, and seems so remote from the brutal England of luxury and destitution that Hogarth was soon to paint as to be a dream concealing the grim reality. But this was reality, too, for men like Walton, whose simplicity was anything but artless, and it is a singular honour for the Anglican Church to have produced it for so long.

Sir Thomas Browne (1605–1682) was altogether different from Walton. A physician and archaeologist, interested in everything, he was himself the most astonishing curiosity of his Norwich collection. He seemed an intellectual through and through compared with the simple Walton, and as perfect an eccentric as the other was conventional, though of equally good stock. He asked every kind of question, physical, metaphysical, physiological, fantastic—questions that do not seem to have ruffled the smooth surface of Walton's almost too serene intelligence. But the same superior good sense was merely more evident in his case, though his religion —which at first sight and to judge from his works was as rational as his thought could be adventurous—was surely, in its well-Christianized Platonism, if not more mystical, at least more obviously "otherworldly".

The satisfaction he derived from Anglicanism, as compared with the excesses of Puritanism which were as foreign to him as to Walton, was just as thought out and just as decided, though in his case he spoke of it. But with him as with Doctor Johnson, who, we would imagine, was as truly rational as Sir Thomas Browne wrongly thought himself to be, there were curious nostalgias for, and as it were presentiments of, the truth of Catholicism—however unattractive its externals as seen in their continental contemporaries must have seemed to them.

His *Religio Medici*[25] reveals his attachment to dogmatic and ecclesiastic Christianity as being as firm as his horror of vain theological disputes, and a sense of the supernatural present everywhere behind creation as being of the type that would more readily fall into credulity than agnosticism, despite his very positive and —in its way—critical intelligence. The enduring charm of his personality comes primarily from his sense of the one thing needful which never for a moment deserts him, just as his mind never tires in its curiosity about the most diverse realities and speculations that throng the great world of creation and the microcosm of human thought. The deepest intuitions and oddest fancies of a mind that could never be commonplace are expressed in this work, clothed in extraordinary prose in which sprightly solemnity and grandiose humour go hand in hand. It has been well said of this amazing toccata that it makes Taylor's organ-like sonorities sound like a piano.

The cast of mind of this magnificent old eccentric (who was writing like a centenarian sage at the age of thirty) was typically Anglican in its humanity, and it united the most serious spirituality with extreme originality (not to say "crankishness") and a humour that defies all criticism.

After Walton's *aurea mediocritas* and Sir Thomas Browne's Tyrian purple, Anglican lay piety was never perhaps more purely expressed than in Nicholas Ferrar (1592–1637). A businessman in the City, and one of the promoters of the colonization of Virginia,

[25] *Religio Medici* was first published in 1642 without Browne's authorization, and re-published the following year with his consent. His *Works* appeared in 1686, and *Posthumous Works* in 1712, with an anonymous Life. *Christian Morals*, edited by J. Jeffrey in 1716, re-edited in 1756 with his Life by Samuel Johnson. Complete modern edition of works and correspondence by G. Keynes, 6 vols., 1928–1931. Many current editions, notably that of *Everyman's Library*, republished many times since 1906 with an introduction by C. H. Hertford. On Browne's life see O. Leroy, *Le chevalier Thomas Browne, médecin, styliste et métaphysicien*, Paris, 1931.

he travelled across Southern Europe where he came into contact with semi-Erasmian and semi-Quietist circles in Spain and Naples —and returned home more attached to Anglicanism than ever. But he left life in the world and withdrew to a quasi-monastic retreat, to which he was also able to convert his family, including sons, sons-in-law, nephews and nieces. Here he ended his life in the odour of sanctity (but no less persuaded for that that the Pope of Rome was Antichrist!) just as Cromwell's troops were about to plunder and consign to the flames what they called his "nunnery". Ferrar was perhaps the most engaging of the early Anglican figures. We know the fascination he exercised over Henry Shorthouse whose delightful—though inaccurate—novel *John Inglesant* did more than any hagiography to popularize the hermit, or rather the patriarchal monk, of Little Gidding. Nearer our own time, T. S. Eliot in the last of his *Four Quartets* makes a poetic pilgrimage there as if to one of those frontiers where poetry is absorbed in mysticism.[26]

At Little Gidding we have left the temperate slopes of Wiltshire and East Anglia where the reasonable, conversable Anglican piety of Walton and Browne had established itself. In this rural manor everyone led a life of almost Cistercian austerity. The kindly girls, of a comfortable and cultivated middle class, played their part to the full—doing the most humble tasks, when they were not cleaning up the village children between a catechism class and visiting the sick. The most strict fasts and vigils were kept by the family. In the carefully restored little chapel, where the horrified Roundheads were to destroy the abominations of a worship judged to be far too Papist, they added prayers for each hour of the day to the daily chanting of Mattins and Evensong, and took turns at night to recite the whole psalter, with pauses for silent prayer during which Mr Ferrar improvised on the organ. The only recreations they allowed themselves, apart from work in the garden, were book-binding, manuscript illumination and fine handwriting—notably of a synopsis of the Gospels which King Charles I admired some days before his fate was sealed not far away at the battle of Naseby.

And yet this "monastery", where they meditated on Juan Valdès translated by the master of the house, was very Anglican through the family life that was pursued there in an atmosphere of biblical piety and polyphonic music, and where women and girls provided the touch of delicacy—as, for instance, Ferrar's young niece Mary Colet, whose life of union with God in dedicated virginity came to a premature end on the Continent. In this type of Anglicanism

[26] The two best studies of Ferrar are A. L. Maycook, *Nicholas Ferrar of Little Gidding*, London, 1938, and B. Blackstone, *The Ferrar Papers*, London, 1938. F. Chapman re-edited in 1905 *The Hundred and Ten Considerations of Signior John Valdesso*, translated by Ferrar (1st ed., 1638).

people lived for nothing but to be alone with God, and the love of Christ penetrated all other love to the point of submerging it.

The inhabitants of Little Gidding themselves were too reserved to describe their inner experience and the mystical light that shone in the lamps which they held as wise virgins. And anyway they felt no need to do so. For Nicholas Ferrar had himself brought out a volume of poems and meditations in which his best friend had expressed their spiritual ideal to perfection. This was George Herbert's *The Temple*, with its prose companion, *The Country Parson*.

The Anglican Poets: Herbert, Vaughan, Traherne, Crashaw

George Herbert (1593–1633), younger brother of Lord Herbert of Cherbury—viewed as the founder of deism—belonged to an aristocratic family from the Welsh border.[27] A brilliant pupil at Westminster school, then at Trinity College, Cambridge—of which he was later a fellow—he then became master of rhetoric, then Public Orator of the university. Worldly ambitions and politics held him back for some time from fulfilling his mother's ardent wish that he should take holy orders (his mother was a friend of Donne and had become Lady Danvers by a second marriage). And it seems to have been poor health—which was to shorten his life—that finally decided him to receive the diaconate in 1628. He married the following year and was ordained priest and became rector of Bemerton, near Salisbury, in 1630.

He spent the two remaining years of his life in this rectory, leaving it only for brief excursions to the cathedral town to which his love for choral liturgy and music drew him. As he had written the preface to Ferrar's translation of a treatise by Juan Valdès, Ferrar edited and wrote the preface for his sacred poems, *The Temple*. These poems are seen more clearly in the light of the perfect "country parson" which was the title he gave to his manual. But above all they throw light from another world on the daily monotony of a life of service in which no detail seemed too humble for his attention.

In this ideal Anglican parish, the clean, well-kept church attached great importance to the pulpit and the parson's stall where the liturgical prayers were said. But the altar standing between the two was used for the eucharistic celebration at most five or six

---

[27] *The Temple* was brought out by N. Ferrar in 1633. In 1652 *Herbert's Remains*, edited with a biography by B. Oley, also included *A Priest to the Temple* and *Jacula Prudentum*. There is a modern edition of the complete works by F. E. Hutchinson (1941), who has also published an excellent study on Herbert in *XVIIth Century Studies presented to Sir Herbert Grierson*, London, 1938. Many popular editions.

times a year (though it was used for the first part of Mass, up to the Sunday morning sermon after the Gospel). Herbert would have liked a monthly eucharistic celebration, but does not seem to have found this realizable.

So he concentrated his efforts on regular attendance at Vespers, where the second lesson, before the *Magnificat*, was followed by catechism, not only for the benefit of the children but of all the parishioners. During the week, however, the parson went morning and evening to the church to recite Mattins and Evensong even if there was no attendance. If he had a family, the family should accompany him (Herbert himself was married and counselled no less to his colleagues, if they were not capable with God's help of remaining celibate).

Visits to parishioners, and especially to the poor and the sick, were seen as an almost liturgical act in which prayers and exhortations led either to spontaneous confessions or to catechetical questions from the parson to his flock; and these alternated with long hours devoted to the study of the Bible and its commentators— Fathers of the Church and Schoolmen—as well as of moral theology; and to personal prayer. But if we are to understand exactly what these various activities, and especially personal prayer, meant to the faithful parson, we must enter the *Temple*.

The first thing that strikes us is the way in which this unified life, regularly illumined by prayer and charity, was in fact the fruit of a conquest of self that was always painful and always had to be repeated. This explains the outburst of impatience in the poem, *The Collar*, with its single touch of final serenity brought about by an intervention from above, but homely nonetheless:

> I struck the board, and cry'd, "No more;
>   I will abroad."
> What, shall I ever sigh and pine?
> My lines and life are free; free as the road,
>   Loose as the winde, as large as store.
>   Shall I be still in suit?
> Have I no harvest but a thorn
> To let me bloud, and not restore
> What I have lost with cordiall fruit?
>   Sure there was wine
> Before my sighs did drie it; there was corn
>   Before my fears did drown it;
> Is the yeare onely lost to me?
>   Have I no bayes to crown it,
> No flowers, no garlands gay? all blasted,
>   All wasted? . . .

> But as I rav'd and grew more fierce and wilde
>   At evr'y word,
> Methought I heard one calling, "Childe";
>   And I reply'd, "My Lord." [28]

This irresistible sense of Christ's inescapable domination goes
side by side with the certainty that Christ dwells in those on whom
he has laid his hand irrespective of their personal unworthiness.
Seldom has this double nature of the priest—his anguish and his
unique consolation—been better expressed than in the poem *Aaron*:

> Holinesse on the head,
> Light and perfections on the breast,
> Harmonious bells below, raising the dead
>   To lead them unto life and rest:
>   Thus are true Aarons drest:
>
> Profaneness in my head,
> Defects and darknesse in my breast,
> A noise of passions ringing me for dead
>   Unto a place where is no rest:
>   Poor priest, thus am I drest.
>
> Onely another head
> I have, another heart and breast,
> Another musick, making live, not dead,
>   Without Whom I could have no rest:
>   In Him I am well drest.
>
> Christ is my onely head,
> My alone onely heart and breast,
> My onely musick, striking me ev'n dead,
>   That to the old man I may rest,
>   And be in Him new-drest . . . [29]

When the parson makes room within himself for Jesus, Jesus
becomes his master by associating him with his passion, but once
he abandons himself to this, the Master is no more than a perfume
of sweetness in the accepted sacrifice:

> "My Master," shall I speak? O that to Thee
> "My servant" were a little so,
>   As flesh may be;
> That these two words might creep and grow
> To some degree of spiciness to Thee! [30]

[28] *Chandos Classics*, p. 214.
[29] *Ibid.*, p. 238.
[30] *The Odour, ibid.*, p. 239.

Thus the priest's yearning towards fidelity becomes a humble yet impatient expectation of the encounter and the consummated union with his Master who is also his all:

> Come, Lord, my head doth burn, my heart is sick,
>   While Thou dost ever, ever stay;
> Thy long deferrings wound me to the quick,
>   My spirit gaspeth night and day:
>   O, show Thyself to me,
>   Or take me up to Thee! ...
>
> With one small sigh Thou gav'st me th' other day
> I blasted all the joyes about me,
> And scouling on them as they pin'd away,
>   "Now come again," said I, "and flout me."
>   O, show Thyself to me,
>   Or take me up to Thee! ...
>
> We talk of harvests—there are no such things
>   But when we leave our corn and hay;
> There is no fruitful yeare but that which brings
>   The last and lov'd, though dreadfull day:
>   O, show Thyself to me,
>   Or take me up to Thee! ...
>
> What have I left, that I should stay and grone?
>   The most of me to heav'n is fled;
> My thoughts and joyes are all packt up and gone,
>   And for their old acquaintance plead:
>   O, show Thyself to me,
>   Or take me up to Thee! [31]

The eucharistic meal alone—in its union with the suffering Saviour—anticipates the awaited encounter with the triumphant God, and encourages us to go on seeking him in ceaseless strife:

> Welcome, sweet and sacred cheer,
>   Welcome deare;
> With me, in me live and dwell:
> For thy neatnesse passeth sight,
>   Thy delight
> Passeth tongue to taste or tell.
>
> O what sweetnesse from the bowl
>   Fills my soul,
> Such as is and makes divine!
> Is some starre—fled from the sphere—
>   Melted there,
> As we sugar melt in wine!

31 *Home, ibid.*, p. 161.

... Doubtlesse neither starre nor flower
                    Hath the power
Such a sweetnesse to impart;
Onely God, Who gives perfumes,
                    Flesh assumes,
And with it perfumes my heart.

But as pomanders and wood
                    Still are good,
Yet being bruis'd are better scented;
God, to show how farre His love
                    Could improve,
Here, as broken, is presented.

... For with it alone I flie
                    To the skie;
Where I weep mine eyes, and see
What I seek for, what I sue;
                    Him I view
Who hath done so much for me.[32]

The effect of Herbert's type of piety on his flock can be seen in
one of his lay readers, Henry Vaughan.[33] Vaughan's poetry was
to become very personal, but at first it grew like ivy over the pillars
of the *Temple* built by Herbert. It then as it were crystallized in
Silex Scintillans, a poem that showed that the mystical spark was
brighter, if less sustained, in the disciple than in the gentle illuminations of the master.

A physician, who had first been drawn towards law on leaving
Jesus College, Oxford, and then joined the king's army, Henry
Vaughan (1622–1695) shared Walton's love for nature as revealing
divine glory. But as he was Welsh (Silurist, as he liked to call himself) the nature he loved was not at all the smiling countryside
round Winchester, but the streams and woods of a remote valley
where everything was redolent of fairyland. This was the valley of
the Usk where he lived and wanted to die, and the whiteness of
its orchards in springtime was a recurring image in his work (in
Welsh, white is often used to suggest magic). *Olor Iscanus*, the
Swan of Usk, was the title of his first collection of poems—a series

[32] *The Banquet, ibid.*, p. 264.
[33] Vaughan produced *Poems* in 1646, *Silex Scintillans* in 1650 (re-issued with
considerable additions, 1655), *The Mount of Olives*, 1652, *Flores solitudinis*, 1654,
Hermetical Physics, 1655, *Thalia rediviva*, 1678. The best modern edition of his
works is that of L. C. Martin, 2 vols., Clarendon Press, 1914. The best study
on him is F. E. Hutchinson, *Henry Vaughan, A Life and Interpretation*, Oxford,
1947. See too E. Holmes, *Henry Vaughan and the Hermetic Philosophy*, Oxford,
1932, and the essay on him in E. I. Watkin, *Poets and Mystics*, London, 1953,
pp. 272 *et seq.*

of translations from Latin, from Ovid, through Ausonius and Boethius, to an obscure neo-Latin Polish poet, Casimir.

In the two slim volumes of his *Silex* we find not only echoes of his former book, but his absorption in Herbert's *Temple* (which he made his breviary), as well as what was essentially his own. *Silex* is steeped in the imagery of alchemy borrowed from his twin brother Thomas,[34] a clergyman whose mystical leanings were enveloped in an impenetrable theosophical esotericism. With Henry, on the other hand, the image of natural transmutations is just a familiar medium for describing the latent presence of the other world that reveals itself in the inmost recesses of this one and will one day flood it with its light. This ever more lucid perception and ever more intense hope constitute the keynote of his work. His poems are often no more than commentaries in the margin of Herbert's, even their titles sometimes being the same. But his vision leaps out of his poems with more rapture than his master's, and yet with a simplicity still more homely if this is possible. It is a vision that often reminds us of the Rheno-Flemings and above all of Eckhart (whom he would not have known) because of a familiarity going side by side with etherial mysticism—and this not only on account of the occult images and neo-Platonic speculations that give it form. But his God is always the Father and it is always in Christ alone that he finds him.

Nothing is more characteristic than the opening and conclusion of *The World*:

> I saw Eternity the other night
> Like a great *Ring* of pure and endless light,
>   All calm, as it was bright,
> And round beneath it, Time in hours, days, years
>   Driv'n by the spheres
> Like a vast shadow mov'd, in which the world
>   And all her train were hurl'd . . .
>
> Yet some, who all this while did weep and sing,
> And sing, and weep, soar'd up into the *Ring*,
>   But most would use no wing.
> O fools (said I) thus to prefer dark night
>   Before true light,
> To live in grots, and caves, and hate the day
>   Because it shews the way,
> The way which from this dead and dark abode
>   Leads up to God,

[34] There are some poems by Thomas Vaughan (1621–1666) that Grossart published with those of his brother in a 4-vol. edition published in 1871 (in vol. 2). His prose works were edited by A. E. Whaite in 1919, *The Works of Thomas Vaughan: Eugenius Philalethes.*

A way where you might tread the Sun, and be
    More bright than he.
But as I did their madness so discusse
    One whisper'd thus,
This Ring the Bride-groome did for none provide
    But for his bride.[35]

The death of his first wife and young brother William hastened
the consummation of his hope: to be drawn into the Lord's Ascension:

They are all gone into the world of light!
    And I alone sit lingering here!
Their very memory is fair and bright,
    And my sad thoughts doth clear....

Dear beauteous Death, the jewel of the just,
    Shining nowhere but in the dark;
What mysteries do lie beyond thy dust,
    Could man outlook that mark!

He that hath found some fledg'd bird's nest may know,
    At first sight, if the bird be flown;
But what fair well or grove he sings in now,
    That is to him unknown.

And yet, as angels in some brighter dreams
    Call to the soul when man doth sleep,
So some strange thoughts transcend our wonted themes,
    And into glory peep.

If a star were confined into a tomb,
    Her captive flames must needs burn there;
But when the hand that locked her up gives room,
    She'll shine through all the sphere.

O Father of eternal life, and all
    Created glories under Thee!
Resume Thy spirit from this world of thrall
    Into true liberty!

Either disperse these mists, which blot and fill
    My perspective still as they pass;
Or else remove me hence unto that hill,
    Where I shall need no glass![36]

The soul's flight to God is but a return to its native country.
Whence the final poem concerning memories of childhood—an extraordinary foreshadowing of Wordsworth's ode, though Words-

---

[35] *The World* in Part 1 of *Silex Scintillans.*
[36] Second part of Ascension Hymn at the beginning of Part 2 of *Silex Scintillans.*
5*

worth seems not to have known this piece. But with Vaughan the nostalgia is not for human childhood but for an earlier one, the ageless youth that God holds in store for us all in eternity:

> Happy those early days when I
> Shin'd in my angel-infancy!
> Before I understood this place
> Appointed for my second race,
> Or taught my soul to fancy aught
> But a white, celestial thought;
> And yet I had not walked above
> A mile, or two, from my first Love,
> And looking back (at that short space)
> Could see a glimpse of His bright face; ...
> Some men a forward motion love,
> But I by backward steps would move;
> And when this dust falls to the urn,
> In that state I came, return.[37]

It was to this new and wholly supernatural childhood that another mystical poet of Anglicanism devoted all his poems. We know only the broad outline of Thomas Traherne's life (1637?– 1674). The son of a Hereford shoemaker, he was a student of Brasenose College, Oxford (thanks, no doubt, to the generosity of some rich patron), and for a time rector of a Herefordshire parish before ending up as chaplain to Sir Orlando Bridgman, Lord Keeper of the Seals, from 1667 to 1672. It was not until 1896 that the manuscript of his *Centuries of Meditations* and the poems that accompany it were found in a small second-hand bookshop, and they were brought out a few years later by Bertram Dobell.[38] Traherne was one of those great poets in prose whose verse by comparison seems almost flat. Since his belated discovery he has been praised, by Aldous Huxley among others, as one of the few mystics whose mystical experience has the effect of heightening rather than diminishing his appreciation of the created world. And it is true that the new way in which things are seen by an eye rejuvenated and regenerated by faith has seldom been better expressed. But this never-ending *Benedicite omnia opera Domini Domino* does not benefit from being so repeatedly pressed home (so different from Herbert whose full fragrance, like that of certain perfumes, only comes forth after being pressed in the hand—to use

---

[37] *The Retreate* in Part 1 of *Silex Scintillans.*
[38] First edition of *Poems* by Dobell in 1903 and of *Centuries* in 1908. Traherne himself prepared the publication of *Christian Ethics* which came out in 1675, a year after his death, and *A serious and pathetical Contemplation of the Mercies of God*, 1699, re-edited for the *University of Toronto* Studies by R. Danielle, 1941. The classic work on Traherne is G. I. Wade, *Thomas Traherne*, Princeton, 1944.

one of his own favourite similes). All evil is so totally banished from Traherne's jubilant vision that the continual praise soon rings false. We wonder how the perceptive author of *Christian Ethics* could have managed so successfully to ignore sin and suffering. Only the third of the *Centuries*—allusively autobiographical—pays even fleeting tribute to the existence of evil, and even here it is forgotten, or almost forgotten, as soon as recalled. This voluntary blindness coming from wilful innocence makes us suspect either his sincerity or his perception.

This type of uncertainty is also to be found in Richard Crashaw's (1613–1649) ravaged mysticism, though for a different reason. A Londoner, and son of the Puritan preacher of the Temple (of whom we shall speak again), he was educated at Charterhouse and Pembroke Hall, Cambridge, before becoming a fellow of Peterhouse, the most Laudian of the colleges. He was passionately fond of poetry, music and painting and a frequent visitor to Little Gidding. Here the flowery and exalted preacher that he was must have aroused the girls' smiles and blushes by the extravagant "mystical" madrigals he addressed to them, accustomed though they were to the metaphysical preciosity of the day.

All the tears, bitter potions, wings and flames that we found in Herbert—the necessary apparatus of the poetic school stemming from John Donne—are to be found in Crashaw, but run to seed. His conceits are the most baroque liquefactions and incandescences of the whole of English literature. This High Church Anglican's *Saint Teresa* has often been compared to Bernini's. But the sort of clammy sensuality in which the erotic imagery is drenched is more embarrassing in Crashaw if this be possible, and quickly leaves an after-taste of insipidity. It is the shamelessness of innocence, but an innocence that has passed maturity without ever reaching it. This falsely sensual liquor can only burn on a sea of sugariness, just like Traherne's falsely angelic will-o'-the-wisp. The psychoanalysts who detect a longing for the mother's breast behind Crashaw's orgy of pseudo-nuptial images are probably not far from the truth.

This semi-mystical poet was nevertheless a very touching figure, certainly very sincere, if a little hysterical in his way. Uprooted from his Anglo-Catholicism by the Puritan fury, he pursued a wretched existence wandering across Holland, France and Italy, in poor health and practically penniless. In spite of his conversion to Catholicism (probably in 1645) and the patronage of Henrietta Maria, he obtained a canonry at Loreto (the ideal place for him) only to die there.[39]

[39] Richard Crashaw published *Epigrammatum sacrarum Liber* in 1634, *Steps*

Protestants and Catholics are agreed in viewing his conversion to post-Tridentine Catholicism as the only possible course for a temperament such as his. This seems rather a hasty judgment. E. I. Watkin has had the curiosity to make a close study of the prose and poetry of Richard's Puritan (and very anti-Roman and anti-Catholic) father, William. All the son's characteristics of imagination, style and piety are foreshadowed in the father; all that is missing is the touch of genius.

Puritan Mysticism: Francis Rous

Here an important fact must be noted: that the hot-house mysticism that seems to many people a characteristic essential and proper to post-Tridentine Catholicism—like baroque taste in general—was nevertheless widely shared in the spiritual world of the Puritans. This passionate mysticism was not necessarily as equivocal in Catholicism as Crashaw's poetry might lead us to suppose; nor was it among the Puritans of the same period. The staggeringly bad taste on both sides of the fence should not conceal the purity and potential wholesomeness of an authentic love of God made man. In the vicinity of a rationalism that was already more than a threat, this love certainly showed its ardour in astonishing and disturbing ways, but love it undoubtedly was.

A number of Cromwell's chaplains figured among the eminent representatives of this vehement mystical feeling for Christ, and, surprising as it may seem, they were closer to many aspects of the Jesuits and Visitandines of the period than were the traditional Anglicans—at least so far as we can discover. How is this paradox to be explained? Much more easily than might be supposed.

The Anglo-Saxon Puritans of the seventeenth century were Calvin's most direct spiritual descendants. Their faith derived from him far more than did the scholasticism of the Dutch theologians such as Gomar, and the Dordrecht synod. But they were heirs whom Calvin would have viewed with some consternation. They diverged from him primarily by the marked pessimism with which they viewed the "world"; this gave their "discipline" its streak of gloomy asceticism, a streak unknown to the "discipline" that was Calvin's dream, for all his authoritarianism and rigorism. But this

---

to the Temple in 1646 (second augmented edition, 1648). His Carmen Deo nostro was published in Paris in 1652. The standard modern edition of his works is by L. C. Martin, 1927. See Austin Warren, Richard Crashaw, A Study in Baroque Sensibility, Louisiana State University, 1939, and the pages on him in Mario Praz, The Flaming Heart, New York, 1958. Cf. E. I. Watkin's two essays, Richard Crashaw and William Crashaw and his Son, pp. 136 et seq. in his Poets and Mystics.

outer shell of their religion, which made such a deep impression on their hostile contemporaries (one thinks of the satire in *Hudibras*), concealed a delectable content that was still further removed from Calvin whose intellectualism was so dry even when at its most passionate.

Calvin, in his doctrine of sanctification, was undoubtedly the first to introduce the explicit possibility of a *fruitio divina* anticipating eternal beatitude. But it is at least doubtful whether this, as he understood it, could be interpreted in any sort of mystical sense. Following Judaistic literalism, he seems rather to have had in mind a healthy enjoyment of the goods of this world already bestowed by God on his elect in so far as they were truly faithful. And although some of his expressions seem to allow for a foretaste of purely spiritual beatitude too, he does not seem to have been touched by a love of Christ the man in St Bernard's or St Francis's sense—a love that was so striking in the Puritans long before the advent of Pietism, and quite independently of orthodox Lutheran mysticism of whose very existence they were unaware. Not that we may doubt Calvin's love for Christ—but it was a cerebral love, not the spiritual love in which St Bernard wanted carnal love of the Saviour to reach its culmination. With the great spiritual writers of Puritanism, on the other hand, an evangelism still very much tinged with a late medieval love of Christ—evocative of Gerson and the *Imitation*—gave colour to the most Calvinistic themes.

All the Anglican spiritual writers mentioned above were viewed by the Puritans as mere "Arminians"—that is to say humanists who misunderstood the radically supernatural quality of grace. Here again (as Jardine Grisbrooke brought out so well in connection with the rejection by the Scottish Calvinists of the eucharistic liturgy of the *Prayer Book*), it was the persistence of the Zwinglian spirit that shocked the Puritans, much more than details of the supposedly idolatrous Catholic liturgy retained by Cranmer and the Caroline divines. They viewed with horror the rejection, or at least the excessive spiritualization, of Christ's real presence. And it is worth noting that even Herbert's moving poem on the subject (quoted above) projects the realism of his Christic mysticism on to the Eucharist rather than drawing the realism from it. The poem is concerned with the spiritual banquet, but there is nothing in it to show any direct inspiration from Communion. And even with Andrewes we find no doctrinal formulation of the real presence that goes beyond the ambiguities of Alexandrian symbolism—even though, according to Brightman, he rounded off Cranmer's eucharistic liturgy with "devotions" borrowed from ancient liturgies, and in spite of the lights, incense, ornaments and ceremonial that he re-introduced into his private chapel.

The Puritans, on the other hand, while not going so far as to believe that Christ whole and entire, with his humanity and divinity, was to be found in the consecrated species, most certainly believed that eucharistic communion received with faith brought about sub-stantial union with Christ. From this they drew a very realistic mysticism of Christ—one that easily became emotional if not car-nal, and completed the unconscious Pelagianism lying behind their passionate struggle towards some sort of tangible sanctification.

This supernaturalism of intention, though affirmed in a factual incarnationalism in which they tended to imagine the reality of grace in such a palpable way that they unknowingly naturalized it, was not so very far removed from many of the Counter-Reforma-tion tendencies. So we should not be surprised that it produced similar fruits or so unhesitatingly drew on the same sources. Our Puritan friends, like Crashaw's father, could rant against the Jesuits as they liked, but their prayers so closely resembled those of the Jesuits that the osmoses that we shall be obliged to point out, how-ever improbable a priori, were not at all exceptional.[40]

One of the most striking examples of all this was Francis Rous (1579–1669). He was a layman from Cornwall who became provost of Eton under the Commonwealth and ended up as Speaker in the House of Commons. He wrote a commentary on the Song of Songs that is surprising from many points of view.

We should note that plenty of other Puritans wrote commen-taries on this text, but they usually did so in the spirit of Origen's Homilies, where it is the Church that is the bride of Christ and not the soul that is the bride of the Word as in the great Commentary. Such was the case with Richard Sibbes's The Spouse (London, 1638). Although he says that "all Christian favours belong to all Christians alike" and that "every Christian soule is the Spouse of Christ, as well as the whole Church" (ibid., pp. 13–14), he in fact only applies this to the reception of the Eucharist and from it deduces a mystical moralism rather than an experimental mysti-cism.

But this is not the case with Rous's treatise, Mystical Marriage, or Experimental Discourses of the Heavenly Marriage between a Soul and her Saviour.[41] He himself explains the principle of the nuptial mysticism of which Christ, God made man, is the object: the soul's uncleanness does not allow it to unite itself with God

---

[40] On Puritan piety in general see Gordon S. Wakefield, Puritan Devotion. London, 1957.
[41] Published in 1635.

unless there is a mediator. But there is a "pure counterpart" to our nature, and "that pure humanity is immediately knit to the purest Deity". So, just as Jesus Christ is one with God by personal union, so the human soul can be made one with God by "mystical union".[42]

Certainly this union will only be fully consummated in eternity. Life on earth is no more than the time of betrothal. But, as Gordon S. Wakefield[43] rightly points out, we should not forget that to the Puritan a betrothal was a solemn contract whereby the parties belonged mutually to each other in a way that was in principle irrevocable. Thus mystical betrothals implied renunciation of all that belonged to the old man. But the possession of Christ obtained in return was the possession of a new universe at the same time as a new possession of the universe. For was he not "all lights in one light, all glories in one glorie, all beauties in one beauty, all joys in one joy"? Moreover, the soul "hath him by whom the worlds were made, and therefore she hath all the worlds made by him".[44]

This possession should be made manifest in the soul by an active obedience as the fruit of union. It cannot stay idle, for the enjoyment of it presupposes "doing and suffering". In a word, it is normally from the height of tribulation that the soul will reach the summit of union.[45] To persecution and other external trials are added those inner trials that arise when the soul believes itself to be abandoned by the Bridegroom and handed over to the ghosts of its former lusts. But these trials are necessary so as to purify the soul, and so that the soul may strip itself of all pride and discover how the love of Christ surpasses any sensual experience we may think we have of it. As Rous says in a magnificent phrase: "When the wine of natural joy is spent and there is nothing left but the water of affliction, then doth Christ turn this water into wine."

When Christ returns, the soul will not only cling closer to him, will retain his presence more surely and thus be able to enjoy it more intimately and for longer,[46] but it will also discover that Christ was with it, and closer than ever, in the time of trial, as a means of preparing the soul for ultimate union. For Christ and his love "are thine when thou seest or feelest not that they are thine ... He and his love are better than the seeing and feeling of him and his love; ... better for thee that they are thine, than that they appear to be thine; ... therefore at all times and in all estates, even in

---

[42] *Mystical Marriage*, pp. 8 and 9.
[43] *Op. cit.*, p. 103.   [44] *Mystical Marriage*, p. 73.
[45] *Ibid.*, p. 79.   [46] *Ibid.*, p. 113.

darkest desertions and greatest sufferings, trust in him whose love turns all things to good unto his beloved, even death unto life."

All this is remarkably close to Luther's teaching on justification by faith. But at the same time there could be no better way of showing how all that is most positive in this teaching opens out naturally into St John of the Cross's mysticism of the purifying nights of the soul.

During the Beloved's "desertions", the soul should "sigh and pray and read and hear", preparing itself by these earthly works "as a bride that looks for her husband". During this time its waiting should be concentrated on the place and time when the fulfilling presence will return and remain, remembering that it is lodged for the moment in a house of clay and has no converse with its Bridegroom except through the cracks effected by the Spirit, whereas in the homeland nothing will ever separate them again. Following a line of thought very like St Bernard's, the Bridegroom's "visitations" must then be viewed as a comfort and a "stocke of confidence" against times of aridity which will maintain and deepen the longing for eternity.[47]

When the supernatural light shines it does nothing to remove the light of reason, but, when its light supervenes, reason readily makes way for it and yields to it. Thus the more Christ comes into the soul by the Spirit, "the more spiritual he doth make her; yea, the more he doth melt a soule in himselfe; the more he doth turne her will into his will, and the more doth he increase his own image in her; and we know that his image is righteousness and true holiness".[48]

The book ends in prayer the aim of which is to dispose the soul to yield to these visitations and thus to prepare itself for the perfect and definitive union:

> By often visitations, put thy own image and beauty more and more on my soule and then love thy own beauty which thou hast put on her and let my soule love thee infinitely for being infinitely more beautiful than that beauty which thou hast put on my soule and therefore infinitely more lovely than that which thou lovest in my soule.

Once more we come up against the infinite distance between Christ and the soul, even when saved, justified and sanctified, the absolute and permanent dependence of the soul on Christ that Luther strove so hard to maintain in the face of a pantheistic interpretation of mysticism in which God and the soul become indistinguishable. For all that, the similarity of Rous's terms and those

---

[47] *Ibid.*, pp. 202–203.   [48] *Ibid.*, pp. 255–256.

of St John of the Cross is so marked—as E. I. Watkin has pointed out—that the conjunction cannot be due to mere coincidence.[49] And there are no grounds for supposing that the meaning Rous gave to the terms was significantly different from the saint's (from whom he probably borrowed them). The following prayers show clearly that for Rous, as for the Spanish mystic, God's transcendence in eternity as in this life—and even though union with Christ is unrealizable this side of death—in no way prevents the full reality of the transforming union even in the present.

> Let the soule drink plentifully that she may be mounted up in a divine ecstasy above her carnal and earthly station.

And he makes the soul say to the Bridegroom in its supplication:

> Let the measure sometimes be not only full but running over to a spiritual drunkenness but not unto drowning: for these ecstasies and excesses of love shall somewhat increase my ability of loving thee. For when my understanding, will and affections are all overflown, overcome and amazed, then shall my wonder gaze on thee and my very faintings shall be inflamed towards thee and melt me into thee.

As he says again of the soul and the Christ-Bridegroom:

> The spirit of union is fire, and fire turns that into itself to which it is united . . . He and she are met in the heats of a spiritual conjugation and the excesses of a fruitive union.

It would be hard to find a more complete expression of the most traditional Christian mysticism, and impossible to show better how this mysticism, far from being in opposition to the true notion of salvation acquired by faith alone in the sole grace of God in Christ, is no more than its fulfilment in the faithful soul.

Yet if we were tempted to imagine that the theme of the mystical marriage between Christ and the Christian soul was incapable of sinking into bad taste and turbid emotionalism outside the framework of actual Catholics or Catholics by desire, like poor Crashaw, then we should read a few pages—or even a few lines—of the Scottish Puritan, Samuel Rutherford. Here we find as much slumbering in the arms of Christ as we could wish, and swooning on his breast, and the exchange of languorous and sophisticated kisses. All that is lacking is a touch of real poetry which, at least in Crashaw, makes up for these tasteless bits of nonsense.[50]

---

[49] *Poets and Mystics*, p. 154. Watkin compares this doctrine of Rous's with verse 36 of the *Cantico espiritual* and its commentary.
[50] See Gordon S. Wakefield, *op. cit.*, p. 107.

Thomas Goodwin and the Sacred Heart

There was another spiritual writer of the same period whose spirituality was as pure and uplifted as Rous's but possibly even nearer to its contemporary Catholic counterpart. In this case any possible interplay of influences would have worked in the opposite direction. We are referring to a synthesis of the devotion to the Sacred Heart which irresistibly reminds us of Paray-le-Monial ... but a good half-century before Margaret-Mary Alacoque. This occurs in Thomas Goodwin's *The Heart of Christ in Heaven towards Sinners on Earth.*[51]

Goodwin was born in Norfolk in 1600, and after being expelled from Cambridge by Laud became Cromwell's chaplain and one of the most influential preachers in the Long Parliament (and one of the most insistent on the need to purify the English Church of all traces of "popery").[52]

We can best explain the theme of his book in his own words:

The purpose of this Discourse is to lay open the Heart of Christ, as now He is in heaven—how it is affected and graciously disposed towards sinners on earth that do come to Him, how willing to receive them, how ready to entertain them, how tender to pity them in all their infirmities, both sins and miseries ...

The drift of this discourse is therefore to ascertain poor souls that His Heart, in respect of pity and compassion, remains the same as it was on earth, that He is as meek, as gentle, as easy to be entreated, so that they may deal with Him as fairly about the great matter of their own salvation, and as hopefully and upon as easy terms obtain it of Him, as they might if they had been on earth with Him and be as familiar with Him in all their requests, as bold with Him in all their needs.[53]

The first part of his treatise thus shows us that the "gracious dispositions of Christ's Heart towards us" are always the same; the second part shows why this is so; and the third gives an outline of how this consoling mystery operates.

The first part consists of a commentary on the discourses after the Last Supper according to St John. Goodwin is concerned to establish that the love Christ showed his disciples right to the end —a divine love but incarnated in a heart just like our own exclud-

---

[51] Published in 1652,

[52] Thomas Goodwin's works were published in 5 vols. from 1681 to 1704. They were reprinted in 6 vols. in 1861. See the study on him in John Brown, *Puritan Preaching in England*, London, 1900. E. I. Watkin has devoted one of his best chapters to him in *Poets and Mystics*, pp. 56 *et seq.*: *A Puritan Devotion to the Sacred Heart*.

[53] This quotation may be found in Watkin, *op. cit.*

ing the sin—is the love with which he intends to love us for ever.[54]
According to Goodwin, the promise of the Holy Spirit concretises
this permanent disposition of the Heart of Jesus towards us which
he revealed to his disciples as the meaning of his whole work.[55]

The promise to answer prayer and Jesus's own prayer after the
Last Supper are seen as the supreme witness which puts the seal
on the revelation of Christ's Heart. And his appearances after the
resurrection reveal not only its permanence but its definitive flowering in the sanctified, glorified body of the risen Christ.[56]

Just as the Holy Spirit's promise had affirmed the disposition—
and the definitive disposition—of Christ's Heart in our regard, so
the realization of this promise makes it as if tangible to us, particularly in eucharistic communion.

The second part of Goodwin's work is intended to enlighten us
on the deep reasons for the humanity that the Son of God took on
himself for ever. Why did he want to have a fully human heart,
and retain it even in his glory? Goodwin finds the explanation in
the Epistle to the Hebrews: "We have not an High Priest which
cannot be touched with the feeling of our infirmities, but was in
all points tempted like as we are, yet without sin." God's love, in
effect, is communion, which must extend to us to make us enter
into it. In this way God, in his Son, takes on himself our human
heart so that this heart, in us, can love as he loves.[57]

The Holy Spirit, who should dwell in our hearts, dwells first and
foremost in the Heart of Jesus, and it is through this Heart that we
have been shown what man's heart should become when subsumed
into it.[58] And even now, if the Holy Spirit is to produce the same
effect in us, he must dwell in his Heart, irradiating it more than ever
with tenderness and compassion which always remain just as
human in their supernatural condition. It is thus that divine love,
in the risen and glorified Christ himself, as in us, should not destroy
but increase the natural affections. From Christ to us, and for ever,
divine love thus becomes like a Bridegroom's love, who loves, in
his Bride, his own flesh.[59]

So—and we can find similar views in Bérulle—just as Christ
has his divine fullness in his personal union with the Godhead, he
wants for himself a human fullness in his union consummated with
all mankind.[60]

But then Goodwin asks himself: "But was not the son of God as
merciful without the taking of our nature?" His answer is magnificent: He could have been, but the incarnation gives a human

---

[54] Watkin, *op. cit.*, p. 62.
[55] *Ibid.*, p. 63.
[56] *Ibid.*, pp. 63–64.
[57] *Ibid.*, p. 65.
[58] *Ibid.*, p. 65.
[59] *Ibid.*, p. 66.
[60] *Ibid.*, pp. 66–67.

character to his love which allows us ourselves to love him in a human way, with a love that echoes his, and indeed is his.[61]

The third part consists of a theological justification of this doctrine by a speculative analysis of the continuance right into the glory of heaven of all that is essential to the manhood Christ took upon himself. It rests on a solid and positive basis drawn from all tradition. The central problem that would later be raised by the whole spirituality of Paray-le-Monial—of how the glorified Christ can still be affected by our suffering and sins—is resolved with a delicacy that could hardly be surpassed.

Abbé Bremond, who was probably introduced to this book by his friend Alexander Whyte, perceived all its purity and beauty and was greatly struck by its containing a sort of anticipatory synthesis of all the objective aspects of the Paray-le-Monial apparitions: the physical Heart of Jesus as presented to sinners even in its glorification. He felt it necessary to add: "It would nevertheless be absurd to attribute to Goodwin the slightest influence over the Paray-le-Monial movement."[62]

And indeed we ourselves do not see any channel by which these resemblances—sometimes reaching identity—can be explained. And yet it might be over-cautious to assume *a priori* that influences are to be entirely ruled out. As we shall see, even the most anti-Roman Puritans saw no harm in reading the spiritual works of the "papists" and deriving all possible profit from them. Were the French clergy who sent a note of congratulation to the Anglican Bishop Bull for his *Defensio fidei nicaenae* incapable of also reading the Puritans? It is not self-evident.

And even if in this particular case the similarities are a coincidence, the coincidence is far from fortuitous. Agreements of this kind in spiritual works of roughly the same period are at least a sign of the community of religious thought and culture that went much further than people have hitherto realized.

The Theology of the Covenant from Perkins to Ames

Works such as those of Rous and Goodwin represent high-water marks in Protestant spirituality and, we have no hesitation in adding, in Christian spirituality as a whole. But in seventeenth-century Puritan spirituality works of this kind were not so much exceptions as exceptionally successful examples of a wide current of thought. And as such they raise a problem.

However faithful they were to the great religious intuitions of

---

[61] *Ibid.*, p. 67.
[62] P. 641 of *L'Ecole française* (vol. III of *Histoire littéraire du sentiment religieux*).

the Reformation and especially to Calvin at his best in his doctrine
of sanctification, coming after Luther's doctrine of justification, we
can find nothing in these works to contradict, or even to disagree
with, Catholic faith. We must go further: whatever their individual
doctrine on other points, when these Protestants were dealing with
spirituality they expressed a faith whose substance had become
Catholic again. In other words, the spiritual and intellectual universe within which Luther, and even Calvin, had thought out their
faith had apparently disappeared. That world—heir to late medieval thought, to Ockham's Nominalism, Scotist voluntarism and exaggerated Augustinianism, the world in which biblical realism had
seemed condemned to vaporization in ultra-spirituality, and the
transcendence of the Christian God to destruction in an equally
radical monism or dualism—that shattered world was no longer
theirs.

What then had happened? We must not imagine that a change
of such magnitude was the product of a mere intellectual revolution. Here as elsewhere, the logic that subtends thought was, as
Newman puts it, less the cause of change than the barometer indicating its presence in the atmosphere. The changes themselves were
undoubtedly mainly the outcome of a fertilization by the Bible
which refashioned thought by giving it new life. But this does not
mean that philosophical reflection did not play its part by helping
the implicit to become explicit. In fact during the first part of the
seventeenth century, Puritan theological thought was recast in a
way the importance of which we are only just beginning to realize.
The man who has shed most light on this is the distinguished historian of American Puritanism, Perry Miller, in his crucial work
The New England Mind.[63] For he established the importance for
Puritan culture—whose focus was to become John Harvard's university in Massachusetts—of the adoption by the English Puritan
theologians of the previous generation of what was called Ramist
logic.

It is an amazing thing that no important study has yet been devoted to Ramus in France. Ramus was a Frenchman who was
almost entirely unknown in his own country, but his intellectual
influence in the English-speaking world equalled, if it did not sur-
pass, that of Descartes; and, incidentally, he was one of Descartes's
precursors and possibly one of his sources.

His real name was Pierre la Ramée (1515–1572). He was one
of the first royal lectors at the Collège de France and one of the
most regretted victims of the criminal insanity of the massacre of

[63] Perry Miller, *The New England Mind; the XVIIth Century*, New York, 1939,
re-issued in 1954 and 1961.

St Bartholomew. An early partisan of the Reformation, he was a grammarian and a logician and had no intention of assuming the mantle of a metaphysician. But like many other logicians before and after him who would set out from an analysis of language, he prepared the way for a metaphysical revolution. For the Protestants who followed him he sounded the death-knell of the Scotist and above all Ockhamist notion of *potentia absoluta* whose ghost Luther had never been able to lay, and which Calvin had carried to its logical conclusion with his theology of law and predestination and, finally, the Word of God.   ,

In this way Ramus undoubtedly linked up with the liberal humanism from which Zwingli and the non-Calvinist reformed Churches proceeded, and he consciously struck at the root of the idea of an irrational authority which the greatest reformers had so closely identified with their notion of the Word of God. But the genius for compromise which is supposedly so typically Anglo-Saxon was to produce a dynasty of theologians who wanted to be Calvinists to the extent of detecting "Arminianism" all over the place, yet were capable of combining Ramist logic with all that was best in Calvinist theology.

Ramus was a ferocious anti-Aristotelian. But like the medieval nominalists themselves, and following an interpretation that links up with more than one modern historian, he saw in Aristotle's system not the moderate realism that St Thomas read (or wanted to read) into his conceptualism, but a radical, or at least a seminal, Nominalism. Such a position seemed to him to do no more—pure agnosticism apart—than open up thought to a blind submission to some arbitrary authority, and this he was unprepared to accept at any price. Whence a neo-realism based on a doctrine of participation, in which the reality of a structure common to thought and being was revealed in language.

The theologian William Perkins (1558–1602) had introduced Ramist logic into his treatise on sacred eloquence, which was to dominate Puritan preaching for a number of generations. But Perkins, while rejoicing in the Calvinist doctrine of the divine will, "absolute rule for both justice and reason"—understood in the voluntarist sense that what God wills becomes "reasonable and just by this very fact"—was unable to foresee the complete reversal of the terms of this equivalence for which his introduction of Ramist logic prepared the way.[64]

This reversal became plain in the work of his pupil, William

---

[64] First edition of his *Complete Works* in 1600. See Perry Miller, *op. cit.*, pp. 335 *et seq.* Cf. appendices on Ramus and on the "federal" school.

Ames (1576–1633), *Medulla Sacrae Theologiae*.[65] He was the father of the theology of the Covenant which was to be developed with him or after him by John Preston, Richard Sibbes and many others both in old and New England. According to this view God made a first covenant with Adam which was the basis of the religion of works and rested on the law inscribed in our nature. Had it not been for the fall, the covenant would have led Adam to perfection. The fall, however, brought about a new compensating covenant, based on faith, which began with Abraham and reached its perfection in Christ. It saves those who believe, not by doing away with the law of nature, immutable in itself, but by giving to faith, in the grace of the mediator, the power to accomplish what had become beyond the capacity of nature.

In this way all arbitrariness in the divine will disappeared. Faith was no longer in opposition to reason, and grace no longer condemned nature. Rather, faith restored perverted reason just as grace healed vitiated nature.

The only weakness in this neo-realism—the weakness of all Platonist-type systems of logic or metaphysics of participation—was that it was so successful in re-establishing the harmony of grace with nature, of faith with reason, that it ran the risk of leading to sheer identification. This was soon to show itself among the Cambridge Platonists, and, more, among the Oxford latitudinarians gathered round Lord Falkland, and especially in the tolerance of all possible opinions as preached by William Chillingworth (1602–1644) on the basis of a purely rational faith. And it was to come fully into its own with the naturalistic deism of Lord Herbert of Cherbury.

But before reaching that point we pass through a position of equilibrium, unfortunately very unstable. This we find at its best moment in the rational but still completely Christian spirituality of yet another of Cromwell's chaplains, Peter Sterry, before the flowering of the Cambridge Platonists' religious thought. But the worm of rationalism was already gnawing at the flower of a spirituality of inner enlightenment.

Peter Sterry (1613–1672)

Peter Sterry, chaplain first to Robert Greville, second Lord Brooke, and subsequently to Cromwell, was one of the most famous Puritan preachers among those with independent leanings.[66] He

---

[65] Franeker (Holland), 1623; translated into English: *The Marrow of Sacred Divinity*, 1642 (perhaps there had already been an edition in 1638 which was lost).
[66] See V. de Sola Pinto, *Peter Sterry, Platonist and Puritan (1613–1672)*.

was at the opposite pole from the austerity generally ascribed to the Puritans owing to the freedom with which he drew on classical literature to illustrate his thought, and to his inclination to explain the great myths of antiquity in terms of allegory and as dark echoes of the teaching of the Bible. The Puritan master of the next generation, Baxter, stigmatized Sterry and with him the whole group of Cambridge Platonists (mostly, like himself, from Emmanuel College), for being "a mixture of Platonism, Origenism and Arianism", and far more rationalistic than scriptural.

In fact Sterry was a Platonist more by the general atmosphere of his thought than by any study of, or fertilization by, Platonism; and like the best among the Platonists, he wanted to be and thought he was a perfect Calvinist. But with him Calvin's autocratic God turned into a sovereign "poet", in all the original richness of that word. By that we mean that the ideal beauty of God's love and goodness was the source of all reality. In this divine beauty, "freedom and necessity meet in unity". Reciprocally, in man, reason as he understood it was what Coleridge was later to understand by imagination: the faculty which unites in itself the spiritual world and the corporal world.

Thus he says:

If thou hadst any taste or glimpse of the glory of God in thy soul, thou wouldst feel a sweet peace within thee, with thy God, with thyself and with all things. The soul that dwells in this love thinks no evil of God, of itself, of anything but is at peace with all, hath sweet thoughts of all. For God is its eye by which it sees and its heart by which it thinks.[67]

It follows that:

Holiness and happiness are both one thing in God and the soul. Each is an elevation above all inferior corrupting or corruptible things and an habitation in the Supreme Good.[68]

For:

All the goings forth of Wisdom in thy spirit are peaceful and pleasant. If wisdom enlighten thy way, all the outgoings of thy soul into things and all the appearance of things to thy soul will be like a sweet tune or pleasant dance.[69]

In order to arrive at this point all we need is for faith to open us up to Wisdom in mystery which is the Wisdom of Christ as St Paul preached it to us:

Comprehend all, thyself and all, in the incomprehensible

---

[67] *The Rise, Race and Royalty of the Kingdom of God in the Soul of Man*, 1683, p. 88.
[68] *Ibid.*, p. 134.   [69] *Ibid.*, p. 165.

mystery of God. There see, hear, taste, enjoy Him as beauty itself, sweetness itself, music itself, joy itself in all. See, hear, taste, enjoy all as that beauty, that music, that sweetness, that joy in Him.[70]

For this Wisdom in mystery brings us to the discovery of divine love in all things:

> Divine love is the most universal and importunate beggar. It cometh to the door of every spirit. It knocketh. It presseth in.[71]

Revelation, when accepted, becomes a universal enlightenment:

> The love presence of God is a light of glory shining round about thee.[72]

Coming down to us, however far we may be from it, God's love will draw us up to itself:

> Mercy is the circle of Divine Love as it cometh forth from heaven and eternity, goeth down to the lowest depths of time and the creation, then ascendeth again, till like the sun it return thither where it first arose. Poor broken spirits who lie mourning as outcasts, hope evermore in the eternal love, wait for it. The love of God will find you out. It will meet with you and take you in its way. For Divine Love is eternal. It encompasseth heaven and earth, time and eternity . . . All motions in the heart of God and in the creature, of grace and nature are founded upon the unmovableness, the unchangeableness of eternal love. O blessed love, O blessed God who is this love![73]

This love which is the source of all things in the creature is, in fact, God's very being:

> The heart of God, the divine Nature is all love. All the wonders of God are wonders of love. What joy is this to understand that all that we cannot understand in the nature of things, which is as a thick darkness round about us, is a glorious mystery of Divine Love! That all that everywhere, of every creature, of every providence of the Creator Himself in which our spirits are swallowed up and lost, is an abyss of love, a great and shining deep of Divine Love![74]

And in the end Divine Wisdom upholding all things is revealed as "the music of love".[75] Hence the irrepressible conclusion:

> Abide in the Father's love by spiritual joy. Joy is love flaming. One saith, that laughter is the dance of the spirits, their freest motion in the harmony, and that the light of the heavens is the

---

70 *Ibid.*, p. 282.   71 *Ibid.*, p. 308.
72 *Ibid.*, p. 319.   73 *Ibid.*, pp. 324–325.
74 *Ibid.*, p. 327.   75 *Ibid.*, p. 334.

laughter of Angels. Spiritual joy is the laughter of Divine Love, of the eternal Spirit, which is love, in our spirits.[76]

As Watkin points out,[77] random texts such as these give an impression of Puritan spirituality that could hardly differ more from the impression given of it by its narrow exponents in the following generations. It is not hard to believe that Sterry (who was present at Cromwell's Christian deathbed) played his part in a first attempt at an extension of toleration even towards Catholics, and this in the Protector's last years and before the Stuart restoration. But we may well fear that behind this mysticism of heavenly harmony, where divine Wisdom is so naturally wedded to human reason, there already lay an element of latitudinarianism; in other words the transcendent meaning of revelation had been in some way effaced. Such fears seem all the more justified when we turn from Sterry to his fellow-pupils of Emmanuel College, the Cambridge Platonists.

The Spirituality of the Cambridge Platonists: John Smith and Henry More

The group of Cambridge Platonists was composed of moderate Puritans who had never wished to break with the Anglican Church. But it is difficult to decide whether the *pietas anglicana* with which their Plato-saturated Calvinism had certainly come to terms was due more to their devotion to tradition or to their indifference to external forms.[78]

Their common master was Benjamin Whichcote (1609–1685).[79] He was a pupil, fellow and tutor at Emmanuel—the college that has been called "the great nursery of Puritan thought"—and a humanist in the tradition of Erasmus and Hooker. When reproached by his own tutor, Tuckney, with leading his pupils to Plato, Cicero (the Cicero of the *Tusculanes*, of course) and Plotinus, his answer was that he spent much more time on Calvin, Perkins and Theodore de Bèze. In fact, as Tuckney again complained, Whichcote had taken the sentence from the Book of Proverbs (20. 27), "Man's spirit is a lamp the Lord gives . . .", as his motto, and it became the motto of all his school. For him man's spirit was

---

[76] *Ibid.*, p. 390.
[77] *Poets and Mystics*, pp. 59–60.
[78] On the Cambridge Platonists in general, see F. J. Powicke, *Cambridge Platonists*, 1930; G. P. H. Pawson, *Cambridge Platonists*, 1930; W. C. de Pauley, *Candle of the Lord*, 1937; E. Cassirer, *Die Platonische Renaissance in England und die Schule von Cambridge*, Leipzig, 1932, as well as the chapter devoted to them in Douglas Bush, *English Literature in the earlier Seventeenth Century*, pp. 340 *et seq.*
[79] His *Select Sermons* were published based on his hearers' notes in 1698. His complete works were published in Aberdeen in 4 vols. in 1751. A selection of them in E. T. Campagnac, *Cambridge Platonists*, 1901.

essentially *recta ratio*. But Whichcote justified himself by pointing out that *recta ratio* could only be found where there was *recta fides*. As he saw things, there could be no conflict between the two, for God was perfect reason and goodness, and reason and goodness were natural to man despite his fall which had gone against his very nature. Hence nothing could be genuinely religious without being rational, and nothing could be genuinely rational without being religious. However, since the fall, man's reason, like his natural religion, needed to be reinforced and restored by revelation, in other words by Christ, both as principle of life within us and as Saviour outside us.

At first sight this doctrine merely makes grace a part of nature; as has been said, it is a natural supernaturalism. But if we go deeper into the meaning Whichcote ascribed to the terms he used, we see that his thought was subtler and patient of a far deeper and more satisfying interpretation. For by "reason" he did not mean merely the logical and critical faculty, but that capacity for attaining truth that belongs, according to Plato, only to the soul taken in its entirety, or even to man taken in his entirety. This, like many similar expressions used by the Greek Fathers, can be interpreted as a vocation and native disposition (but supernatural, in the sense in which we use the word today) for knowing the Truth in its divine plenitude—a disposition which the fall would have irreparably deprived of its capacity for fulfilment had it not been for the gift of revelation and grace.

We come across plenty of quotations from Whichcote and his disciples, and notably John Smith, which leave us in no doubt that this is the way things should be interpreted. "Reason", which Christ's grace does no more than restore, is the equivalent of *nous* in writers like Gregory of Nyssa or Evagrius: that delicate point or spark of the soul of which the mystics spoke, made for union with God but unable to attain that union unless his penetrating and absorbing presence is given, or given back, to it by the Holy Spirit.

Unfortunately our Christian Platonists remained the children of their time, so we find in them a ceaseless tendency to slip from the theologically orthodox meaning of their *recta ratio* into the meaning current in their epoch. Whence the unavoidable risk of ending up—as happened with Lord Falkland's group—in a rational Christianity, in the sense of a Christianity watered down to natural religion—"within the limits of reason", as Kant was to put it.

It is here that we put our finger on the permanent temptation of those Christian systems of theology which take refuge in Platonist realism. Though such Platonism is excellent for expressing the creature's participation in the life of the Creator, it provides no safe criterion for preventing such participation from turning into pure and simple fusion. Even the notion of stable and relatively autonomous natures is lacking, together with the very possibility of conceiving them. In particular it is impossible to maintain an unbreakable distinction between God's infinity and the finiteness of creatures.

The reconciliation of reason and revelation, as Whichcote epigrammatically formulated it in his *Aphorisms*, was worked out systematically by a pupil who became a fellow of Emmanuel in his turn. This was Nathaniel Culverwell (1619–1651?), in his *Discourse on the Light of Nature*.[80] But it remained for Ralph Cudworth (1617–1688), another student and then fellow of Emmanuel, and subsequently Regius Professor of Hebrew and Master of Christ's College (Milton's *alma mater*), to develop Cambridge Platonism into a complete world system. *The True Intellectual System of the Universe* (1678) is an affirmation of the reality of mind and its priority over things, and, under the guidance of divine providence, of the transcendence and immutability of the rational laws of morality. To this last problem Cudworth also devoted his posthumous work (which only saw the light in 1731), *Treatise concerning eternal and immutable Morality*. In addition Cudworth was the author of a celebrated sermon on the religion of the heart,[81] preached before Parliament in 1647.

Yet it is to John Smith[82] that we must look for the richest spiritual developments of which the thought of the Cambridge Platonists was capable—developments that in their turn provided it with its most substantial nourishment. For him, as for Whichcote, knowledge and love of God must be translated into an imitation that informs our whole life. But no one was as fitted as he for defining and giving life to the notion of the inner "rational" light which was the mainspring of this school of Christian Platonism.

By his own account Smith lived on Doctor Whichcote. But in fact he was a man of such prodigious learning that one of his colleagues at Queen's, Simon Patrick, future Bishop of Ely, described him in his funeral panegyric as a living library and a walking museum. An important characteristic of his learning was his first-hand knowledge of the Bible and of Judaism, drawn from the

[80] Published in 1652.

[81] His *True Intellectual System* was re-edited with abundant notes by J. Harrison, in 3 vols., in 1845. The most recent study on him is by Lydia Gysi, *Platonism and Cartesianism in the Philosophy of Ralph Cudworth*, Bern, 1962.

[82] The *Select Discourses*, with Simon Patrick's sermon, were edited by John Worthington. Bibliography given by R. C. Christie, *Bibliography of John Worthington* (Chetham Society, N.S., vol., XIII, 1888). Good studies on him by Rufus M. Jones in his *Spiritual Reformers in the XVIth and XVIIth Centuries*, 1914, and by Watkin, *Poets and Mystics*, pp. 238 *et seq.*

original Hebrew and "Chaldean" (as it was then called) texts—as
well as of Plato and Plotinus. The outcome was a wealth of religion
in his thought going hand in hand with intellectual clarity and a
fine command of language. These qualities, added to the fact that
the only work by him that has come down to us is a volume of
Select Discourses (published in 1660), guarantee him a relative survival outside specialized circles such as his friends and colleagues
could hardly hope to attain.

He left Emmanuel for Queen's at an early stage and there he
ended his short life (1618–1652).

In a vein that was not only Platonic but even more pronouncedly
Alexandrian, Smith saw the whole universe in terms of a symbolic
manifestation of the presence and goodness of God:

> There is a twofold meaning in every creature, a literal and a
> mystical, and the one is but the ground of the other ... God made
> the universe and all the creatures contained therein as so many
> glasses wherein he might reflect His own glory. He hath copied
> forth Himself in the Creation ... How to find God there and
> feelingly converse with Him and being affected with the sense of
> the Divine Glory shining out upon the creation, how to pass out
> of the sensible world into the intellectual is effectively taught ...
> by true religion: that which knits and unites God and the soul
> together can best teach it how to ascend and descend upon those
> golden links that unite, as it were, the world to God ... That
> Divine Wisdom that contrived and beautified this glorious struc-
> ture can best explain her own art and carry up the soul back
> again in these reflected beams to ... the fountain of them. ...
> When good men are thus conversing with this lower world and
> are viewing the invisible things of God in the things that are
> made, in this visible and outward creation, they find God many
> times secretly flowing into their souls and leading them silently
> out of the court of the temple into the holy place.[83]

But in opposition to this is fallen man's tendency to concentrate
solely on the earthly aspect of creatures and draw from it merely
egotistical and sensual enjoyment. Hence man must endeavour to
emerge from this fog that blurs his vision of the world and darkens
the invisible sun that gives it light (*ibid.*). This essential purification should detach us from all impatience and violence, from all
self-seeking and self-assertion, as well as from all prejudice. God
is both light and life: so we cannot contemplate his light save by
preparation through a purified life.[84] This is a purely Platonic view.
But Smith rounds it off with the statement that such purification
is the outcome of true religion.

---

[83] *9th Discourse*, chap. viii.   [84] *1st Discourse*.

The ninth Discourse, from which we have quoted, explains fully the connection that he sees between "reason", or inner light, and revelation:

> God hath stamped a copy of His own archetypal loveliness upon the soul, that man by reflecting into himself might behold there the glory of God ... Reason in man being *lumen de lumine*, a light flowing from the fountain and father of lights ... was to enable man to work out of himself all those notions of God which are the true groundwork of love and obedience to God and conformity to Him.

But owing to the intervention of the fall, man is no longer capable of achieving this without the conjunction of external revelation and inner light. "We cannot see divine things but in a Divine light."[85]

But the goal of one as of the other will only be reached when we attain a knowledge of God that transcends all reasoning in an immediate intuition that can only be a product of his Spirit.

> When reason once is raised by the mighty force of the Divine Spirit into a converse with God, it is turned into sense ... We shall then converse with God τῷ νῷ, whereas before we conversed with Him only τῇ διανοίᾳ. Before we laid hold on Him only with a struggling, agonistical and contentious reason ... We shall then fasten our minds upon Him with such a serene understanding ... as will present us with a blissful, steady and invariable sight of Him.[86]

This, as he expressly points out, is reserved for the life to come, but, as he says, faith even here below can lead us to a real prefiguration of this state, towards which—in proportion as it is "true faith"—it tends. Here we have his conception of the "justice of faith", in so far as it is opposed to "legal justice", as set forth in his seventh Discourse, entirely devoted to the subject. First of all, according to the interpretation of Moses' vision given by St Paul in the First Epistle to the Corinthians, by faith,

> ... Moses-like conversing with God in the mount and there beholding His glory shining out upon us in the face of Christ, we should be deriving a copy of that eternal beauty upon our own souls, and our thirsty and hungry spirits would be perpetually sucking in a true participation and image of His glory.[87]

But this comes about, he says, precisely and only by faith in God who saves us through Christ when it takes the place of all reliance on ourself and our own works and thus prepares the way for the

[85] *Ibid.*   [86] Second section of the same Discourse.
[87] *7th Discourse*, chap. vi.

disappearance of our sensual and egotistic self so that it may be replaced by the new man in Christ.

The faith we are dealing with, evangelical faith, true faith

is begotten of the Divine bounty and fulness manifesting itself to the spirits of men and it is conceived and brought forth by a deep and humble sense of self-indigency and poverty. Faith arises out of self-examination seating and placing itself in view of the Divine Plenitude and its all sufficiency ... And thus "we received the sentence of death in ourselves that we should not trust in ourselves but in Him". The more this sensual, brutish and self-central life thrives and prospers, the more Divine Faith languisheth; and the more that decays and all self feeling, self love and self sufficiency pine away, the more is true faith fed and nourished, it grows more vigorous; and as carnal life wastes and consumes the more does faith suck in a true, divine and spiritual life from the true "life" who hath life in Himself and freely bestowes it to all those that heartily seek for it ... We are told of Christ being formed in us and the Spirit of Christ dwelling in us; of our being made comparable to Him, of having fellowship with Him, of being as He was in this world, of living in Him and His living in us, of dying and rising again and ascending with Him into heaven: because indeed the same Spirit that dwelt in Him derives itself in its mighty virtue and energy through all believing souls, shaping them more and more into a just resemblance and conformity to Him as the first copy and pattern.[88]

It is by this ceasing to rely on ourselves, and by relying only on God in Christ, that we can empty ourselves of ourselves so as to be filled with the divine life. This life is "nothing else but God's own breath" within us, producing in us an "infant Christ, formed in the soul, who is in a sense the shining forth of the Father's glory" (1st Discourse, third section). For Smith, the experience of all this could become so real that it constituted the principal argument for the immortality promised to the soul (cf. chapter vii of the 4th Discourse).

No less intense was the religious aspiration of the last of the Cambridge Platonists, Henry More (1614–1687),[89] a descendant of St Thomas More. But he was much more saturated with neo-Platonism than with Platonism in the strict sense. From his Eton days he had rejected what he called the Calvinist fatalism of his family, who were Lincolnshire Cavaliers. At Cambridge, where he

[88] *Ibid.*
[89] His *Theological Works* can be found in an edition of 1708. His *Philosophical Poets* were edited by G. Bullough in 1931. F. I. MacKinnon brought out a selection, *Philosophical Writings of Henry More*, New York, 1925, which also contains a bibliography.

spent the rest of his life as a student and then as a fellow of Christ's, he began by plunging into scientific studies. But, as he puts it, all he found there was a temptation to scepticism; until he saw the light with the discovery of Marsilius Ficinus, Plotinus, the hermetic writings, the *Theologica Germanica*, and, finally, Jakob Boehme. At first he was filled with enthusiasm for Descartes (who also influenced Cudworth), but the development of Cartesianism into a science of the quantitative and a system of technics deceived the hope he had cherished of finding in it an interpretation of the world that would give its rightful place to the spirit. So he looked more and more to a "philosophy of nature" of plainly occultist inspiration for a way equidistant between atheist materialism and irrational religious "enthusiasm". Along this road he thought he could achieve a reintegration of man, with and within the whole cosmos, in God, source and end of all being.

The fruits of his work came in 1660 with *The Grand Mystery of Godliness*. He defended himself against attacks on his work—made notably by the Master of Peterhouse, Joseph Beaumont—in his *Apology* four years later.

Neither in his learned works nor in his verse had More anything of the luminous beauty of Smith's prose. Yet his somewhat curious output aroused the warm approval of Sir Isaac Newton, and even more unexpectedly of Hobbes, who said that, were he not convinced of the value of his own philosophy, he would have adopted that of Henry More.

Here, in fact, we have an early example of those vitalistic and organicist cosmologies, crossed with mystical aspirations, but rather turbid and more or less fantastic, that were to be multiplied in the *Naturphilosophie* of the German Romantics, before stricter attempts of the same kind were to be made by English thinkers such as Alexander and Whitehead at the end of the nineteenth and the beginning of the twentieth centuries. In spite of some excellent things in his work, and a religious sincerity that was beyond dispute, this eccentric thinker—half-way between a Teilhard de Chardin before his time and a doctor Faust lost in an unbridled mystico-philosophical imagination—achieved little more than bogging Christian mysticism down in a neo-gnosticism.

Puritan Meditation: Dent, Hall and Baxter

These flights of somewhat intellectualized mysticism brought no good news to the mass of the Puritans, and Baxter was soon to express a feeling common among them when he described Sterry and the other Cambridge Platonists as "a mixture of Platonism, Origenism and Arianism". Baxter's own contribution lay in an attempt to reorientate Puritan piety along both more practical and more scriptural paths—understanding Scripture strictly according to English Calvinism at the beginning of the century.

But this Calvinism, as we have already pointed out, was already in process of metamorphosis; and Baxter in his turn, though in a different way from the great Cambridge thinkers, made a decisive mark on this evolution. The irony was that his contribution was the most Catholicizing of all and the one that brought Calvinism closest to Counter-Reformation Catholicism.

For a Protestant piety dominated by justification by faith—faith interpreted according to the Calvinist doctrine of election and predestination and marked by the positive bent of the Anglo-Saxon mind—the problem had quickly become: have I got saving faith? Am I numbered among the elect? Here we see the subjectivist tendency, already so powerfully apparent in many of Luther's expressions, pushed to its logical extreme. Faith in salvation brought by Christ became faith in *my* salvation and, in the last analysis, faith in my faith.

Thus a psychological upheaval occurred that Luther had not foreseen. Whereas the whole of his struggle had been directed towards the achievement of peace-bringing certitude, this subjectivism, this turning inwards, was to produce the exact opposite— thorough-going obsession. According to Luther himself, his intuition regarding salvation by faith (as opposed to salvation by works) had been prepared by Staupitz, when he told him not to look inwards at himself but at Jesus who was crucified for him. But the Puritan insistence on salvation by faith was soon to absorb them in minute self-examination, bearing (at least in principle) not on external works but on inner feelings. But in fact works soon regained their supremacy along this slant, for in the uncertainty that all self-analysis inevitably creates (for we become absorbed and lost in self) works re-emerged as a more tangible criterion by which to judge a man's inner condition.[90]

We can observe this state of mind and its consequences in one of the most popular Puritan manuals of the first half of the seventeenth century, *The Plain Man's Pathway to Heaven*, by Arthur Dent. This book, first published in 1601, had reached its twenty-seventh edition by 1648. It provides us with "eight infallible notes and tokens of a regenerate minde" as the "eight signes of salvation":

A love to the children of God.
A delight in his word.

[90] On all that follows, see Louis Martz's crucial work, *The Poetry of Meditation*, New Haven and Oxford, 1954. See too his subsequent work, *The Meditative Poem*, New York, 1963.

Often and fervent prayer.
Zeale of God's glorie.
Deniall of our selves.
Patient bearing of the cross, with profit and comfort.
Faithfulnesse in our calling.
Honest, just and conscionable dealing in all our actions
and amongst men.[91]

We can well imagine Luther's horror had he been able to read this work, wholly devoted though it was in principle to promoting the central idea of the Reformation, yet contriving by an unforeseen deviation to close up again the very blind alley from which Luther had sought to find a way out.

That Dent's "signes" failed to reassure his numerous readers is amply proved by a Puritan treatise that had an even greater success in the second half of the century—and it was this that led Dent himself to set out on another path. This second treatise was Richard Baxter's *The Saints' Everlasting Rest*. Published in 1650, it was reprinted nine times in the next ten years.

Baxter was born at Rowton in Shropshire. His family was comfortably off, but his father threw it into penury by his passion for gambling. Baxter started out on a worldly career at court but left in disgust after a month. In 1638 he was ordained priest by the Bishop of Worcester, but soon changed over from the royalist and High Church ideas of his family to moderate Presbyterianism. For a short while he was a chaplain to the Parliamentary army, but retired owing to poor health and devoted himself to writing in retirement on the property of his friend, Sir Thomas Rouse. Later he resumed his ministry at Kidderminster where he had already been a curate before his removal by the Act of Uniformity in 1662. He was among those who would have been prepared at the Savoy Conference to accept the institution of bishops, but only within a Church more orientated towards Protestantism than the High Churchmen of the Restoration wanted. After a variety of tribulations, bad health and activity in the ministry, he died in peace in 1691.

His two most popular works were his *Reformed Pastor* (1656)— a more Protestant equivalent of Herbert's *Country Parson*—and *The Saints' Everlasting Rest*. Here his type of spirituality is seen at its best.

The everlasting rest of saints is no less than their calm assurance of salvation as produced by justifying faith. But, while extolling this state, the first three parts of the work make no disguise of the fact that, in his experience as a pastor, it is "a truth too evident

[91] Pages 31–32.

that many of God's children do not enjoy that sweet Life, and blessed Estate in the World, which God their Father hath provided for them". There is, he tells us, "a strange disagreement between our Professions and Affections".[92]

What is the cause of this? He gives an excellent analysis: a false concept of grace, one that puts it in opposition to the activities of the will and makes us simply sit and wait for it in a fatal state of sloth; while the conviction that many are called but few are chosen plunges our souls into anxiety: is our soul of this small number?

According to Baxter there is only one remedy for this:

> He that wants Assurance of the truth of his Graces, and the comfort of Assurance, must not stand still and say "I am so doubtful and uncomfortable that I have no minde to duty", but ply his duty, and exercise his Graces, till he finde his Doubts and Discomforts vanish.[93]

But how is this to be achieved? Here we come to the fourth part of the book, to which, as Baxter assures us, the rest is but a pre-amble.[94] And the fourth part is nothing else than a treatise on systematic meditation, passing from intellectual considerations to the excitation of the heart's affections so as finally to liberate the efficacious will.

He has no hesitation in saying:

> As the Papists have wronged the Merits of Christ, by their ascribing too much to our own Works; so it is almost incredible how much they [the Protestants] on the other extream have wronged the safety and consolation of men's souls by telling them that their own endeavours are onely for Obedience and Gratitude, but are not so much as Conditions of their Salvation or Means of their increased Sanctification or Consolation. And while some tell them that they must look at nothing in them-selves for Acceptation with God, or Comfort ... others tell them that they must look at nothing in themselves, but onely as signes of their good Estates: this hath caused some to expect onely Enthusiastick Consolations, and others to spend their days in en-quiring after signs of their sincerity ... Had these poor souls well understood that God's way to perswade their wills, and to excite and actuate their Affections, is by the Discourse, Reason-ing, or Consideration of their Understandings, upon the Nature and Qualifications of the objects which are presented to them [in the Bible]: and had they bestowed but that time in exercising holy Affections, and in serious Thoughts of the promised Happi-ness, which they have spent in enquiring only after Signs, I am

---

[92] 4th part, pp. 61 *et seq.*
[93] 3rd part, p. 168.   [94] 4th part, p. 148.

confident, according to the ordinary workings of God, they would have been better provided both with Assurance and with Joys.[95]

Thereafter he embarks on a détailed description and warm recommendation of the best method of meditation as he sees it; and, with endearing honesty, he makes no attempt to hide from us that he has taken this method from a Puritan of the preceding generation, Joseph Hall, who had been Bishop successively of Exeter and Norwich before his suspension by Laud in 1641, and had set forth the method in his book *The Arte of Meditation*, published in 1606. But Hall himself—and Baxter did not hesitate to say so in his turn—had done little more than copy out the method suggested as early as 1494 by Jean Mombaer in his famous *Rosetum* which was the principal source of Garcia de Cisneros and hence also an indirect source of St Ignatius of Loyola's *Exercises*.[96]

Hence the meticulously described development from a state of reflection on the truths of salvation systematized down to the smallest details, to a no less methodical excitation of the affections, beginning with an imaginative evocation appealing to each sense in turn so as finally to set all the springs of the will in motion.[97]

What strikes us here, as compared with the adaptation from Mombaer made by Ignatius in his *Exercises*, is that neither in Hall nor in Baxter do we find any of the clarifications or putting-into-focus so characteristic of the high spiritual good sense of the founder of the Society of Jesus. We find neither the simplification of these psychological procedures nor their extremely free and supple unification, and still less their rigorous subjection to an exercise of faith—as affirmed in Ignatius by his insistence on an invocation of the divine presence and divine co-operation as a preliminary to any and every exercise. Ignatius insists just as much on the necessity of invoking grace, as if all depends on grace alone, as on the necessity of personal endeavour as if all depends on ourselves alone; whereas in their common source, as in Hall, and even more formally and explicitly in Baxter, the whole lay-out and the whole detailed setting-in-motion of the psychological springs come first, in order that prayer may flourish at the end.

Naturally Baxter, like everyone else, speaks of the divine Spirit and attributes to it all the good that there could possibly be in us. But in his view any free and spontaneous action of the Spirit could only generate the "enthusiasm" he holds in such horror. And we would look in vain in his whole book for anything corresponding to the view, so well developed by Smith and so traditional, of the

---

[95] 4th part, p. 5.
[96] See Louis Martz, *op. cit.*, p. 331, n. 1.
[97] Cf. Louis Martz, *op. cit.*, pp. 168 *et seq.*

concomitant need for the external presentation of revealed truth and the purely inner imprint of the light of the Spirit. As he sees things, the inner witness of the Holy Spirit which, according to Calvin, corroborates in the elect of the truth of the Word as heard, can only be envisaged as the very term of a proposition and an understanding of the selfsame Word by the purely psychological means that he sets out to explore and describe. If we glance at the quotations above and compare them with the book as a whole, we seem driven to this conclusion: that God's ordinary action in us is, and is no more than, the judicious releasing of the appropriate springs.

Abbé Bremond caused an outcry when he said that Acquaviva's over-rigid (in his view) interpretation of the method of the *Exercises* had ended by reducing mysticism to an ascetic system with semi-Pelagian tendencies. Whatever our views, there seems no doubt about this: that in the use to which Hall, and above all Baxter, put Ignatius' sources we find pure practical Pelagianism superimposed on a mysticism of *sola gratia*. For here "grace" is no more than a psychological determinism set up by the Creator for the benefit of the elect, and all they need do is discover it and set it in motion so as to obtain assurance and "the saints' everlasting rest".

Bunyan and The Pilgrim's Progress

There could be no better conclusion to a study of the period in which Puritan piety produced its various classics than a reference to its most popular author and most popular book. It is not that Bunyan and his *Pilgrim's Progress*[98] put forward anything original as to doctrine, but they display in its most widespread, because most popularizable, form the average Puritanism that was able to become the religion of the average Englishman.

John Bunyan (1628–1688), originally a tinker (there is no foundation for the theory of his gypsy origin), became a typical example of those non-conformist preachers who won the hearts of the English masses by the combination of a solid practical spirit with warm and simple religion, transmitted in unpretentious language that still retained medieval freshness.

His *Grace Abounding*[99] provides as literal a confirmation as we could wish for of the lucid and honest analysis of the anguish of the Puritan conscience as we saw it in Baxter. However, Bunyan

---

[98] See *John Bunyan, the Man and his Works*, by Henri Talon, London, 1951.
[99] *Grace Abounding to the Chief of Sinners* was re-edited by John Brown, Cambridge, 1907, and *The Pilgrim's Progress* by R. Sharrock, Oxford, 2nd ed., 1950.

seems to have found a way out not by recourse to subtly ordered methods but thanks to the deep commonsense with which he applied Dent's criteria to his own case. Dent's *Pathway to Heaven* (from which we quoted above) was, as Bunyan tells us, one of the two books that made up his wife's whole dowry. This, with the Bible, constituted pretty well all the sources of his teaching. And it was in order to illustrate that "pathway to heaven" that he composed his allegory of the *Pilgrim*. For all its wealth of popular psychology and almost proverbial expressions, we have to admit that this story of a pious "morality play" type with strong medieval overtones (to which it owed its immense success) strikes us as childish and tedious and has contributed not a little to Puritanism's reputation as being the quintessence of boredom. It is a sort of instinctive and simplified equivalent of the systems of meditation worked out by Hall and Baxter. But Bunyan's analysis of the heart and its hidden springs took the form of a sort of animated Epinal print and as such has charmed generation after generation (or else bored it to tears!). We are uncertain which to wonder at most— the factitiousness of the action itself or the guileless art by which it was set in motion.

George Fox and the Friends

Bunyan belonged to one of the extreme groups of "dissenters" with Baptist tendencies such as pullulated in England as early as James I's reign, before being expelled to Holland, thereafter to seek refuge in America. They were to start up again after the Stuart Restoration when the "independents" or "congregationalists" were driven in their turn from the Established Church, which they had looked on as a home under the Commonwealth. But in 1656 Bunyan had come into conflict with sectaries of quite a new kind, ones who displayed no more taste for the various forms of evolved Puritanism than for Presbyterianism, Anglicanism or Catholicism. These unexpected adversaries were the Quakers.

Their appearance on the scene was a phenomenon which revealed more than anything else the crisis to which Puritanism had led, just as the document which discussed this crisis in plainest terms was the autobiographical *Journal*[100] of their founder, George Fox (1624–1691), a work of genius in its way and even blunter in style than Bunyan's.

Fox was the son of a weaver and churchwarden in the little parish of Drayton-in-the-Clay (now called Fenny Drayton) in Leicestershire. There had been an idea of making him a priest, but

[100] First published in 1694.

doubtless owing to lack of funds he was apprenticed to a shoe-maker where he spent more time looking after his master's flock than in the workshop. He gives us an astonishing insight into the spontaneous reactions of a simple and upright soul, in direct contact with the Gospels, when confronted with the unbelievable confusion that the Protestant Reformation in England had by that time reached. In view of the multiplication of Churches, sects and parties alternately in power or persecuted, and of pulpits whence issued endless reciprocal invective, it was hardly surprising that the whole thing appeared as a purely man-made complication and obfuscation of divine revelation. A man who, though uneducated, was drawn by the inner life to read the Gospels would easily have felt an irrepressible need to get away from all this quibbling and bawling. But we would do best to leave the description to young George Fox:

> The Lord said to me, "Thou seest how young people go to-gether into vanity, and old people into the earth; thou must forsake all, both young and old, and keep out of all, and be as a stranger to all." Then at the command of God, on the ninth day of the seventh month, 1643,[101] I left my relations, and brake off all familiarity or fellowship with old or young.[102]

So he led a life of wandering from town to town looking for a spiritual master and failing to find one. One day early in 1646 as he was on the road to Coventry it came to him as if by revelation that what mattered was not whether you were a Papist or a Protestant, but that "the only believers are those who have passed from death into life". On another day,

> it was opened in me that God, who made the world, did not dwell in temples made with hands. This, at the first, seemed a strange word, because both priests and people used to call their temples and churches dreadful places, holy ground, and the temples of God. But the Lord showed me, so that I did see clearly, that he did not dwell in these temples, which men had commanded and set up, but in people's hearts ... His people were his temples and he dwelt in them ... I fasted much and walked abroad in solitary places many days, and often took my Bible, and went and sate in hollow trees and lonesome places till night came on; and frequently, in the night, walked mournfully about by myself: for I was a man of sorrows in the times of the first workings of the Lord in me. Now during all this time I was never joined in profession of religion with any, but gave up myself to the Lord, having forsaken all evil company, and

---

[101] That is, 9 September, as the year then started on 1 March.
[102] Everyman Library, p. 11.

taken leave of father and mother and all other relations, and travelled up and down as a stranger in the earth, which way the Lord inclined my heart . . . seeking heavenly wisdom and getting knowledge from the Lord . . . and was sometimes brought into such a heavenly joy, that I thought I had been in Abraham's bosom . . . Oh the everlasting love of God to my soul, when I was in great distress . . . when my troubles and torments were great, then was his love exceeding great . . .

And when all hope in anything had disappeared, so that I could expect no help from outside and knew not what to do, then, O, then I heard a voice that said, "There is only one, Jesus Christ, who can answer thy needs", and when I heard these words, my heart did leap for joy.[103]

He goes on, and this was to be the keynote of all his preaching:

My desires after the Lord grew stronger, and zeal in the pure knowledge of God, and of Christ alone, without the help of any man, book, or writing. For though I read the Scriptures that spake of Christ and of God, yet I knew Him not, but by revelation, as He who hath the key did open, and as the Father and Life drew me to His Son by His spirit.

This marks the birth of the master-idea of the Quaker movement: that of the inner light by which God alone addresses the soul that wants to follow the Gospel and allows it to understand him; the inner light is enough. Fox refers to the "seed" implanted by God in every soul and which only needs to be awakened; and to the hidden "pearl" that only needs to be brought to light.

There was an obvious risk of illuminism. But what safeguarded both him and his most loyal disciples from this was the certainty —felt with the deep simplicity of upright souls face to face with the Gospel—that each one of them could and should verify his feeling in the assembly of the faithful, or, to put it more exactly, in the love that should knit them together. Know God's life in one another as well as God's power; you must feel and see God's life among you and recognize it between you; know one another by the love that never changes: these were the ever-recurring themes in his letters and sermons.

This astonishing man, who reminds us of Abraham or the first monks and who severed all natural bonds following their example so as to find God in the solitude of perpetual pilgrimage, discovered the meaning of the Church by instinct: as community in love wherein each person is assured that he will hear the Spirit speaking in his heart solely because he is always ready to hear it speaking in others, in a communion of charity with others.

[103] *Ibid.*, p. 13.

So George Fox, who was viewed on all sides as an extreme in-dividualist and persecuted alike by Anglicans, Presbyterians and other non-conformists, even by extremists with Baptist tendencies such as Bunyan, rediscovered the principle of Catholic tradition as, all unknowing, he rediscovered the vocation of early monasti-cism. What was so tragic about the situation was that the Catholic Church should have been in practice inaccessible to him, and in practice unrecognizable as it showed itself at that time to a man of his background. Quakerism, with its gatherings of "friends" having no bond but that of charity, no confession of faith outside the Gospel, and no liturgy other than waiting in silent recollection for what the Spirit might suggest, represented a sort of heroic antici-pation of the Church in heaven: a pure communion of souls in Christ.

It would be impossible to give a picture that did not seem a caricature of the sincerity, uprightness and fervent humility of this small band of souls, distinguished by their great inner simplicity. The astonishing thing was that, despite all the temptations to what Baxter would have called "enthusiasm", these spiritual men and women were able to remain relatively unscathed by the oddities that earned them their nickname of "quakers" or "shakers" (trembling under the supposed inspiration of the Spirit). Intrepid sub-mission to the letter of the Gospel; truthfulness, non-violence, a permanent disposition to give away all their possessions and to devote themselves to the unfortunate with the same humble sim-plicity as their waiting for the Spirit—alike in silence and solitude as in communal recollection: these things were their great safe-guards.

To be sure this exaggeratedly spiritualized Christianity, with no organization, no sacraments, no dogmas even, underestimated both the needs of common humanity and the will to incarnation empha-sized in the Gospel. But the explanation—which probably also ex-plains its miraculous preservation from the corruptions by which it has repeatedly been threatened—lay in the disfigured incarnation presented to it by the Churches divided against themselves as well as cut off from the one Church. Its best representatives kept it alive, in the midst of the Protestant world, as a recall to evangelical authenticity and spiritual fulfilment that could be called prophetic.

It may seem surprising, but is not really so very odd, that Quakerism has provided the environment in the heart of Protestant-ism in which people have been most ready to give a warm and in-stinctive welcome to the highest teachings of the Catholic mystics, from St Teresa of Avila and St John of the Cross to such a man as Fénelon. The temptation to quietism has always been a lively one

6*

in the movement, but it has always been counter-balanced by evangelical charity.

Two outstanding recruits came to help George Fox in spreading and consolidating the "Society of Friends", as he called it. The first was the Scottish theologian Robert Barclay (1648–1690) who in 1676 produced (and in Latin!) his *Apology for the True Christian Religion, as the same is set forth and preached by the People called in Scorn "Quakers"*. The second, William Penn, son of Admiral Sir William Penn, provided his own justification of the peculiarities of Quaker life in a spiritual treatise, *No Cross, No Crown* (1669). But he became even more celebrated by founding the Quaker state of Pennsylvania and by his famous constitution built on the formula that freedom without obedience is confusion, but obedience without freedom is slavery. And indeed Pennsylvania seemed a blessed land indeed compared with New England, where the Mayflower pilgrims had introduced a congregationalist Puritanism and where the theology of the Covenant was to see new developments with Thomas Hooker, Increase Mather and their like, round Harvard university, the great centre of Ramist humanism; for this theology was to be responsible for the Salem witch trials and pave the way for the ferocious conquest of the poor pagan Indians by God's "elect". Even though Quakerism eventually declined into the middle-class humanism of men like Benjamin Franklin, Pennsylvania seemed a sort of haven of peace and light in the spiritual beginnings of the United States.

Jakob Boehme and his Theosophy

Another thoughtful shoemaker, this time in Germany and of the generation immediately preceding that of Fox, had prepared the way for another kind of illuminism, more esoteric than sectarian and far less pure that that of the Quakers. This was Jakob Boehme (1575–1624). Despite the many studies devoted to him, some of the highest value such as Alexandre Koyré's,[104] his personality and writings remain among the most mysterious in Christian history. We are at a loss to understand how this self-taught man, who seems never to have used any language but his local Lusatian dialect, came by all his knowledge, which would appear to have included the Jewish Kabbala, the neo-Platonism of the Renaissance and the hermetic medicine of Paracelsus. His books were only published at a late date and by educated friends such as his first biographer, Abraham von Frankenberg. It may well be that it was

[104] *La Philosophie de Jacob Boehme*, Paris, 1929, where a bibliography will also be found. A translation in 2 vols. of his *Mysterium Magnum* was published in Paris in 1945 with two essays by Berdyaev.

they who introduced him to his many sources of knowledge. This might apply especially to his links with Paracelsus and the Kabbala in the context of a rather strange notion of divine Wisdom which resuscitated while altering certain conceptions of the ancient Gnostics. One wonders how otherwise he could have known all these things.

It is possible that his immediate source was an earlier synthesis of these two same currents—involving the same hypostatized Wisdom—in the Latin work of an alchemist-doctor writing at the beginning of the century: the *Amphitheatrum divinae Sapientiae* of Joseph Kunrath. Doubtless some learned man must have introduced him to this other angel of bizarre thought, and in Kunrath's subject-matter his imagination found its predestined nourishment. We cannot otherwise explain the striking resemblances between his isolated work of genius and that of the frenzied compiler who had assembled all its ingredients beforehand—minus the genius.

In all things Boehme appears as an inspired man and a visionary. He was certainly no liar, in the sense that we find in him an element of ecstatic psychology combined with an extraordinary power of thought, but the materials he worked on could not have come from the Bible or from books of popular Lutheran piety, nor could they have been a creation of his own mind *ex nihilo*. Obviously they must have had a history, and they had another and much more fruitful one when his primitive genius had recast them in its own way. The Görlitz shoemaker had one of those religious and meditative minds to which scholastic statements of Lutheran doctrine on justification by faith seemed mere juggling with words with no satisfactory spiritual or intellectual content. So, like men before him such as Schwenkfeld and Weigel (especially the latter), he tried to proceed further by means of religious experience directly nourished by the Bible and speculation drawn from the most random sources. The central, indeed sole, object of his inquiry was the problem of evil, of its origin, of the higher ends by which its appearance might be justified, and the way it might be reabsorbed by itself co-operating in reaching them. To him the answer seemed provided by an almost apocalyptic discovery of divine Wisdom, an aspect of God that appears in God as another self, whose separation from him is Evil, but the condition of their ultimate reunion, in a conjunction in which God and his creature will live a life of fulfilment.

With his first book, *Aurora* (probably published in 1612), he took possession of his master-idea, that of *Ungrund* (or *Urgrund*), a word that appears to derive from Rhenish mysticism. The word is an equivalent of Eckhart's *"deitas"* and also of the depth of the soul. God and the creature pre-exist in this subsoil of being, in an undifferentiated state that precedes all differentiated existence, from which state they will emerge by a painful tearing-apart which will nevertheless prepare the way for the final and fruitful reunion of the divine Word and Wisdom in Mary, of Christ and his people in the Church, of God and the cosmos in man.

We are not surprised that the Lutheran theologians lost no time in denouncing this strange doctrine as heretical as soon as it started gaining ground. So Boehme made his one and only journey—to Dresden, to defend himself; and thanks to protectors whom he had found even at court, he was able to return unharmed to Görlitz. But on his return he fell ill and died soon afterwards.

No sooner had Frankenberg published Boehme's *Forty Questions on the Soul,* his *Three Principles* and his *Mysterium Magnum* than they made their mark in Germany and Holland and even in England. Henry More, though he hardly ever stirred from his rooms in Christ's, travelled the world tirelessly through bookshop catalogues (like the good Cambridge don that he was) and discovered Boehme's works with something near delight. Sir Isaac Newton was hardly less enthusiastic, and Charles I himself, despite his other preoccupations at the time, was so excited by *Forty Questions* that he immediately commissioned a London lawyer, John Sparrow, to translate Boehme's works, especially the *Mysterium Magnum,* into English. The task was not completed until the Restoration. At the end of the century a mystical blue-stocking, Jane Leade, became so crazy about him that she founded a sect, the Philadelphians, with Boehme as its spiritual light. An eminent physician, Doctor Pordage, thereupon became the first thinker to build a philosophico-scientific system of the world based on Boehme's thought.

But Boehme's greatest disciples were to be found in German romantic thought. Boehme unquestionably lies at the source of Hegel's dialectic; and Hegel's idea of God, realizing himself in the world and ultimately in the collective consciousness of mankind, is, in substance, Boehme's. And Boehme's theosophy—that is, his doctrine of Wisdom—made inroads into Schelling's later philosophy through the intermediary of Franz von Baader.

By this route it reached Russia where Vladimir Soloviev made it the cornerstone of his religious philosophy. It has been taken up yet again, and variously interpreted, in our own time by professional theologians such as Father Paul Florensky and Father Serge Bulgakov. And with Alexander Blok even a literary school was born of a fusion of Boehme's Wisdom and the old, half-

Christianized pagan notion of the earth-mother. Finally Berdyaev's rather gnostic philosophy of creation was inspired by it.

Three particular elements in Boehme's system, together with the kind of savage poetry in which his ideas were first expressed, brought him this immense success. The first of these elements was the directly religious significance that he restored to the universe in contrast to the exaggeratedly platonizing theological and spiritual systems which gave no place to the body or the material cosmos. But more important was the deeply tragic sense not only of human life but of cosmic, and even divine, life. And finally there was the extremely bold way in which the possibility of a communication of the divine life to man and the universe was explained in an effective participation of the Creator in the life of the creature—so remote from the philosophical outlook of the Greeks which plunged the divinity into an inaccessible sphere where it seemed withdrawn from the world and its destiny. There is no doubt that all this responded to certain aspirations of Christian thought and spirituality, which theological systems built on philosophical bases borrowed from Hellenism would always find it difficult really to satisfy.

But, as Boehme's intellectual and spiritual following shows only too plainly, the mainspring of his system lay in a fundamental monism which, whatever its intentions, fused the divine being within earthly being. Hence the markedly turbid and ultimately unacceptable character of his theosophy, whether as religious philosophy or as spiritual nourishment—and this in spite of the undeniable evangelical fervour that animates so much of his writing and especially his smaller work, *The Way to Christ*.[105]

This is not to deny that Boehme has aroused a genuinely Christian spiritual search in many minds; but this has only produced substantial fruit once his system has been abandoned. The best in the later writings of Law is relatively independent of Boehme; and a man like Angelus Silesius only fulfilled himself when, through Boehme, he re-established contact with, and then extended, the great current of Rhenish mysticism.

Much the same needs to be said of Johannes Kelpius (1673–1708), a German who went off to America with the Philadelphians. But he soon withdrew alone to a cave, and later to a cabin, to lead a hermit's life of the greatest austerity. When still very young he attracted a number of disciples who called him "the Master". He died in their midst in his garden, like Epicurus, when he was only thirty-five. His one work, *A short, easy and comprehensive Method of Prayer*, was published only in 1791.[106] It is a real jewel of a book

---

[105] Berlin, 1722.
[106] Reissued with an introduction by E. Gordon Alderfer, New York, 1950.

on the prayer of the heart, which sometimes reminds us of Fénelon and sometimes of pseudo-Macarius. It would be interesting to know something about the sources on which such an isolated man drew for the exceedingly pure doctrine which so obviously reflected his experience.

III

THE EIGHTEENTH AND NINETEENTH CENTURIES

Spener and the Birth of Pietism

THE biggest factor in the history of Protestant and Anglican spirituality in the eighteenth century, both by its influence and the reactions it aroused, was Pietism.[1] It could be said to have left an ineradicable mark on Protestantism. Generally speaking it does not appeal to the taste of modern Protestant theologians, who blame it for leading Protestantism towards both Catholicism and a religious attitude with nothing specifically evangelical about it. As we have said elsewhere, such judgments contain a number of unfair simplifications. If we are to be true to history we must recognize that this movement was far too complex to be judged as a single whole and apart from the multiple tendencies that it displayed.

The movement's antecedents are deeply significant. We find a mixture of the sustained influence of Johann Arndt's work with all the life it had instilled into early orthodox Lutheranism; of the Protestantism of the sects and particularly as it developed in the Dutch conventicles; of English Puritanism and especially as practised in kindred sorts of groups such as the one with which Bunyan was associated; and finally of the Catholic quietism, whether derived from Fénelon or elsewhere, that had been welcomed and somewhat modified in certain French Protestant circles, particularly among the exiles in Switzerland or, again, Holland.

But the founder of the Pietist movement was a Lutheran pastor, Philipp Jakob Spener (1635–1705).[2] Born at Rappoltsweiler in

---

[1] The most comprehensive study of Pietism, though often biased by systematic hostility, is still A. Ritschl, *Geschichte des Pietismus*, 2 vols., Bonn, 1880–1886. But Ritschl introduces too easily into Pietism people who were not really Pietist in the strict sense, such as the Dutch reformed. See too H. W. zur Nieden, *Die religiösen Bewegungen im 18. Jahrhundert*, 1910, and W. Mahrholz, *Der Deutsche Pietismus*, 1921.

[2] See H. Bruns, *Philip Jacob Spener, Ein Reformator nach der Reformation*, Giessen, 1955.

Alsace, son of the castle archivist, he was from childhood under the influence of his deeply religious godmother, Countess Agathe de Ribeaupierre, and of her chaplain Johachim Stoll whose sister-in-law, Suzanne Ehrardt, Spener later married. Arndt's *True Christianity* played no more decisive part in his early reading than translations of the English Puritans, beginning with Baxter.

Spener studied theology at Strasbourg and almost immediately afterwards taught it at Basle, then Geneva, where he developed a deep interest in the quietist sermons of a rather dubious character, Jean de Labadie, a former Jesuit who had left the Catholic Church after being accused of seducing nuns: he was all the rage in Protestant circles at that time, before becoming the object of similar suspicions. But Spener left Geneva before the "Labadist" sect was founded, with its mystical tendencies, and returned to Strasbourg at the end of 1661. In 1662 he paid a short visit to Tübingen after which his ideas began to circulate in university circles in Württemberg. But the characteristic feature of his work only developed later when he was appointed dean of the Frankfurt pastors in 1666—in Strasbourg he had never been more than an independent preacher.

He began with a tussle against the immorality of religious indifferentism among the middle classes. But as he was frowned on by the senate of patricians at an early stage, pretty well all he could achieve was a reform in education. He was determined that catechetical instruction should be a formation in solid piety as well as doctrinal teaching. With this in mind he gave fresh life to the practice of confirmation as an introduction to first communion and a personal renewal of the baptismal vows (this had been re-established in Strasbourg by Bucer in the sixteenth century). At the same time he concentrated his sermons on the Christian's need for a new birth, understood as a renewal of the whole of existence by a living faith.

But it was not until 1669, in a sermon preached on the seventeenth Sunday after Trinity, that he embarked on positive action for the foundation of the Pietist movement. He put it to his more fervent parishioners that instead of their all-too-frequent Sunday occupations of drinking and card- or dice-parties, they should hold edifying meetings with pious reading. Hence arose the *collegia pietatis* which gave the movement its name. In the early days the meetings took place in Spener's own house, and there was no more than a discussion of the sermon after a re-reading of the text. The meeting ended with the reading of some pious work and a hymn.

By 1675 the essence of the meetings lay in Bible readings followed by discussions in which the practical application of what had been read to the lives of each was the main concern. That same year saw the publication of Spener's crucial work, the *Pia Desideria*. This book made a modest appearance as a preface to a new edition of Johann Arndt's *Sermons*.[3]

This gave rise to the facile assumption that the foundations of Pietism had been laid by Arndt; a view to a large extent erroneous. Arndt had never thought of anything but a solidly doctrinal Christianity, and if he had criticized the theology of his time, it was in order to bring it back from controversy and abstract scholasticism to a theology aimed at spirituality—though none the less theological for that, whereas Spener, while remaining faithful to the main lines of Lutheran orthodoxy, concentrated almost exclusively on practices of piety in which doctrine played a secondary part.

First and foremost he advocated meetings for Bible-reading meditated in common from an entirely practical point of view, such as he was in fact already organizing. He expressed the formal wish that they should take place in each household, round the father of the family. For he insisted strongly on the universal priesthood of the faithful and in particular on the duty of all the truly faithful to teach and exhort their brothers exactly in the manner of pastors and, if need be, instead of them (he never concealed his poor opinion of the clergy of his time).

This he justified by the crucial statement that Christianity was as much a matter of practice—of practice penetrating all existence —as of doctrine: indeed, more so.

In accordance with this view he wanted theological students in their turn to be educated in piety and a really Christian way of life in preference to a purely intellectual formation accompanied by only moderately devout lives. Moreover, he said, there should be a radical change in preaching: its aim should no longer be an eloquent display of scholarly knowledge, but conversion. Hence the new edition of Arndt's sermons.

The repercussions were enormous, but soon opposition began to build up. The *collegia pietatis* into which, as Spener himself admitted, illuministic and, worse, pharisaical tendencies had rapidly made their way, were the main butts of criticism. The Darmstadt consistory proposed prohibiting them as early as 1678. Spener himself was accused of crypto-Catholicism, and his Alsatian origins made him suspected of sympathizing with France in the war against the Emperor.

In 1686 Spener seems to have been protected from these attacks by his appointment as preacher at the Saxon court in Dresden.

---

[3] The sum total of Spener's writings were published at Halle in 5 vols. between 1700 and 1711: *Theologische Bedenken*.

At more or less the same moment a *Collegium Philobiblicum* had been founded at the university of Leipzig under the inspiration of the famous theologian, J. B. Carpzov, with the assistance of professors who included August Hermann Francke. This was a much more academic affair than what Spener had in mind, but he gave warm encouragement to its organizers none the less; and in the event this college soon changed over from exegetical studies to edification of its members.

This change-over from studies to edification was the result of Francke's exalted "conversion"—to which we shall return. As groups of more or less exalted laymen multiplied in the town, the theological students rose in revolt against what had been the official teaching and went so far as to burn their textbooks and notebooks. Confronted with what had been let loose, Carpzov turned against Pietism, and Francke had to resign his post and leave Leipzig.

Meanwhile Spener, under the patronage of the Electress, remained in Saxony until 1691—though already by 1689 he had turned the Elector against him by his admonishments.

He found refuge for the remainder of his days in the parish of St Nicholas in Berlin. But the storm now raised against him and his disciples gave him no respite. He nevertheless persuaded Frederick III, Elector of Brandenburg, to create a faculty of theology in the university of Halle, which he filled with his disciples. It was here, round the hot-headed extremist Francke, that Pietism entered on its second phase, and controversy became rampant.

Halle Pietism: Francke

August Hermann Francke (1663–1727)[4] was born in Lübeck and began his career as an outstanding exegetist with a high reputation in Hebrew and Greek philology. But after his conversion he began developing a view of biblical exegesis that ignored scientific and theological problems in the interests of direct edification. It was to him that Pietistic circles owed their insistence on conversion which they interpreted as a very definite type of psychological experience: without it, no one deserved to be called a Christian.

Spener, previously, had emphasized the idea of rebirth as a transformation of the whole of life. But he had not identified this with any particular experience, to be given a date and a specific character of its own. Francke, on the other hand, set up his own experience as a norm.

This experience occurred while he was preparing a sermon on

[4] See E. Beyreuther, *August Hermann Francke*, *Zeuge des lebendigen Gottes*, Marburg, 1956.

the text in St John's Gospel, 20. 31, "These things have been written that you may believe that Jesus is the Christ, the Son of God, and, believing, that you may have life in his name."
Here is his description of what happened:

> I saw all my past life unfold before me, as we see a town from the top of a churchtower. My sins came before me so distinctly that I could have counted them; and I soon discovered their main source: my unbelief, or rather my supposed faith that only served to deceive me about myself ... Then all my doubts vanished as if by magic; I had the grace of God in Christ in my heart and I could call God my Father. All sadness and all anxiety were lifted from me and my soul was invaded by a torrent of joy.[5]

Driven from Leipzig, as we have seen, he set up as pastor of Graucha. But he was soon teaching at Halle university at the faculty founded under Spener's influence; he had adopted Spener as his spiritual guide and Spener tried unsuccessfully to moderate his zeal. One of Francke's most important activities at Halle was the school for poor children that he opened in his residence, to which he added an orphanage in 1698. His school grew rapidly, and many of the children formed by him joined the clergy and so increased the number of his students.

As he grew to play the part of a patriarch among his innumerable disciples, he exercised nothing less than a censorship over the Church, owing to his narrow views on conversion. His whole teaching was devoted to preparing for and producing conversions. Those who did not adopt his views were debarred from both teaching and the ministry. The most sensational of the disputes in which he became involved on this account was with the philosopher Christian Wolff, one of the fathers of the Enlightenment. In the end Francke managed to persuade Frederick-Wilhelm I to remove Wolff from his post and banish him from the town.

But Francke then came up against an adversary less easy to dispose of—Valentin Ernst Löscher, the outstanding exponent of orthodox Lutheranism. Löscher had been appointed professor at Wittenberg in 1698 when he was only twenty-four. In two successive editions of his *Timotheus verinus*, first published in 1711 and then in a much augmented form in 1718, he provided the first systematic criticism of Pietism, and especially of Halle Pietism.

His criticism was the more telling owing to its moderation—it did justice to Spener and his disciples—and the fact that it came from an undisputed heir of early Lutherans such as Johann

---

[5] This text may be found in the autobiographical fragments published in his *Pädagogische Schriften*, edited in 1885 by H. Kramer. Francke's main work is *Offentliches Zeugnis von Werk, Wort und Dienst Gottes*, Halle, 1702.

Gerhard. Indeed Löscher was much more in the tradition of Arndt than were many of the Pietists such as Francke himself and especially his vehement disciple Joachim Lange. It was against Lange that many of Löscher's thrusts were aimed, and Lange made a reconciliation between Löscher and Francke impossible, much as Löscher wanted this.

Löscher had already made it plain in his *Edle Andachtsfrücht*, published in 1702, that he had no intention of making an indiscriminate attack on religious experience and mysticism—far from it: his aim was solely to distinguish between authentic experience and adulterated forms of it. In the confusion between faith and sense-experience, and the tendency to replace the objective data of faith and the sacraments by an emotional subjective event, he discerned at least latent indifference regarding all established doctrine and, in a more general way, loss of sight of the Church and its ministry as institutions. Having pointed out these essential lacunae, Löscher could readily put his finger on the illusions contained in the idea of a conversion as produced at a given moment and patient of a *ne varietur* definition. The consequence, as he pointed out, was a sort of renewed "chiliasm", that is to say the immediate expectation of a kingdom of God on earth which it would be within our power to produce. He also attacked "precisianism", or the condemnation of unimportant trifles such as innocent distractions; "perfectionism", or the idea that perfection is attainable here below; and finally the more or less pharisaical sectarianism to which all this inevitably led.

Löscher laid great stress on what was, as he saw it, the central error of Pietism: the confusion between justifying faith and piety. In doing this his sole intention was to defend genuine Lutheranism as he understood it; but what he was really defending was the dogmatic element and the mysterious element—transcending all possible experience—contained in the most traditional faith.

Gottfried Arnold (1666–1714)

The dangers in Pietism so pertinently denounced by Löscher—the dissolution of all defined dogmatic faith and its substitution by unverifiable sentiment—were brought to light in no uncertain manner by another of Spener's followers, Gottfried Arnold.[6]

Arnold was a Saxon whose master was one of the many Halle professors with whom Francke had come into conflict, Christian Thomasius, the jurist. Thomasius declared that piety (like juris-

[6] See E. Seeberg, *Gottfried Arnold, Die Wissenschaft und die Mystik seiner Zeit*, Meerens, 1923. W. Nigg has devoted a study to him in his *Heimliche Weisheit*, pp. 320 *et seq.*

prudence as he saw it) was a matter of pure instinct totally independent of theology.[7] Hence the amazing theory that he developed in the four volumes of his *Unparteiische Kirchen- und Ketzerhistorie*, published in Frankfurt in 1699–1700. Whenever the Church started dogmatizing, so he held, it fell into decadence, and the only way out lay in the fact that each generation produced simpleminded men whose instinctive reaction (bullied by authority) constituted a prophetic reaffirmation of the one pure Christianity, primitive and free from all ratiocination.

It was a road that led to a full-blown theory of the infallibility of heretics, as Auguste Lecerf, the Calvinist theologian, ironically remarked. But this fantastic version of Church history enjoyed wide success. It showed Protestantism as having been a constant phenomenon since the beginning, and provided it with a sort of continuous tradition very similar to the one on which the Gnostics had prided themselves. The final outcome was an apologia for Jakob Boehme who was described as a new Luther. Spener himself (as Löscher had pointed out) had been only too indulgent towards Boehme's mystagoguery; but now, in the name of Pietism, his works were being proclaimed as far superior to the whole traditional dogmatic system simply because they were supposed to have been written by a simple and uneducated man.

The equivocal situation that this kind of religion tended to beget can be seen in another book by Arnold, his *Sophia*.[8] Here Madame Guyon became as it were the last incarnation of Boehme's Wisdom. For, said Arnold, Christianity was a matter of feeling, or more exactly of the passivity of man as sensitive to God's influx. So piety had to appear as an essentially feminine reality, and women were by nature its most perfect exponents. Hence an unexpected exaltation of monastic piety in the ancient Church, and the contemplation at which it aimed in solitude being explained by a mere desire to "feel oneself" (*sich fühlen*) before God, in which the whole of piety consisted. Hence, also, the exaltation of the themes of virginity and nuptial mysticism, but in a context of such dubious sentimentalism and naïve eroticism that it was enough to compromise them for good and all in the eyes of healthy-minded Protestants.

Württemberg Pietism

In Württemberg, on the other hand, a moderate Pietism

[7] On Thomasius, see Pierre Grappin, *Le XVIIIe siècle* in *Histoire de la littérature allemande*, ed. F. Mossé, Paris, 1959, pp. 338–339.
[8] G. Arnold, *Geheimnis der göttlichen Sophia oder Weisheit*, Leipzig, 1700.

developed, fully integrated into the Lutheran Church and by and large productive of positive results.[9]

We have already seen how Spener spent several months in Tübingen in 1662 and won much sympathy in university circles. In that ancient university he found no disciple as passionate as Francke, but there were a few serious, cultivated and judicious men who profited by all that was best in his influence. They included Johann Wolfgang Jäger, Johann Christoff Plaff, Andreas Adam Hochstetter and Christoff Reuchlin.

The Stunden, as the collegia pietatis were called in Swabian regions, were much more balanced and avoided illuminism and extreme sentimentalism as well as pharisaical and separatist tendencies.

Soon after they were set up in 1680, the consistorial authorities introduced a series of progressive measures aimed at eliminating sectarian tendencies by institutionalizing some of Spener's guiding ideas—such as the renewal of religious instruction and confirmation, a reform in preaching and confession, and little by little all the articles of ecclesiastical discipline. One of the most beneficial of all these reforms was a ducal rescript of 1695 on biblical studies. It set its seal on an ideal of biblical theology which, unlike Francke, attempted to reconcile spiritual preoccupations with a solid exegetical and theological education. The outcome was to be an educated and pious clergy having a wide influence on both the peasants and the middle class. In Württemberg, as elsewhere in the eighteenth century, only the aristocracy remained largely sceptical and libertine in outlook.

A typical product of Swabian piety was Johann Albrecht Bengel (1687–1752),[10] who was possibly the most learned exegete of his century. He was born at Winnenden, studied at Tübingen, for long was pastor and professor at Denkendorf, and died at Stuttgart covered with ecclesiastical and academic honours but retaining a purely evangelical piety and simplicity.

His Gnomon (1742), a series of learned notes on the New Testament, is a real mine of solid biblical theology, a classic of Protestant exegesis at its best. Bengel drew on the Fathers as well as on scripture and can be said to have renewed in Protestantism the sense of an exegesis at once doctrinal, scientific and highly attractive. The two lines that Nestle was later to use as epigraph in his

---

[9] See Ritschl's chapter on the subject.
[10] See G. Geiss, *Johann Albrecht Bengel Gottesgelehrter und Ewigkeitsmensch*, Giessen, 1953.

edition of the Greek New Testament expresses Bengel's spirit exactly:

Te totum applica ad textum,
rem totam applica ad te.

The phrase comes from Bengel's own preface to his *Novum Testamentum Grecum Manuale* which appeared in 1734.

But for all his solid knowledge and pure piety, Bengel was not entirely free from the oddities of Pietism; nor were these confined to him. He became one of the most convinced advocates of the millennary ideas that had such a curious resurgence throughout all Europe at this time (we only have to think of some contemporary Jansenists, such as the abbé d'Étemare). The excellent Bengel died in the firm conviction that he had proved by irrefutable exegesis[11] that Christ's coming would occur on 18 June 1836, and that after a thousand years of reign on earth and a second thousand years for the reign of the saints in heaven, the end of the world and the Last Judgment would occur punctually in 3836. But for all this innocent oddity, Bengel remains one of the holiest souls and one of the most respectable men of learning whom Protestantism has produced.

Zinzendorf's Moravian Brotherhood

A very peculiar brand of Pietism came with the Moravian Brotherhood, reorganized and transformed by Nikolaus-Ludwig Graf von Zinzendorf (1700–1760), one of the most astonishing figures of the eighteenth century.[12] It has recently been suggested, and not without good reasons, that Zinzendorf did not belong to the Pietists strictly speaking.[13] True, though a pupil in the Halle schools and directly influenced by Francke, he regained his freedom and even vigorously criticized Pietism. Moreover, some of the most important characteristics of his spirituality had already be-become apparent before he went to Halle. However this may be, Zinzendorf and his movement cannot be dissociated from Pietism, as they had too many elements in common with it and a powerful influence over its future development.

Zinzendorf came of an aristocratic Austrian family that had emigrated to Saxony owing to its devotion to Lutheranism. His father, a high official in the Saxon administration, died a few weeks after the child's birth (in Dresden), leaving him to be brought up

---

[11] *Erklärte Offenbarung*, Stuttgart, 1750.
[12] Mgr Cristiani has devoted a good study to him in the final volume of the D.T.C.
[13] See G. Hoek's recent studies, *Zinzendorfs Begriff der Religion*, Uppsala-Leipzig, 1948, and E. Beyreuther, *Studien zur Theologie Zinzendorfs*, Neukirchen, 1962.

by his maternal grandmother at Gross Hennersdorf in Upper
Lusatia. As he owed his formation to women whose piety was
marked by Arndt's type of Lutheranism, though obviously coloured
by feminine feeling, Zinzendorf developed a warm piety towards
Jesus at an early age, accompanied by some rather unusual ecstatic
characteristics. This could hardly be better expressed than in the
account he himself has left us of a decisive experience in his childhood:

> In my eighth year I spent a whole night awake, and I thought
> of an old hymn that my grandmother used to sing to me before
> I went to bed. I entered into a state of meditation and then of
> speculation that was so deep that I almost lost consciousness. All
> the subtlest arguments of the atheists fixed themselves in my
> mind of their own accord, and they took hold of me and pene-
> trated to my very depths . . . But because my heart was turned to
> the Saviour and I was devoted to him with a delicate righteous-
> ness and I often thought that were it possible that there should
> be a God other than him, I would prefer to be damned with my
> Saviour than be happy with another God, the speculations and
> arguments that assailed me without pause had no other effect
> than to cause me anguish and take away my sleep, without hav-
> ing the slightest effect on my heart.[14]

According to his own comments on this episode, all that he was
later to call his "theology of the heart" founded on "the religion of
the Saviour" was there in seed.

> What I believed, I wanted; what I thought, was hateful to me:
> and at that instant I made a firm resolution to use my reason in
> human things as far as it would go, and to instruct myself and
> make myself as cultivated as possible, but in spiritual things to
> remain sincerely attached to the truth as grasped by the heart,
> and in particular to the theology of the Cross and the blood of
> the Lamb of God, so that I might put it at the basis of all other
> truths and immediately reject all that I could not deduce from it.
> And so have I remained to this day.[15]

Two years later he was sent to the Paedagogium at Halle. There
he seems to have been deeply unhappy, misunderstood by his
fellow-pupils and masters with the apparent exception of Francke
himself. But his First Communion in 1715 was marked by a lively
fervour towards the Eucharist that never left him. When he moved
on to the university of Wittenberg, he wanted to take up theology,
but his family insisted on his studying law. He accepted this with
resignation but spent most of his time reading the Bible, Luther's
works and the writings of the Pietists. He would have liked—an

---

[14] *Reden*, vol. I, Vorrede.   [15] *Ibid.*

intention that lasted long—to reconcile Lutheran orthodoxy with Pietism.

In 1719–1720, still impelled by his authoritarian tutor-uncle whose only thought was for his career, he went travelling, notably in Holland and France. It was during these travels that he had a new spiritual experience renewing and deepening the one of his childhood. This occurred in a museum in Düsseldorf where he saw an *Ecce Homo* with the inscription, "This have I done for Thee; what doest thou for Me?" and he had a vivid impression of hearing Christ himself saying these words, and to him.

> I felt that there was little that I could answer to this question, and I implored my Saviour to force me to suffer with him, should I not consent to do so voluntarily.[16]

But meanwhile he was experiencing another influence hardly less important for his future thought—that of the new religious circles to which he had been introduced by his travels. At Utrecht he came across some particularly fervent Calvinists. In Paris he made the acquaintance of some Catholics, beginning with Cardinal de Noailles. This rather blundering prelate made a permanent impression on him which we may find surprising. For his own part the Cardinal was equally moved by the piety of the young German aristocrat, and despite Noailles' failure to convert him they kept up their link. A little later Zinzendorf dedicated his French translation of Arndt's *True Christianity* to the Cardinal.[17]

As a result of his travels he reached the conclusion that the "theology of the heart" could unite all sincere Christians. The outcome would be the ecumenical utopia of a single Church in which Lutherans and Calvinists would be united with Catholics, and where differing traditions (*tropoi*, as he called them)—whether liturgical, spiritual or even theological—would be reconciled while retaining their individuality.

On his return to Germany he embarked on a romantic adventure. It began when he asked for the hand of his cousin, Theodora, but when he learnt that his young friend, the Count of Reuss, was also in love with her, he stood aside. Everything turned out well and he himself married his rival's sister, Erdmute-Dorothea. At the same time he entered the Saxon civil service as "Hof- und Justizrat". Shortly after his appointment to this post and a few months before his marriage he inherited from his grandmother the lordship of Bethelsdorff in Upper Lusatia, and used his rights of patronage to appoint Johann Andreas Rothe, the religious poet, as pastor. He

---

[16] *Ibid.*   [17] Published in Paris in 1725.

did not foresee the extent to which these events would lead him along the path of his religious aspirations.

In May 1722 Rothe introduced him to a Moravian carpenter, Christian David, who asked for permission to establish himself and several companions on Zinzendorf's new estates. This little group belonged to a branch of the Utraquists of Bohemia. They had emigrated to Poland under Ferdinand I, where they were converted to Lutheranism. They then returned to Bohemia and Moravia under Rudolph II, but had to go into exile again after the Battle of the White Mountain.

In the seventeenth century they had had as their bishop Johann Amos Comenius, or Komensky (1592–1670), an interesting and original type of religious humanist who died in exile in Amsterdam.[18] Hostile to both the Papacy and the Empire and a partisan of ecumenism before his time, Comenius had been in close touch while in Holland with the English non-conformist emigrés who were to sail in the *Mayflower* to found New England. At one time he had even been thought of as a possible president of Harvard University which was soon to be founded. When he died, there was no successor to the leadership of the Bohemian Brotherhood— which was what the "Moravians" were commonly called at the time—and the group seemed on the point of dissolution.

Zinzendorf welcomed them, and they established themselves in the Huttenberg which they renamed Herrnhut. Zinzendorf had little to do with them at first, as he was actively engaged in turning his castle into a spiritual centre and was starting one thing after another without noteworthy success: the foundation of a college for the nobility, of an orphanage, and of a periodical (*The Socrates of Dresden*) which was to bring rationalist unbelievers back to the faith.

Meanwhile, as Moravians continued rallying to Herrnhut, followed by inevitable disagreements among themselves, Zinzendorf proposed them a charter in 1727 which they accepted; and the next year he obtained permission to resign from the civil service so that he could devote himself to them entirely.

At first their chapel was no more than an annexe of the Lutheran parish where Rothe was still pastor. But that same year (1727) the Moravian community was formally reconstituted by an agreement reached by its members and came to look like a sort of family monastery. Marriages only took place with the approval of the

---

[18] Père Congar, in an article he devoted to him (*Catholicisme*, vol. II, 1950), does not mention his mystical allegory written in Czech in 1620 after the Battle of the White Mountain when he had just lost his wife and children. English translation by Lutzow, *The Labyrinth of the World and the Paradise of the Heart*, London, 1905.

group of directors elected by the community. Children had to be educated away from their families in two boarding-schools from an early age. All life was strictly regulated, with daily services, morning and evening, the "brothers" and "sisters" being divided up into a number of "choirs" sufficient to take turns and make collective prayer unceasing.

Zinzendorf came under attack from both strict Lutherans and Pietists. He began by answering that he was merely combining Wittenberg theory with Halle practice. But at Halle the main reproach made against him was that he had failed to undergo "conversion" on the model canonized by Francke and, moreover, that he had never provided personal witness to what was called the *agon poenitentiae* (or *Busskampf*), that is to say a deep conviction of sin suddenly effaced by grace. Full of good will, Zinzendorf tried to force himself to undergo this experience, but later had to confess how contrived it had been. He wrote:

> What is called *agon poenitentiae* cannot be other than a sort of spiritual convulsion . . . I admit that it is infinitely better for a child to suffer convulsions while teething than to die in the same process, but I maintain that there has never been a doctor such a slave to system as to forbid children to grow their teeth without convulsions.

He also wrote, mincing his words even less:

> There is only one race in the world that I cannot abide and which is antipathetic to me, and that is those miserable Christians who give themselves the name of Pietist which no one else accords them.[19]

By 1732 he foresaw that sooner or later he would have to leave Saxony with the Moravians who had now become his disciples, so he set out on preliminary missionary expeditions—first to Greenland, then, in 1735, to Georgia (it was on this latter expedition that Wesley came into contact with the Moravians). In 1736, despite his repeated professions of loyalty to the Confession of Augsburg, Zinzendorf and his followers were banished from Saxony on the grounds that, by introducing a new sect, they had contravened the Treaty of Westphalia. He established his community at Wetterau, near Frankfurt, in a place that was later called Herrnhag, and himself began travelling again, going as far as Livonia to found a group of Brothers.

On his way through Berlin on his return in 1738 he was consecrated bishop by Jablonsky[20] whom a community other than the

[19] Quoted by Cristiani, *ibid.*
[20] See Père Congar's study on Jablonsky in the encyclopedia, *Catholicisme*, vol. V, 1962.

Herrnhut one had chosen as its bishop and who had previously consecrated one of the missionaries sent out to Georgia. It was from this time and under Jablonsky's influence (he was a follower of Comenius and corresponded with Leibniz) that Zinzendorf devoted himself first and foremost to promoting Christian unity—according to his own views which were pretty chimerical, it has to be admitted.

In 1741 a Moravian synod gathered in London proclaimed Christ as "Universal Priest" (literally "General Presbyter") of Christians and Zinzendorf as *Scharnier* (or hinge) of their union. Some while after he went to Georgia, renouncing his title of bishop among the heathens who called him simply "Brother Ludwig"; but the pious expedition did not have the success he had hoped for.

Back in Germany the following year, Zinzendorf was uneasy about the legal recognition that the Moravians had meanwhile obtained, both in Prussia and Wetterau, as a new independent religious body, and he had himself appointed by them "Servitor Plenipotentiary of the Community" (which meant in practice dictator, as Cristiani notes). He persuaded the Moravian synod held at Marienborn in 1745 to ratify his theory of "religion of the heart" and the organization of the *tropoi paideias* which were to bring about the symbiosis between the different Christian Churches and sects, which was his dream.

In 1747, however, he was able to return to Saxony with full freedom to take his community with him on condition it subscribed to the Augsburg Confession. But when in 1749 the English Parliament recognized the Moravian Church under the name of *Unitas Fratrum*, he established himself in London, which then became his home and the centre of his activities pretty continuously until 1755. He had to return to Saxony now and again owing to the enormous debts he had accumulated there.

In 1752 he lost his son at the age of fifteen, who he had hoped might develop into his successor. In 1756 his wife died. Despite his grief, he remarried the following year. But three years later he himself died—uttering those words of disarming frankness in which his Pietist enemies saw the wrong-headed Christian who (so they said) had never recognized the tragedy of sin: "I am wholly devoted to the Lord's will, and he is pleased with me."

It would be hard to find anyone in Christian history so puzzling to sum up as Zinzendorf. His sincerity and the touching ardour of his piety and love for Christ seem beyond dispute. But there was an element of unreality and megalomania in his grandiose and over-simplified schemes for Christian reunion. His personal theology in particular, in which he attempted to define what he meant by

Herzenreligion, went beyond the limits of extravagance. To none of the spiritual teachers who concentrated on devotion to the Saviour's humanity does P. Bulgakov's remark seem more appropriate: this is not a matter of Christianity but Jesuanity.[21]

For to Zinzendorf our real heavenly Father to whom we address the Lord's Prayer was exclusively God made flesh in Jesus Christ. He was not the Our Father of eternity and the creator of the universe. Not that Zinzendorf denied the Trinity, but he had his own views on it: the Father was more our Grandfather than our Father, and the Holy Spirit was more or less our Mother. From this Father and this Mother was born, through the Virgin, our Father and Brother, the Lamb of God.

Attempts have been made to see a sort of renewal of gnostic theology in these expressions. But although Zinzendorf may have been led to some of his strange formulations by Boehme's and especially Arnold's ideas, it seems more accurate to think of them as the natural outcome of an ever-increasingly sentimental expression of Christianity. Zinzendorf was no speculative theologian, but in all good faith wanted to remain faithful to Christian dogma on the Trinity, the Incarnation and the Redemption, while at the same time presenting it in "cordial" terms more easily acceptable to all pious, if not Pietist, Christians. He was incapable of perceiving the risk he ran of distorting the dogma by such images.

These were drawn from the whole deposit of childish-loving terms, and reached their apogee on his return from America where contact with the "good savages" seems to have made more impression on the lord of Herrnhut than he made on them. It was at that time that God the Father became *Papa*, the Holy Spirit *Mama*, and Jesus *Flämmlein, Bruder, Lämmlein*, and even—two centuries before the Christian working-class movements—*Handwerkgesell*. Sometimes familiarity was pushed even further—to *Galgenschwengel*, or even worse! He made all his disciples adopt the same language in all things, making everything hopelessly silly on the pretext of being like little children, and trailing a false innocence which even dispensed with elementary decency (at least in words).

To this we should add his exalted doctrine of Christian marriage which made him say, among other absurdities, that husbands were only the vice-husbands of their wives who were brides of Christ. But what was most disturbing was his constant evocation of the pierced side of the Saviour, with the streams of blood gushing out in which those new-born to grace could bathe with delight (and, alas, he used the same wording when treating of the theme of the

---

[21] See his *Amerikanisches Reden*, 2 vols., Büdingen, 1796, and his *Londoner Reden*, 2 vols., 1756–1757. See too *Ueber Glauben und Leben*, Berlin, 1825.

Church, for whom Christ was a "Bridegroom of blood"). We find no difficulty in understanding the turbid impression that Moravian mysticism made on contemporaries, and indeed we find it hard not to share it. The least we can say is that the two thousand-odd hymns[22] that he composed—many of them on these themes and in this style—are of a sickly sentimentality that makes this *Pleurakultus*, as it has been called, a mournful equivalent of the worst side of Catholic devotion to the Sacred Heart.

If we were to subject Zinzendorf's life and personality to stringent analysis, as the pastor and psychologist Oskar Pfister has done,[23] we should be forced to admit certain neurotic characteristics. Yet for all that we cannot deny that Zinzendorf's deeply Christian fervour was of greater value than his psychological capacities allowed him to express. Later the Moravians were cleared of most of these equivocal oddities by Zinzendorf's successor and biographer, Bishop Spangenberg; and in any case the impulse they gave to works in the mission-field, to evangelical piety and the earliest aspirations towards unity among Protestant Christians, were a much more important factor than the *Kitsch* they bequeathed to German Protestantism—which was in every way up to its Catholic equivalent.

Anglicanism in the Eighteenth Century and Wesley: Butler and Law

It was from English Puritan sources that Pietism had partly sprung, and it was in England that Pietism was to find its continuation and its greatest repercussion—with Wesley's Methodism and the whole nineteenth-century movement of "revival".

When John Wesley began his work of evangelism, England, spiritually speaking, had reached its lowest level ever. After the mass exodus of the best Puritans under James I and then again at the Restoration, the failure of the Restoration and the accession of William of Orange produced the liquidation of High Church Anglicanism in its turn. Its best spokesmen, such as Thomas Ken, Bishop of Bath and Wells, were driven from the "establishment" by their refusal to betray their oath of loyalty to James II. The little Church that these Non-jurors managed to keep going for a while is very interesting, for it represented a much more decided return to Catholic tradition than that of the Caroline Divines— above all in liturgical usages and the doctrine of the Eucharist. In

[22] *Geistliche Lieder*, edited by A. Knapp, Stuttgart, 1843.
[23] O. Pfister, *Die Frömmigkeit des Gräfen L. von Zinzendorf*, 2nd ed., Vienna, 1924.

this way it certainly prepared the way for the Oxford Movement, though it was destined soon to die out in isolation.[24]

The High Church tradition survived in Anglicanism, but until the middle of the nineteenth century it was more a refuge of political and religious conservatism than a spiritual focus. After the expulsion of James II the mass of Anglicans fell into a latitudinarianism of a more and more rationalizing kind, accompanied by spiritual laxness and almost complete indifference to the headlong de-Christianization of society. And the Non-Conformists on the fringe of the official Church remained mere sectaries whose Puritan inspiration had been more or less extinguished.

Yet all spiritual preoccupations were not dead in the Anglican Church. In the eighteenth century Christian Platonism produced two of its most original exponents. These were the Irishman George Berkeley (1685–1753), Bishop of Cloyne,[25] a powerful religious philosopher of intrepid spirituality and for all that completely free from all temptations to pantheism or dualism, and Joseph Butler (1692–1752), one of the great philosophical apologists of Christianity.

Butler was born at Wantage in Berkshire of a Presbyterian family that had turned to Anglicanism. He went to Oriel College, Oxford (where a century later Newman was elected fellow), and devoted the long years of his peaceful parish life at Stanhope, in Durham, to his famous *Analogy* (1736). He was promoted as Bishop of Bristol and then of Durham, and died at Bath while travelling—which explains why his grave is in Bristol rather than Durham.

His *Analogy,* like his few sermons that have been preserved,[26] reveals a religious philosopher deeply influenced by Alexandrian Christian Platonism, but one who pushed the analysis of moral conscience and of the various branches of human thought to their limit. Both in his deeply theological concept of conscience as in his vision of the natural world as inseparable from the supernatural world—to which all contemporary thought tended to be

[24] See P. A. Tavart, *The Quest for Catholicity,* New York, 1964, and Jardine Grisbrooke, *Anglican Liturgies of the XVIIth and XVIIIth Centuries.*

[25] A Berkeley bibliography may be found in all the histories of philosophy. But it has been insufficiently noted how (even more than with Malebranche) his philosophy from many points of view is but a transposed spirituality. His thesis of immaterialism is constantly presented in a caricatured way, but Newman believed that, if one takes the trouble really to understand it, it is irrefutable. Professor Collingwood comes to the same conclusion in the lucid pages he has written about him in *The Idea of Nature.*

[26] See *The Analogy of Religion . . . also Fifteen Sermons,* ed. by Joseph Angus towards the third quarter of the nineteenth century (no date given) with a biography. Gladstone re-edited Butler's works in 1896. Church has devoted an excellent essay to him in *Pascal and other Sermons,* 1895, pp. 25 *et seq.*

opposed—he was to be the most fertile stimulant of all Newman's thought and of a crucial part of his religion. It is painful to see such a great mind and such a deeply religious prelate coming into unyielding conflict with Wesley.

Wesley derived what was best in his early religious inspiration from the High Church traditions strictly upheld by his father, though both his father and mother were of non-conformist origin. He was also indebted to one of the most curious figures in the Non-juror group, William Law.[27] Law (1686–1761) was the son of a Northamptonshire grocer and a student and fellow of Emmanuel College, Cambridge, from which he was expelled for refusing to take the oath of allegiance to William and Mary. He then became tutor to the future father of Gibbon the historian who, with his sceptical and trenchant turn of mind, paid no small compliment to his father's master when he called him a worthy and pious man who believed what he professed and practised what he preached. After Edward Gibbon's premature death in 1737, Law retired to his native village of Kingscliff which he thereafter rarely left. There he served as chaplain to Hester Gibbon, the historian's aunt, and to Mrs Hutcheson, her widowed friend, who became his disciples. They spent their income on works of charity inspired by him.

Law first became known as a brilliant controvertialist in the defence of traditional Anglicanism, but on his retirement he devoted himself to meditation and writing pious works.

The first of these, *A Serious Call to a Devout and Holy Life*, was published in 1729. Its success was so great that we can only compare it to that of the *Introduction à la Vie dévote* in France at the beginning of the seventeenth century. Law's aim was similar: to show (though this time not to a woman, but to young people of both sexes of the best contemporary society) that there was nothing absurd or outlandish about devotion and a life lived in accordance with it: on the contrary, such a life and such devotion were worthy objectives for the most refined hearts and minds and could be pursued in perfect harmony with life in the world, if not with every type of worldly life. Doctor Johnson had no hesitation in attributing his earliest religious convictions to this book, and its influence over young John and Charles Wesley was even more decisive.

But when Wesley came to know the author personally he was bitterly disappointed to find that he had already moved away from this book's sane and balanced outlook. The explanation was that

27 His *Collected Works* appeared in 12 vols. starting in 1762. See M. Grainger, *William Law and the Life of the Spirit*, 1948; A. W. Hopkinson, *About William Law*, 1948; and J. B. Green, *John Wesley and William Law*, 1948. Numerous editions of *Serious Call*, including Everyman Library.

in 1733 Law had discovered Jakob Boehme and was so impressed that his first aim in his solitary retreat—which also became the first aim of the two devout women following in his footsteps—was to dig deep into his works and assimilate his doctrine. Thenceforward Law's output was almost entirely confined to treatises on Boehme's mysticism, such as *The Way to Divine Knowledge* and *The Spirit of Love* (1752). Though these works contain passages of high spirituality, there is something definitely extravagant about them. Boehme's bizarre genius here turns into a very British kind of mild dottiness which suggests that, in the touching and faintly comic trio of Law and the two pious Egerias, Law was by no means the least old-maidish of the three. This, anyway, seems to have been the impression that Wesley came away with after his last pilgrimage to Kingscliff.

John Wesley and Methodism

John Wesley (1703–1791),[28] was, as we have seen, the son of a High Church Anglican ecclesiastic, though his mother, Susanna, remained the loyal daughter of Doctor Samuel Annesley, a preacher who in his time was called the St Paul of Non-Conformity. His paternal family belonged to the gentry and had produced a number of clergymen. Wesley was born at the rectory of Epworth in Lincolnshire and went to Charterhouse and Christ Church, Oxford, where he was ordained deacon in 1725. The following year he was elected fellow of Lincoln where he became tutor and reader in Greek. He was ordained priest in 1728.

He and his brother Charles and several of their companions immediately became outstanding for their ascetic zeal and piety. At that time his favourite reading was *The Imitation* and Jeremy Taylor. He retained Taylor's Arminianism, with its ferocious opposition to Calvinist predestination, to the end. In 1727 and 1728, when he absented himself from Oxford so as to help his father in the parish of Epworth, the pious meetings held in the university by his brother and their friend George Whitefield won them the nickname of "methodists"—which stuck. He returned to Oxford in 1727, the date of the publication of Law's *Serious Call*,

---

[28] Wesley's works were edited in 14 vols. starting in 1872. The poetic works of the two brothers, John and Charles, occupy 13 vols., of another edition published in 1868 onwards. Nehemiah Curnock edited the *Journal* in 8 vols. starting in 1918, and the *Letters* were edited in 8 vols. by John Telford starting in 1931. A biographical study, over-emphasizing perhaps Wesley's misadventures of the heart, but excellently documented, came out in 1937 and there have been many subsequent editions: G. Elsie Harrison, *Son to Susanna, The Private Life of John Wesley*. In 1876 Richard Green drew up the first complete bibliography of all the works of the two brothers: *The Works of John and Charles Wesley*.

and immediately became a great admirer of Law, though later he was disillusioned by Law's immersion in Boehme's mysticism, as we have seen. In 1773 he expressed in his *Journal* his solidly British and commonsense reaction to Boehme:

> ... to whom I object not only that he is obscure (although even this is an inexcusable fault in a writer on practical religion); not only that his whole hypothesis is unproved; wholly unsupported either by Scripture or reason; but that the ingenious madman over and over contradicts Christian experience, reason, Scripture, and himself (Entry for July 12).

After his father's death in 1735 his zeal found a better outlet in a missionary enterprise in Georgia on behalf of the Society for the Propagation of the Gospel. At that time Wesley was a High Churchman of the strictest type—he recited the divine office daily with great devotion, fasted, went regularly to confession, and celebrated the Eucharist at least once a week. He had a vigorous antagonism to Non-Conformity. Yet in his Christianity there must surely have been an exclusive ascetic element accompanied by a strong dose of rigorism and intolerant dogmatism.

All this was thoroughly shaken up by his missionary expedition, though his basic convictions were not as much altered as one might have supposed. To begin with the expedition was marked by a setback, even by ridicule. For just when his strictness was shocking his companions and arousing rather bitter opposition, he fell in love—vainly and rather absurdly with a girl of a very different type from himself. These burning mortifications were combined with the impression made on him, in his travels, by a group of Moravians at a moment when a storm was endangering both the boat and its passengers.

Back in Oxford he began to be attracted by these sectaries whom previously he had viewed with some contempt. Also he felt uneasy in a confused way and dissatisfied with himself. He resumed contact with the Moravian missionary, Peter Böhler. Böhler, though initially without much success, tried to convince him that true Christianity was not so much a matter of correct doctrines and practices as of the heart's adherence to Jesus, Saviour of the weak and the sinful. He himself described in his *Journal* the inner event that was to determine his spirituality and preaching for the rest of his life. It occurred on 24 May 1738, in London:

> In the evening I went very unwillingly to a society [Moravian] in Aldersgate Street, where one was reading Luther's preface to the Epistle to the Romans. About a quarter before nine, while he was describing the change which God works in the heart through faith in Christ, I felt my heart strangely warmed. I felt

I did trust in Christ, Christ alone, for salvation; and an assurance was given me, that he had taken away *my* sins, even *mine*, and saved *me* from the law of sin and death. I began to pray with all my might for those who had in a more especial manner despitefully used me and persecuted me. I then testified openly to all there what I now first felt in my heart...

No text is more important for a grasp of the new-style Methodism, or Wesleyanism, that emerged whole and entire from this inner conversion and early testimony.

We cannot bring out better than Wesley himself the way in which his conversion echoed Luther's experience; the very words used to describe it are in a direct line from Luther's famous formulation. But Wesley's interpretation—and it was immediate—can be distinguished by various essential shades of meaning from the one that had produced Lutheranism.

In the first place we are not only dealing with the spiritual experience of illumination but with a change of heart, a conversion. Nothing is more characteristic of this fact than Wesley's first and immediate inspiration, which was to pray for all those against whom at that very moment he was nursing feelings of resentment. And indeed he was never thereafter to be tempted to dissociate justification by faith from a changed life. Little of a Calvinist though he was, he made his own, and immediately, the Calvinist doctrine of sanctification as inseparable from justification. But, for the first time in the reformed tradition, the two aspects were bound organically together by the assurance of a wholly inner action of the Holy Spirit in the souls of believers, and this not after the fashion of the more or less sectarian "enthusiasts" with whom Wesley was to be somewhat confused, but in a deeply traditional and substantially Catholic sense.

Wesley soon entered into violent conflict with Calvinism, which his friend Whitefield was carrying forward into a "conversionism" even more exalted than his own. And the reason why he declared his horror of Calvinist predestination at that very moment was that, when he saw it combined with the preaching of the transforming conversion, he was afraid—and not unreasonably—that it would bring with it a fatal illusion. For if justifying faith became faith in one's own justification, the result would be either the chimera of a perfection suddenly conferred by conversion, or else an attitude of negligence towards "working for one's salvation in fear and trembling", as the apostle said. Of course he accepted all the Lutheran expressions on the faith that assures *me* of *my* salvation; but he explained that this assurance was only valid in and for the present moment, and that it should thus uphold us in the hope of the grace of perseverance (which is never our right), and also in the effort of constant prayer and progressive sanctification (by obedience to faith) without which we could not hope for it. In this way not only did he attain to Catholic doctrine, but even to those forms of it—such as Molinism—which allow the greatest scope to human freedom. Moreover, St Ignatius Loyola was for him, as he put it, one of the greatest men in Christian history.

From the moment on 24 May 1738 that Wesley had his decisive experience (commemorated by a plaque in Aldersgate Street fixed, ironically enough, to the frontage of one of the largest City banks!) all his preaching was aimed at arousing something similar in his fellow-countrymen. The English of that most pleasure-seeking and easy-going period—so terribly depicted by Hogarth—but also of the Industrial Revolution that was to change the face first of England and then of the whole world, soon came to realize that a voice of ardent and prophetic conviction was re-echoing from the pulpits of the Established Church. Nothing so direct and popular had ever been heard, at least not for a long time.

But the voice soon caused scandal, for it gave a sharp shock to the comfortable intellectual and spiritual attitudes of good society. The fact that it drew all sorts of people to church who had lost the habit of going was hardly likely to appease Wesley's colleagues regarding a style of Christianity so alien to them. Soon they forbade him their pulpits, so he began preaching anywhere, even out of doors, though not without some hesitation at first. As he was anxious not to cause a schism and add yet another sect to the nonconformist movements from which all his former convictions separated him, and acting less by preconceived design than by force of circumstances, he began making it his normal practice to preach far away from any existing church. This meant that his apostolate came to be directed not towards the parishes in the old cities (which were becoming more and more aristocratic and middle-class), nor towards the rural areas (where the best in ecclesiastical life had anyway been preserved), but towards the suburbs and shanty towns that were springing up everywhere with the development of the mines and heavy industry. The ecclesiastics responsible had by and large done nothing for these uprooted masses, overwhelmed by poverty and alcoholism and the worst degradations.

Wesley, with his group of faithful friends such as his brother Charles and Whitefield, was the first churchman whether Protestant or Catholic to become aware of the need for a mission to the new pagans of the modern world, a mission no less urgent than the one he had previously been engaged on in distant lands.

He himself has left an account of his decisive conversation with the Bishop of Bristol who was none other than Joseph Butler, the wisest and holiest bishop of the period, but who for long now had looked at the world from the interior of his book-lined study. Butler showed himself as unable to see in Wesley, with his highly unconventional preaching to the de-Christianized masses, anything but another "enthusiast", that is to say a fanatical illuminee and an incipient sectary.

Yet on the whole Wesley seems to have been viewed less as a new type of "dissenter" than as a crypto-Catholic or an active partisan of the Stuarts—two things rather easily confused at that time. This double accusation was not entirely without foundation because, in addition to the fact that he had inherited from his father, not to mention William Law, very lukewarm feelings for the House of Orange, he preached a religion that had a closer resemblance to that of Catholic missionaries than anything else being preached at that time, either from Anglican pulpits or in nonconformist chapels.

At an early stage there arose a controversy among the Methodists that has lasted till this day. Did Wesley retain his High Church convictions after his conversion and involvement in his new ministry? That he never accepted the Calvinism inherited from the Puritans is amply proved by the dispute that arose between him and Whitefield and only ended in a makeshift compromise. For the rest, he seems to have broken with his earlier ecclesiastical ideas only with regret and under pressure of circumstances. He came to oppose the High Church doctrine on regeneration by baptism only in as much as he saw it standing in the way of his preaching on conversion. And it was only at the very end of his life and because he despaired of obtaining regular ordinations that he, a simple priest, ordained ministers and even consecrated bishops for the American mission. Even then he took a firm stand behind the idea, taken from St Jerome and which a Thomist would not have disclaimed in principle, of the unity of the priesthood and the episcopate.

His acceptance of lay preachers as assistants to the small band of priests who helped him was also wrung from him by force. When Thomas Maxfield, a worker converted by his sermons in the streets of Bristol, began preaching himself, Wesley at first forbade it. It needed an awakening in his mother of her non-conformist background to make him change his mind. She pointed out to him that this man had surely been called by God to preach just as much as he had himself.

It was thus that the new-style Methodism was slowly built up, not as the product of innovating ideas as such, but in a spirit of cautious pragmatism, and preserving as long as possible the links with the Church of England that this Church's dignitaries would have preferred to see severed. But this was not the feeling of the priest who caused them so much worry by trying to awaken the Sleeping Beauty of whom they were the guardians—guardians somewhat sleepy in their turn.

This pragmatic spirit was equally observable in the prudence with which Wesley, while preaching conversion—and a conversion, if not sudden, at least matured by a decisive experience—avoided basing the notion too closely on his own experience, in this way escaping Francke's fatal mistake. As the Methodists, who took up the expressions we find on every page of Wesley's sermons, were to put it, a "converted" Christian was one for whom God's gifts had become the object of truly personal interest: that is to say, assurance of forgiveness and adoption into God's family. But they insisted that conversion could not by itself become a guarantee of final perseverance. It was always possible to fall from this state of grace and, having savoured the heavenly gift and participated in the Holy Spirit, to perish spiritually. Hence the emphasis on constant effort towards total sanctification for which conversion was no more than the point of departure. The goal was Christian perfection, a perfection relatively accessible here below if our faith and the generosity of our response to grace were sufficient. This perfection, they went on to say, was one and the same thing as a life so really crucified with Christ that one could testify in one's turn, "I live now, not I, but Christ who liveth in me."

In this state ignorance, error and frailties were not lacking, but these faults were no more than "involuntary sins" which maintained in us the constant need to be purified in Christ's blood but without separating us from his friendship. This is something with which, in another terminology, Catholics are familiar in the distinction between mortal sins and venial sins (or imperfections), or yet again in the "daily sins" of the best of the faithful to which St Augustine referred (and Wesley did not fail to quote him).

All this, then, marked a return to Catholic doctrine in its deepest and most traditional form, but powerfully revived by the most positive Protestant intuitions and expressed in a simple and popular language with great vigour and communicative conviction. From this point of view and without exaggeration Wesley can be viewed as a reformer of the Reformation itself who should perhaps be put on the same plane as its greatest initiators. If he lacked Luther's intellectual power and original religious genius, he proved himself an incomparably more efficient apostle and pastor than anyone else when it came to producing a real spiritual revival in his disciples.

We can say that never, since the beginning of the Christian mission in England, had there been such an effective movement of religious and moral revival.

The efficiency of the movement was much helped by the way the Methodists were organized in "classes" of a dozen people, each under a "leader" whose task it was to keep a friendly watch over their spiritual development and the organization of their contribution to the missionary effort. The attempts at authoritarian "discipline" among the Calvinists and Puritans were replaced by a much more flexible effort towards spiritual solidarity among the simplest of Christians. They were carried along in the wake of the best among them, not by dictatorial or oppressive means, but by mutual education which on the whole, and despite weaknesses and deviations for which Wesley was always on the watch, was thoroughly successful.

The educational side of Methodism explains one curious phenomenon. Though in the first generation the Methodists were recruited from among the masses and those lowest in the social scale, before long they became a typical and representative denomination of the middle classes, and even of the upper middle class. How did this happen? Simply because Methodism proved to be an incomparable means for professional education, and especially for education to responsibility, so that its adepts raised themselves in the social scale as a matter of course, while never losing the religious convictions that had played an essential part in their promotion.

Wesley's peculiarly practical and concrete spirit can be found behind all this. His emphasis on a Christianity that should involve the inner man, while remaining fundamentally social, begot a movement—beginning with the masses—of Christian solidarity directly inspired by charity, not the condescending charity of the "paternalist" type, but real charity in which both rich and poor recognized one another as equals and brothers in Christ.

In spite of the fanatically anti-Roman prejudices that dominated England at this time, Wesley was perfectly well aware that what he wanted corresponded with the highest aspirations of the Catholics—and Catholics not only of the ancient Church but of the Church of his time. Anxious to provide his disciples with solid spiritual reading, he thus became, within Protestantism, one of the great popularizers of his beloved *Imitation* as well as of Teresa of Avila, Ignatius of Loyola, Francis de Sales and Fénelon. Apart from the Quakers—who turned their attention almost exclusively to mystical writers—no one did so much to rebuild the bridges on the spiritual plane between Catholicism (old and new) and a renewed Protestantism.

John and Charles Wesley and Methodist Hymnology

Methodist piety can be appreciated at its best in what was at once its favourite means of expression and its most active agent of propaganda: the abundant output of hymns in which John Wesley found more than a collaborator in his brother Charles.[29] For while John usually confined himself to felicitous translations and adaptations from German and above all "Moravian" hymns, Charles soon proved himself to be an original religious poet, able to express the great themes of Methodist preaching in a really popular way, but no less inspired for that, and showing lively but normally very wholesome feeling. We find in these hymns all the freshness and depth of the discovery of God's love for us in Christ—a discovery felt so keenly in this spirituality that it cut through all the artificial barriers set up by Protestant systematization to the spontaneous flowering of genuine Christian mysticism. The revelation of divine love in the cross which in return arouses a total love for Jesus and, through him, for the Father has hardly ever found franker and warmer expression so felicitously conveyed to the humblest of Christians.

Hymn-writing had already been a practice in England before the time of the Wesley brothers. The Non-juror Bishop Ken left three fine prayers, for morning, evening and night, for his Cambridge students. But the best-known practitioner had been the "independent" preacher, Isaac Watts (1674–1748), who had added to the versification of the psalms by Sternhold and Hopkins and others, not only psalms transposed or elaborated into Gospel language (of which the most famous is his paraphrase of Psalm 90, "O God our help in Ages Past"), but also original hymns which rapidly gained popularity. Their chief merit was their great simplicity both as to words and rhythms. But some have real beauty, especially when they echo the radiant imagery of the Apocalypse and the blood of the Lamb—his favourite themes. The one inspired by St Paul's epistle to the Galatians, 6. 14, on the Christian's crucifixion to the world, certainly deserves the place it has been accorded as a classic of English Protestant piety:

> When I survey the wondrous Cross
> On which the Prince of Glory dy'd
> My richest Gain I count but Loss,
> And pour Contempt on all my Pride.

[29] Tom Ingram and Douglas Newton have published a good study on this subject as preface to their excellent anthology, *Hymns as Poetry*, 1956.

> Forbid it, Lord, that I should boast
> Save in the Death of Christ my God;
> All the vain things that charm me most,
> I sacrifice them to his Blood.[30]

Charles Wesley's hymns brought an intensely personal note to the most jubilant expressions of faith, and this possibly gave them even more influence than his brother's sermons. At the very least we must quote "Jesu, Lover of my Soul", in which the Methodist interpretation of justifying faith finds its best translation into words of intense love for Christ and the ardent desire for effective holiness that it presupposes:

> Jesu, Lover of my Soul
>   Let me to thy Bosom fly ...
>
> Thou, O Christ, art all I want,
>   More than all in Thee I find:
> Raise the Fallen, chear the Faint,
>   Heal the Sick, and lead the Blind.
> Just, and holy is thy Name,
>   I am all Unrighteousness,
> False, and full of Sin I am
>   Thou art full of Truth and Grace.
>
> Plenteous Grace with Thee is found,
>   Grace to cover all my Sin;
> Let the healing Streams abound,
>   Make, and keep me pure within:
> Thou of life the Fountain art:
>   Freely let me take of Thee;
> Spring Thou up within my Heart,
>   Rise to all eternity.[31]

Hardly less interesting is the hymn he composed for the anniversary of his conversion. Here we find the strongest expression of what this meant for a Methodist:

> Glory to GOD, and Praise, and Love ...
>
> Sudden expir'd the legal Strife,
>   'Twas then I ceas'd to grieve,
> My second, real, living Life,
>   I then began to live.
>
> Then with my *Heart* I first believ'd,
>   Believ'd with Faith divine,
> Power with the Holy Ghost receiv'd,
>   To call the Saviour *mine*.

---

[30] *Hymns as Poetry*, p. 97.   [31] *Ibid.*, p. 121.

8—H.C.S. III

> I felt my LORD's atoning Blood
> Close to *my* Soul applied;
> *Me, me* He lov'd—the Son of God,
> For *me*, for *me* He died!...
>
> He breaks the Power of cancell'd Sin,
> He sets the Prisoner free:
> His blood can make the Foulest clean,
> His blood avail'd for *me.*
>
> He speaks; and listening to his Voice,
> New Life the Dead receive,
> The mournful, broken Hearts rejoice,
> The humble Poor *believe.*[32]

Later the poet William Cowper, in collaboration with John Newton, a converted slave-dealer who became rector of the parish of Olney, published a famous anthology which carried on in this spirit: *Olney Hymns.* Newton gave expression to a solid, heartfelt, if rather blunt Christianity, but Cowper, who lived under an obsessive threat of madness, provided memorable words for a faith reaching out through anguish:

> GOD moves in a mysterious way,
> His wonders to perform;
> He plants his footsteps in the sea,
> And rides upon the storm.
>
> ...Ye fearful saints fresh courage take,
> The clouds ye so much dread
> Are big with mercy, and shall break
> In blessings on your head.
>
> Judge not the LORD by feeble sense,
> But trust him for his grace;
> Behind a frowning providence,
> He hides a smiling face.
>
> His purposes will ripen fast,
> Unfolding ev'ry hour;
> The bud may have a bitter taste,
> But sweet will be the flower....[33]

In this tradition of piety, with its very strong emphasis on experience, this piece may serve to remind us that men "awakened" by Methodism were well able to discern a higher experience of grace in the deepest depths of darkness as much as in the brightest spiritual joys.

[32] *Ibid.*, p. 125.
[33] *Ibid.*, p. 166. There is an interesting study on Cowper's religious poetry in ford Brooke, *Theology in the English Poets*, 1874.

One of the most striking of the "evangelicals", who extended the influence of Methodism within the clergy of the Established Church while absolutely refusing to go into schism, was A. M. Toplady. One day, shortly before his early death, he was sheltering from a storm in a crevasse in Burrington Combe and composed the hymn which was to have the most lasting success of all:

> Rock of Ages, cleft for me,
> Let me hide myself in Thee!
> Let the Water and the Blood,
> From thy riven Side which flow'd,
> Be of Sin the double Cure,
> Cleanse me from its Guilt and Pow'r.... [34]

Reformed Spirituality in Holland: Tersteegen

The presence of English non-conformist refugees in Holland during the reigns of James I and Charles I had had a deep influence on Dutch Calvinism. The theology of the Covenant as developed by William Ames in particular found an echo,[35] and was taken by Johannes Cocceius[36] of Leyden university as the basis of his notion of the history of salvation (*Heilsgeschichte*). This became the kernel of a renewed biblical theology in which he stressed the mystical character of the prophetical experience destined—with the New Testament—to blossom into a mysticism of Christ and the Holy Spirit.

Not long afterwards the French Protestants who had emigrated to the Netherlands on the revocation of the Edict of Nantes showed themselves no less open to Fénelon-type mysticism than the Lutheran Pietists in Germany. This applied not only to the disciples of the dubious Labadie (of whom we have already spoken), or to prophesying illuminees such as Pierre Poiret (that tireless translator of the more or less authentic mystics),[37] but also to preachers and thinkers of deep biblical inspiration and broad but solid Calvinist theology. These included Elias Saurin (1639–1703)

---

[34] *Hymns as Poetry*, p. 156.

[35] See W. Goeters, *Die Vorbereitung des Pietismus in der Reformierten Kirche der Niederlande bis zur Labadistischen Krise, 1670*, Leipzig, 1911.

[36] See G. Schrenk, *Gottesreich und Bund im älteren Protestantismus vornehmlich bei Coccejus*, Gütersloh, 1923.

[37] Born in Metz, 1646, and died in Rhynsburg, 1719. First drawn to painting, then won over to philosophy by reading Descartes, thereafter studying theology at Basle before becoming pastor to the small communities of French exiles in Germany and Holland, Poiret was a figure it is hard to pronounce upon. A blind admirer of quietism in all its most extreme forms, he enthused ceaselessly over false mystics like Antoinette Bourignon, or doubtful ones like Armelle Nicolas. Yet he was also an indefatigable propagator, in Protestant circles, of the Catholic mystics, and his *Paix des bonnes âmes* (Amsterdam, 1687) contains some fine passages. See W. Nigg, *op. cit.*, pp. 299 *et seq.*

who was called with some reason the Bossuet of Protestantism, with his *Traité de l'Amour de Dieu* published in Utrecht in 1703, and the controversialist Pierre Jurieu (1637–1713) with his *Platique de la Dévotion ou Traité de l'Amour divin*, published in Rotterdam in 1700.

Hasso Jaeger[38] has made an excellent analysis of the rather curious complex of sympathetic feelings aroused by Fénelon in Protestants of this kind who were little inclined to come to terms with any sectarian tendencies, and in Lutherans such as Löscher. In their eyes pure love and trusting abandon to God's will was in harmony with justification by faith and not works, and they also saw in Fénelon's trials a similarity to the misunderstandings encountered by Luther. Moreover, Fénelon's submission to the Church's authority was reassuring, for they were always afraid of irrational and anarchical individualism. So these reformers, steeped in biblical humanism and aspiring to a deep and intense spiritual life, found in Fénelon's views the mysticism of the Gospels for which they were groping—something they could never have recognized in an accepted Catholic school of thought nor among discredited Protestant "enthusiasts".

Thus at the end of the seventeenth century in Holland there were not only the sectarian movements of German or English origin whose career was in decline, but an official Protestantism having a substantial thread of pure and holy evangelical spirituality nourished by all that was best in the culture of the universities.[39] This was the thread on which Gerhard Tersteegen drew—perhaps the greatest and most complete spiritual writer that Protestanism has produced.

The Mysticism of Gerhard Tersteegen (1697–1769)

Gerhard Tersteegen was born at Moers, a small town to the west of Duisburg that was taken from the Netherlands and brought under German domination at the beginning of the eighteenth century. He was born on 25 November 1697, the eighth and last child of a Protestant weaver. Though his father died when he was ten and he had to earn his living at an early age in his father's trade, when he left his excellent school after nine years of study he knew Greek, Latin and Hebrew as well as German, Dutch and French.

The nearby town of Mülheim, where he then settled, had recently had several pastors educated in Holland such as Theodor Underijk,

[38] *Op. cit.*
[39] One of the most representative works of this piety sustained by a solid culture which marked Dutch circles at this time was *De pietate cum scientia conjungenda*, by G. Voet, Utrecht, 1634.

a pupil of Cocceius at Leyden, and Wilhelm Teelinck, who for some time had been a colleague of William Ames at Franeker university. There, in a Pietist circle founded by Underijk and renewed by Ernst-Christoph Hochman, a former student of Francke's at Halle and a friend of Arnold, Tersteegen met Hochman himself and Wilhelm Hoffmann,[40] who became his friend and spiritual father.

Helped by these influences and his wide reading,[41] his spiritual personality was freely formed by intense meditation. Soon, though without abandoning his trade, he began exercising great spiritual influence which was increased still more by numerous journeys and a large correspondence. It was increased still more by his translations—such as that of Bernières de Louvigny published in 1727—and by his own works of which the principal are his *Weg der Wahrheit* and the poems collected in his *Geistliches Blumengärtlein*.[42]

The first impulse of the spirituality that his work unfolds can be seen at its most direct in the consecration of himself to Christ, written with his blood on Ash Wednesday, 1724.

O my Jesus, I consecrate myself to thee, my only Saviour, my Spouse, Jesus Christ, so as to belong entirely to thee for all eternity. With all my heart and from today I renounce all the rights and all the power that Satan unjustly gave me over myself, for thou hast ransomed me by thy agony, thy struggles and thy sweating of blood in Gethsemane, thou hast shattered the gates of hell for me and hast opened the heart of thy Father, full of charity; so that, from today, all my heart and all my love shall be given thee in return; that, from this moment and for all eternity thy will and not mine shall be done. Command, govern, reign in me. I give thee all power over me and I promise thee with time and help to shed the last drop of my blood rather than willingly disobey thee or be unfaithful to thee. I give all of myself to thee, sweet friend of my soul, and I want to belong to thee for ever. May thy Spirit never leave me and may thy mortal agony always sustain me. Yes, amen, may thy Spirit seal what here thou art promised in all simplicity by thy unworthy slave, Gerhard Tersteegen.[43]

---

[40] See H. Forsthoff, "Wilhelm Hoffmann, der geistliche Vater Tersteegens", in *Monatschrift für Rheinische Kirchengeschichte*, vol. II (1917).

[41] See F. Winter, *Die Frömmigkeit G. Tersteegens in ihren Verhältnis zur französische-quietistischen Mystik*, Neuweid, 1927.

[42] His *Gesammelte Schriften* were reissued in 8 vols, Stuttgart, 1844, and his *Weg der Wahrheit* at Bâle-Stuttgart in 1905. On him, see W. Blankennagel, *Tersteegen als religiöser Erzieher*, Cologne, 1934; A. Pagel, *G. Tersteegen, Ein Leben in der Gegenwart Gottes*, Giessen, 1960; C. P. van Andel, *Gerhard Tersteegen* (thesis at Utrecht, 1961). F. Weinhandl has written a well-documented introduction to his good anthology: *Gerhard Tersteegen, Gott ist gegenwärtig*, Stuttgart, 1955.

[43] We note echoes of Luther's famous text, quoted p. 72.

Tersteegen's mysticism was too deeply rooted in the Bible, in St Paul and St John, for his attachment to Christ ever to fall into vague sentimentality—the constant threat of Pietism. Moreover, it was built on an exact and deeply traditional doctrine of the soul. Everything in it was governed by the idea of God's presence which he expressed in the powerful and sober lyricism peculiar to him, as in the poem *Gott ist gegenwärtig*:

> God is present! Let us adore
> And walk before him in fear.
> God is in our midst. Let everything in us fall silent
> And do reverence to him.
> Whosoever knows him, whosoever says his name,
> Lower your eyes,
> Come, consecrate yourself to him anew....[44]

As he saw things, God's presence should be found in the *Eindruck*, that is to say the impression produced in the depths of the soul by the Holy Spirit. This has nothing to do with feeling. It is *Vernunft*, "reason" in Eckhart's sense, or the *nous* of Evagrius, or the fine point of the soul in St Francis de Sales, which alone can feel the presence genuinely. *Vernunft* lies within us as a sleeping power, however, until such time as the Holy Spirit, who created it for himself, awakens it.

> There must of necessity be a capacity within us for recognizing God and spiritual things in an essential and actual manner. And this capacity lies in pure reason which has been presented to us closed and disused until such time as God gives us the intelligence by which we may recognize Truth itself so intimately and essentially that we ourselves are drawn into the true God (I John, 5. 20).[45]

The way that leads there is by *Betrachtung*, that is to say "consideration" of the divine Word which, in a soul entirely given over to it by living faith penetrating all existence, will blossom out into *Beschauung*, or acts of contemplative intuition, and then into *Beschaulichkeit*, or a state of contemplation of God living in us, by the fact of our union with Christ and our participation in the Spirit that has become fully effective.

Tersteegen was as intransigent as St John of the Cross about the danger of becoming attached to extraordinary experiences. Yet he said that if the man who followed this path thought only of giving himself over to the divine will in a more and more detached way, then he would be preserved from falling into illusion.

[44] 3rd book of *Geistliches Blumengärtlein*.
[45] Page 58 of the Bâle-Stuttgart edition.

It must be admitted that the way of pure faith—the way by which the soul, following the commitment of the spirit to Jesus, lets itself be led outside itself and all created being so as to attach itself to God in spirit and in truth and serve him and partake of his communion—this is the surest way, the truest and most indispensable way; whereas the way by which souls experience extraordinary gifts, visions, ecstasies and revelations or other supernatural communications is subject to many pitfalls and misunderstandings. We should not however assume that all souls that have passed by such ways have been deceived and led astray. Not at all: God knows how and by what road he leads each one of us, and what he requires of each, and the man whose hand he holds goes safely everywhere. He who preserved St Paul, by means of Satan's thorn in the flesh, from the pride into which he might have fallen as a result of his revelations, knows a thousand other ways by which to lead our souls safely along crooked roads when they seek only him.[46]

What has to be avoided is that the soul should turn in on its experience and thus subtly become attached to itself rather than to God alone:

It is also an irksome curiosity of reason when sincere souls are always wanting to see everything and analyse whether God is acting within them, wanting to know and feel whether everything is all right, and will be all right, and how far they have already advanced, etc.—which does no more, most of the time, than increase their lack of faith and self-love. It would be much better to put oneself unreservedly and trustingly in God's hands, follow him faithfully in grace and try to cling to him for today. For it is certain that the man who wants to see everything and understand everything, whether this or that, will not get far. The more the ways of God are divine, the more incomprehensible they become. In the end we have to learn to put ourselves into his hands and lose ourselves in him. Blessed are those who do not see and yet believe (John 20. 19).[47]

Thus for the first time in Protestantism we find a really lucid critique of faith in one's faith, of faith in one's justification, becoming the object of faith. On the one hand, there is no faith that can give us assurance of salvation unless it is translated into an effective fulfilment of the divine will:

But he who loves him will keep his Word (John 14. 23). So we must be attentive to his Word, and keep it, not externally in Scripture, but we must hear it in our hearts and obey its operation and direction ... Faith is the inner certainty of the truth of

[46] *Ibid.*, pp. 77 et seq.   [47] *Ibid.*, p. 72.

invisible and future things that concern us. He who believes in his heart that a living and omniscient God is in heaven, and that his Word is the truth, according to which he will be judged, he is the man with saving faith. "All right," someone may say, "and nothing else is necessary to faith; then the matter is settled, because I have believed all that since my childhood and I believe it still." But look, do you believe in this huge business with your whole heart? The faith of the heart is the work of the Holy Spirit. So prove this faith in your works. "What works?" you will say, "Works count for nothing." Answer: Certainly it is not works that will earn us heaven, but faith and works go together and follow one another step by step, or else one doesn't really believe what one says, but only thinks one believes it.[48]

On the other hand justifying faith is not the faith that assures us of our salvation as ours, but the faith that delivers us to Christ by turning us totally away from ourselves:

Justification by faith is not the belief that I am justified, it cannot give me the assurance that my sins have been forgiven me. Though God sometimes provides such assurance, it is all the same false and dangerous to make faith and justification coincide absolutely. Faith that justifies consists in this, that a poor and humble sinner believes he finds forgiveness, help and salvation in Christ alone, that he draws near him with all the strength of his heart (John 6. 35) and gives himself over entirely to him (2 Cor. 8. 5). Justification is inextricably bound up with this faith; God gives more or less assurance of it, sooner or later, according to his good pleasure and the soul's needs: of that we can be certain. But we ought to believe not only once, but always, and we should be anchored in faith and tested in it, in this way our justification will be the stronger and the higher ... Show me thy faith in thy works (James 2. 18). Justifying faith unites us to Christ our Head and is the foundation of a new life. This should show itself. He who is justified should prove it outwardly with evidence, always seeking to become more just (Apoc. 22. 11).[49]

But perhaps even more with Tersteegen than with St John of the Cross, it is the poems[50] that best express the spirituality of total renunciation or dispossession fed by a nostalgia for the rediscovered presence—a spirituality which, while not ceasing to tend towards and sigh after the heavenly fatherland, exults even here below in the first fruits of the spirit. We find this nostalgia very much to the fore in Tersteegen's famous pilgrims' hymns, *Kommt, Brüder, lasst uns gehen*. But the equally well-known invocation to the Holy

---

[48] *Ibid.*, pp. 73–74.
[49] *Ibid.*, pp. 111–112.
[50] Cf. G. Wolter, *Gerhard Tersteegens geistliche Lyrik*, Marburg, 1929.

Spirit, *O Gott, O Geist, O Licht des Lebens*, expresses the invasion of the spirit with the same vigour:

> O God, O Spirit, O Light of Life,
> Our torch in the shadow of death.[51]

When he reached the end of his earthly life and felt his strength ebbing away, he thought of Gerhardt's hymn for a child's evening prayer, and said that God was treating him like a mother who undresses her child before he abandons himself to sleep in her arms. He died on 3 April 1769, at two in the morning, with these words on his lips, "Poor wretched Lazarus that you are! And yet the angels do not disdain to bear you away."

The End of the Eighteenth Century, and the Beginning of the Nineteenth

We could almost end our history of Protestant spirituality with Tersteegen, and we would gladly do so. It was a spirituality of rare purity and elevation. But in substance his spirituality had again become entirely Catholic. By this we mean that there was practically nothing in what he wrote that might not have been written just as well by a Catholic, and one of the surest and greatest at that. He was nevertheless a genuine product of Protestantism as regards both the biblical wealth and flavour of his spirituality and the fact that it was the most coherent development of Luther's and Calvin's great spiritual intuitions. Only, with him, these intuitions seemed as if spontaneously reintegrated into Catholic tradition precisely because they had been restored to their biblical substratum and cleansed of all admixture with any body of thought fundamentally foreign to, and incompatible with, revelation.

After Tersteegen Protestant spirituality marked time within the diminishing repercussions of the Pietistic and Wesleyan revival—such as the Swiss and French revival at the beginning of the nineteenth century or the more popular revivals at the end of it, for instance in Wales. Or else it disintegrated into the type of religious philosophy of which Schleiermacher was the leading light. This prepared the way for a rediscovery of natural religion—not without interest but basically having nothing specifically Christian about it.

At the same time there began a transposition of Christian dogma into those idealistic philosophies that filled the German nineteenth century. They were no more than laicized theologies in which, as once happened with the Gnostics, Christian notions were emptied of their real content.[52] This was replaced by an immanentist panthe-

---

[51] Both may be found in most of the anthologies of German hymns.
[52] See Stanislas Breton, *La Passion du Christ et les philosophies*, Teramo, 1954.

ism which alternated with a radical dualism in accord with a system of dialectics that could be seen at work much earlier, but now blossomed forth unrestrictedly for the first time.

In places where this religious liberalism and romanticism was not dominant, we find a whole series of movements—more or less conscious, more or less bold—for a return to the traditional Church, among which the most famous, if not the most interesting, was the Oxford Movement. It could be said that what was best in the religious vitality of nineteeth-century Protestantism started moving in the direction that was to culminate in contemporary ecumenism; in a word, towards a reintegration of Protestant spiritual aspirations within the body of Catholic doctrine and reality.

Outside this last tendency; outside "liberalism" and the immanentist religious philosophy that no longer really belonged to authentic Christianity; outside sects and sectarian movements lost in a blind alley, there were various attempts at a Neo-Protestantism of which the most outstanding was led by Karl Barth; the idea here was to give Protestantism fresh life by a return to the Reformers. But these attempts only avoided reintegration into the Catholic tradition by their explicit rejection of all mysticism and, at least in practice, by losing interest in spirituality. When they maintained this attitude they fell sooner or later into some form of neo-liberalism such as that of Bultmann who has never stopped, and not unreasonably, proclaiming himself a faithful disciple of the early Barth. When they diverged from this attitude, like the Barth of the latter volumes of his *Dogmatik*, they returned—unwilling though they were to admit it—to substantially Catholic positions.

Religious Romanticism

There is no question of providing even a short analysis of religious Romanticism here, particularly as it developed in Germany. But we cannot end our study without making some comments on it. Earlier on we mentioned the ambiguities of Romanticism. In its reaction against the Enlightenment and the rationalism that accompanied it, it brought into relief spiritual realities which elude rationalising reason (using the word spiritual in its widest sense). It also prepared the way for a discovery of the depths of the soul which even today has been far from exhaustively explored.

Hence it was the product alike of Pietism and related movements as of the occult currents connected with Boehme and his emulators or disciples. But this only shows what a mixture it essentially was—capable of promoting a rediscovery and a deepening of Christian spirituality and mysticism, but also of promulgating bogus forms of spirituality and equivocal or downright misleading mystical systems.

Albert Béguin's fine book, *L'Âme romantique et le rêve*,[53] contains an initial inventory of these ambiguous assets, associated with the names of Hammann, Oetinger, Jung-Stilling, then the Schlegel brothers and Novalis; and the studies undertaken by Alexander Dru on the Catholic renaissance in nineteenth-century Germany and France[54] help us to evaluate and place this renaissance more accurately in its context. But these works are only a beginning and should be supplemented by similar research into English pre-Romanticism and Romanticism, from Cowper through Wordsworth and Coleridge to Keats and Shelley and well beyond.

Then we should see exactly how much the modern religious revival, both Catholic and Protestant, owes for better or worse to this cultural movement. We had to draw attention to this question for future research. But to embark on it here and now would involve us in another history and another book, on a larger and more complex scale than the one we have undertaken.

The Protestant "Revival" in the Nineteenth Century

In England and the other English-speaking countries the Wesleyan movement has extended right up to our own time, both in Anglican "evangelicalism" and in popular revivals of a more or less sectarian kind. But it can hardly be said to have renewed itself. The themes have remained the same and their treatment is wearing thin—apart from a few exceptional personalities none of whom can be said to be really creative.

As regards Anglican "evangelicals", we have already mentioned the names of Toplady, Cowper and John Newton in connection with hymns written under Methodist influence. To these we should add Calvinist "evangelicals" such as Romaine, and above all Thomas Scott[55]: Newman has told us of the deep impression these two made on him at the time of his first conversion. But if "evangelical" piety was kept alive (though not strictly speaking developed) the largest credit must go to Charles Simeon,[56] the Cambridge preacher at the beginning of the century, and Handley Moule,[57] Bishop of Durham, at the end.

[53] 1st edition, Paris, 1939.
[54] See the volume that has already come out, *The Church in the XIXth Century: Germany 1800–1918*, London, 1963.
[55] William Romaine (1714–1795) had not the warmth of conviction of *The Force of Truth* (1779), the autobiography of Thomas Scott (1747–1821) which reveals a much less rigid Calvinism.
[56] See Stephen Neill, *Anglicanism and the Anglican Communion*, London, 1960.
[57] Moule is mainly known for his life of Simeon (1892).

On the Continent, first in Geneva and then in the French-speaking reformed Churches, repercussions of Wesleyanism continued to be felt in what has been called the "revival". Wesleyanism provided all that was most living in those Churches up to the beginning of the present century and drew them out of a spiritual lethargy that closely resembled a death agony.

The initial blow was struck by a Scottish evangelist, Robert Haldane, who reached Geneva in 1817. Here he found a welcome among a group of students called "friends" ("*amis*") who were thirsting for spiritual renewal. They had come under the influence of the Moravians and the questionable though fervent and sincere Madame de Krüdener, friend and inspirer of Emperor Alexander I. Among these "friends" was Empeytaz, for a time secretary to Madame de Staël. He was one of the earliest propagators of the "revival", which he achieved through his *Cantiques Chrétiens* published that same year (1817) and largely borrowed from the Moravians.[58]

Others who propagated the movement in Switzerland, the Rhine Valley and Protestant France were César Malan, Paul-Ami Bost and Emile Guers. They produced many further hymns translated from or inspired by Pietist or Wesleyan hymnology. But the most shining personality in the group was the evangelist Félix Neff,[59] a sergeant-instructor in Geneva who was converted by César Malan and devoted himself to propagating the Gospel among the Vaudois round Briançon.

These various personalities and their literary works are very engaging, but there is no trace of originality to be found in either (except, perhaps, for the popular gusto of Neff's correspondence). They were no more than honest popularizers of a by-product of average Pietism and simplified Wesleyanism.

The two most outstanding figures in French-speaking Protestantism in the nineteenth century—both touched by the spark of the "revival"—were Adolphe Monod,[60] the preacher, and the Vaudois essayist Alexandre Vinet,[61] a friend of Sainte-Beuve to whom the latter was more indebted than he cared to admit. Monod's *Adieux* (addresses to his friends from his deathbed during the last weeks of his life), and Vinet's *Théologie Pastorale* are unquestionably the finest pious writings inspired by the movement. But their value comes less from any sort of really renewed theological

---

[58] There is no critical history of this "revival". But there is a lively account of its main personalities in Gustave Isely, *Les temps où la foi chantait*, 1938.

[59] See *Félix Neff, l'apôtre des Hautes-Alpes* (a biography based on his letters), and Félix Neff, *Lettres de direction inédites*, both published in 1934.

[60] *Les Adieux d'Adolphe Monod* was reissued in Paris in 1929.

[61] His *Théologie pastorale* came out in Paris in 1850. Astier published two vols. of extracts from Vinet: *L'esprit d'Alexandre Vinet*, Paris, 1861.

thinking than from Monod's high spirituality and Vinet's literary culture.

At the end of the nineteenth century there was a second Methodist revival in the English-speaking countries (rather attenuated this time) arising from the efforts of two popular preachers, Dwight Moody and Ira D. Sankey.[62] But the most interesting of these continuations of Methodism, because the most original, was the Welsh revival with its ecstatic quality and torrential emotionalism so well described by Henri Bois and analysed in detail by William James.[63] Here we have a foretaste of the "Pentecostal Movement" which, though simple-minded and popular and not without elements of superstition, has recently shaken up the sleepiest Protestant Churches by a nostalgia for the primitive Church reminiscent of the early fervours of the Mennonites and their like.

The Spirituality of the Oxford Movement

The Oxford Movement, and the fresh life it gave to Anglicanism from 1830 onwards, was a very different story, though its initiators owed no mean part of their early fervour to evangelicalism, even if they never really gave it their full allegiance. Bathed in the air of English Romanticism, and particularly of Walter Scott, the movement was set going by men of a far higher intellectual standing than that of the men of the "revival"—and yet, apart from Newman who passed beyond the movement and separated himself from it, they cannot be said to have had really original minds. But instead of merely continuing a local and recent tradition, they rediscovered —through Hooker, the Caroline Divines and Butler—the great tradition of the Fathers and the Middle Ages.[64]

John Keble was always considered by Newman himself as the author of the movement.[65] This is true not only because of his famous assize sermon preached in 1833 which effectively brought it before the public eye, but because of the ecclesiastical ideal, and more exactly the ideal of the Anglican priest, that he incarnated before putting it into words in the poems of his *Christian Year*

[62] See T. Ingram and D. Newton, *op. cit.*, p. 31, on these two figures.

[63] Cf. Henri Bois, *Le Réveil du Pays de Galles*, and William James, *The Varieties of Religious Experience*, London, 1902.

[64] Newman's *Apologia*, London, 1864, and R. W. Church's memoir, *The Oxford Movement*, 1891, give by far the best account of the Oxford Movement. One of its best histories is by the Swedish Lutheran Y. Brilioth, *The Anglican Revival* (1925). P. Thureau-Dangin, *La Renaissance catholique en Angleterre*, in spite of more recent research, remains excellent from the point of view of a description of the various personalities, while the movement's spirituality is very well conveyed in Christopher Dawson's *The Spirit of the Oxford Movement*, written for the centenary, 1945.

[65] See J. T. Coleridge, *A Memoir of the Rev. John Keble*.

(1827). Though Keble was an accomplished scholar, he was first and foremost a man of prayer and the devoted parish priest of a small rural community. He was the first man since the Non-jurors (whose liturgical and sacramental piety his family had preserved) to bring seventeenth-century Anglicanism back to life, conceived in terms of Catholicism purified by a return to ancient sources. In spite of the minor key and minor quality of his style (Hurrell Froude, the *enfant terrible* of the movement, told him there was something "Sternhold-and-Hopkinsy" about his versifying) he brought to it a sort of new youth by means of his intimate poetry, both typically nineteenth-century and yet tinged with medievalism.

Yet for all his exquisite culture and piety he was a man of many limitations. His letters of spiritual advice are very disappointing[66] and call to mind Newman's disillusioned remark that when you asked Keble for his opinion, all he could give you was his father's or his brother's or his wife's. *Tract 89* was undoubtedly the first solid study on patristic exegesis since Huet, but it betrays, across a first-hand knowledge of the authors, an incapacity to do more than transcribe. The same must be said of his valuable annotated edition of Hooker to which he devoted his most sustained effort. Though it shows great conscientiousness and wide knowledge, it seems almost entirely untouched either by a sense of Hooker's own historical situation or by an awareness of the quite different situation within which he wanted to restore Hooker's thought.

It was only in the best poems of his second collection, *Lyra Innocentium* (1846) that he achieved a fully personal note and one entirely his own. But, as Newman again observed, this poetry of Christian childhood, however limpid and attractive, was really the poetry of a voluntary dream into which one plunges so as to escape the realities one dare not face.

His disciple, Hurrell Froude, would doubtless have developed in a very different way had he lived. This aristocratic ascetic with something of the Cistercian about him, and an intrepid critical faculty and sense of reality, might have turned into a sort of St Bernard without the rhetoric. But his *Remains*[67] are no more than a beginning, cut short before leaving the ground.

As for Pusey, he was learned, good, patient, heavy and boring. His learning in biblical criticism was paralysed by the extreme rigidity and conservatism of his style. He had, of course, an encyclopedic knowledge of the ancient Fathers and a spirituality that developed naturally from a strong Pietistic evangelicalism to

---

[66] *Letters of Spiritual Counsel and Guidance*, ed. by R. F. Wilson in 1870.

[67] These were published by Keble and Newman at the height of the controversy unleashed by the movement, and, showing all the traits in his personality that we have mentioned, they caused an outcry in Victorian England.

devotion nourished on medieval and modern Catholicism—but it became more and more absorbed in meditation on the Passion which was as unpatristic in tone as possible.[68]

Only in Newman do we find Scripture and tradition rediscovered as living realities, with a full grasp of their historical character, so that his return to the sources had no trace of archaism about it, but was used to bring the most pressing problems of the day to life and confront them with the utmost lucidity. Protestants have often reproached him with an inadequate familiarity with the reformers. But this is to forget that all his work—beginning with his work as an Anglican—was in essence pastoral. The Protestantism that he had in mind, alike in his *Lectures on Justification* as in his *The Prophetical Office of the Church*, was the English Protestantism of his time. He was only interested in its earlier or foreign forms in so far as they had contributed to forming the religion he had under his eyes. But the closer we look the more struck we are by the fact that he—who, unlike the other founders of the Oxford Movement, was destined to abandon Anglicanism—never yielded to a facile opposition between a Catholic tradition seen as true and a Protestant inheritance seen as false. What at best was implicit, and often explicitly denied, in Keble and Pusey and still more in the Anglo-Catholicism of the next generation, became conscious and explicit only in Newman: that it was not a mere repudiation of his Protestanism that should bring a Protestant back to the Catholic tradition, but an accurate perception of all that his Protestant faith—in its most genuine aspects—postulated of Catholic reality.

The marked difference between the spirituality of the first generation of the movement as formed by the leading personalities we have just mentioned, and that of the generation that followed, has often been emphasized, and rightly. The "tractarians", as they came to be called (i.e. the authors of the *Tracts*), who launched the Oxford Movement have with reason been compared to the outstanding figures of Port-Royal. Their piety was doctrinal and austere and, even when drawing on modern sources, was rooted in the great theological tradition—above all in Pusey's case—based on the Bible and the early liturgies and dominated by the monastic ideal of "other-worldliness". And through Hooker, Andrewes, Butler, the Non-jurors and a pious bishop of the end of the eighteenth century, Thomas Wilson (all of whom were republished by the tractarians), as well as through the Fathers of the Church, their piety was also far nearer to what was best in Puritan piety (in the moral demands it made and in its religious seriousness) than

[68] See H. P. Liddon, *Life of E. B. Pusey*, London, 1893.

one would have supposed, and nearer to it than the evangelicals of the time.

The later Anglo-Catholics on the other hand, as they advanced behind Ward, Oakeley and Faber, clung to an emotional conception of piety built up around baroque ritualism which, whatever the appearances and the ferocious opposition they aroused, breathed that air of sentimental piety, even of "Jesuanity" (to use Bulgakov's word again) towards which the evangelicals were leaning more and more. They also shared with the evangelicals (to the honour of both) an anguished concern to rejoin and win back the de-Christianized masses.

Perhaps the most interesting and spiritually creative thing that came from the movement was the foundation of a variety of religious communities. Some (Benedictines and Franciscans) aimed at transplanting within Anglicanism the great Catholic orders just as they were though in their most evolved forms, whereas others were more original creations inspired by contemporary needs. Among the latter we should list the Cowley Fathers (Society of St John the Evangelist) started by Hugh Meux Benson; the Community of the Resurrection inspired by Charles Gore (theologian and Bishop of Oxford) and Walter Frere (liturgist and Bishop of Truro); and the Society of the Sacred Mission at Kelham, well known for its missionary apostolate and its pastoral liturgy and for that excellent popular theological writer, A. G. Hebert, who died only recently.[69]

The Rediscovery of the Church through Nineteenth-Century Protestantism

Yet it is an all too common mistake to suppose that the Catholic revival within nineteenth-century Protestantism was confined to Anglicanism. It was a general phenomenon that developed more or less in accordance with the different countries and Churches. It might even be said that the same process within the Lutheran Church, being slower and less spectacular than with the Anglicans, was all the more organic for that and hence more interesting to the theologian and historian.

As we have already pointed out, Lutheran orthodoxy in the seventeenth century had only been able to define and consolidate itself, when faced with reformed Protestantism, by renewing its awareness and appreciation of the most Catholic aspects of Luther's

[69] On all this see Peter F. Anson, *The Call of the Cloister*, London, 1955.

work. For identical reasons this was even more true of the Lutheran revival in the nineteenth century.[70]

In the Churches of the German *Länder* which, under the combined influence of Prussian administration and Schleiermacher's liberal theology, followed and extended Prussian union, i.e. the complete absorption of the Lutheran Church into an ever-increasingly non-dogmatic reformed Church, the Lutheran revival appeared as a vigorous and very positive protest. Its great inspirer was Wilhelm Löhe, a Bavarian pastor whose *Drei Bücher von der Kirche*[71] constituted a glorification of the Church as the body of Christ written in the name of a freshly thought out and revived Lutheranism. By this we are to understand the sacramental and doctrinal Church, in continuity with Christ through the whole Catholic tradition, as mother of the spiritual life of the faithful. Moreover, in his parish at Neuendettelsau, Löhr restored the life of the liturgy and sacramental piety including confession, and became the founder of a system of deaconesses who, as he conceived things, were a genuine monastic community in the service of the Church in the spirit of Basilian monasticism.

In order to safeguard this ideal many Lutherans then emigrated from the German countries where they were threatened by persecution from princes and reformed theologians, taking with them the ideas and practices of Löhr and his kind, such as Kliefoth. Thus they paved the way, especially in the United States, for the foundation of Lutheran Churches of an entirely fresh vigour which increasingly came to think of their Lutheranism not as anti-Catholicism but as a Catholicism both scriptural and liturgical (in the richest sense of this last word).

Similar movements arose in the Scandinavian countries at the same time. There was, for instance, Gruntvig in Denmark, author of one of the most celebrated collections of modern Lutheran hymns, who also inspired a notable surge of social Christianity based on a conception of the Church that was to draw him to the Oxford Movement. In Sweden the same thing happened. There Henrik Schartau's liturgical and pastoral renewal at the parish level prepared the way for ecclesiastical renewal in the twentieth century. Something similar occurred even in France, with F. Horning in his parish of St-Pierre-le-Jeune in Strasbourg, and Louis Meyer in Paris.

Towards the end of the century these aspirations for an apostolic Church, nourished by Catholic tradition on the liturgical, sacra-

---

[70] On all that follows, see Y. Brilioth, *Evangelicalism and the Oxford Movement*, London, 1934.
[71] Stuttgart, 1845.

mental and doctrinal planes, extended to the reformed Churches themselves, though here they would for long remain only sporadic. One of the most interesting cases of this was that of Frederick Denison Maurice, the English Unitarian converted to Anglicanism. Like Gruntvig, Maurice was to be one of the great founders of modern social Christianity. Like Gruntvig, he thought of this from the outset as the natural outcome of the rediscovery of the Church as a concrete institutional reality necessarily embodying genuine Christianity. But in his *Kingdom of Christ*[72] he made his rediscovery a solidly architected theory which, despite certain weaknesses in detail, possibly did more than any other nineteenth-century work to herald the ecumenism that was to come.

The sheer anti-Protestantism into which the followers of the tractarians rapidly drifted drove him away from the Oxford Movement with which he had so much in common. For as he saw things —and with a lucidity without parallel at that time—the Catholic-Protestant either-or was nonsense. If (so he thought) one were to rid the spiritual principles of Protestantism of the formulations and sectarian manifestations that in no way necessarily followed from them, and if one were to cleanse Catholicism of extraneous elements, disfigurements and stultifications which, similarly, were not of its essence, then it would become clear that the most positive Protestant inspiration could only flourish within the body of a regenerated Catholic Church.

[72] 1st edition in 1837. On Maurice see Alec Vidler, *The Theology of F. D. Maurice*, 1948, and A. M. Ramsey, *F. D. Maurice and the Conflicts of Modern Theology*, Cambridge, 1951.

CONCLUSION

Our initial intention was to write an appendix to the third volume of this history of spirituality—i.e. the volume on modern Catholic spirituality. But in the event we have written a whole book; and after consultation with Abbé Cognet we decided that the most suitable place for this work would be before, not after, the intended Volume III.

The cause of this unforeseen development is first and foremost the enormous number of texts that have been published since the invention of printing. And for this same reason Abbé Cognet's study will occupy two volumes instead of one. There has had to be enormous cutting down to keep the present book the size it is.

Not that we ever intended, either in the volumes that have already appeared or in those yet to come, to produce an exhaustive account, and still less to give a complete series of monographs. The critics who attacked us when the earlier volumes came out, and could do so even more justifiably with this one and with those to come, seem to have a conception of history differing from that of the authors collaborating in this work. For we believe that history cannot be a mere accumulating and ordering of all the names and events that bear on the subject under discussion. History has to describe development, and this it can only do by picking out what is of more or less lasting importance or at least represents a salient characteristic. For instance some people have written histories of literature in which as many—if not more—pages are devoted to Pradon as to Racine on the fallacious pretext that his output was larger. Such books only confuse the issue, as the saying goes; they make what should be explained quite inexplicable.

Certainly every selection is open to discussion, and ours as much as anyone's. Critics have every right to take us to task for errors in proportion or judgment. So we would like to define the terms of our selection once and for all, so that we shall be judged not by what we never intended to do but by what was our express purpose.

It will be noted in this volume and in the ones to come that we have ended our account round about the second third of the nineteenth century. This is because we do not believe that history strictly speaking can be written about contemporary events. For that a certain distance is required. Certainly we could give an outline of spiritual development in the recent past and right up to the present. But it would not mean much to people in as good a position as ourselves to judge things on the spot and without specialized research; and it would only make us a laughing-stock to those who come after us.

Yet it was only reluctantly that we made no mention of the brilliant Father John of Cronstadt or the enigmatic and fascinating Sadhu Sundar Singh. But history is about the past, and we cannot call men whom we ourselves might have known, or whom many of our contemporaries in fact did know, as belonging to the past.

Other omissions require some explanation. Readers may be surprised to find no mention in this book of such people as Swedenborg or Emerson. But whether vulgar impostor or (as is more likely) sublime lunatic, Swedenborg belongs only to occultism even though, like many other Gnostics, he played with Christian ideas, and he has no place in our history. Emerson has none either; he is removed by a "transcendentalism" from which all Christian and biblical reality has vanished into thin air.

Other names had to be set aside for other reasons, for instance Oberlin, Elizabeth Fry, Irving, and—though with much hesitation —Kierkegaard. No one can deny that they were Christians. But they belong respectively to a history of pastoral pedagogy, of Christian philanthropy or Christian sectarianism, and finally of religious philosophy. None of them made any distinctive contribution to spirituality in the strict sense.

Others, especially in the nineteenth century, we have regretfully passed over with a mere mention. This in no way means that we think them unimportant. Men like Adolphe Monod, Alexandre Vinet and, a little later, Louis Meyer, were spiritual masters to whom we personally owe our Christian faith more than to anyone. But we came to see that they were no more than echoes of earlier voices, and that in the domain of spirituality they only repeated what had been formulated by others long before.

And this brings us to the important remarks with which we would like to end.

After the high Middle Ages the Catholic Church began to suffer from the progressive estrangement that had developed between the two halves of the Christian world, the half that then spoke Greek and the half that still spoke Latin. In this respect the eleventh century was marked by a gravely revealing incident. But it was not until modern times—not until after the catastrophe of the last Crusade which turned against Constantinople, after the failure of the council in Florence, after the stiffening up at the end of the eighteenth and the beginning of the nineteenth centuries—that the break between East and West became what it is. Yet the very history of the developments in the Christian East, whether Russian or Greek, from the moment when Eastern "Orthodoxy" and Western "Catholicism" began to view one another as foreign, shows this: that the substance of the faith and practice of the Orthodox East has remained in all ways consonant with the substance of the faith and practice of the Catholic West. Nothing proves this better than the fact we have described: that the rebirth of Orthodox spirituality at the beginning of the nineteenth century was produced as much by an assimilation of the highest achievement of the Catholic West as by the accompanying rediscovery of sources peculiar to the East.

To be sure the Orthodox saints have their own special flavour, and one of wonderful variety, just as the Catholic saints do; but it is impossible to say in what way someone like St Seraphim of Sarov is less a brother of, say, the Curé d'Ars than of St Joseph of Volokolamsk, or St John of the Cross less a brother of St Nil Sorsky than of St Ignatius Loyola. Of course in the Orthodox spiritual tradition some developments were more successful than others, some syntheses more satisfactory than others. But exactly the same applies to the Catholic spiritual tradition. We feel that this is no reason for a Catholic to hesitate in venerating not only the life but also the doctrine of the Orthodox saints, just as (again in our opinion) an Orthodox can make his own—and indeed many Orthodox saints readily did so—the doctrine and life of Catholic saints.

On the other hand in the sixteenth century a cleft of quite another kind developed within the Christian West. The promoters of certain principles of spiritual reform, excellent in themselves, contrived from the first to get them inextricably bound up with doctrinal deviations irrelevant to the promoters' essential aim. Then in the next generation, and later more and more, it became evident that the fecundity of their spiritual principles could not really show itself except in so far as their heirs and continuators, whether consciously or not, dissociated these principles from the deviations with which they had originally been bound up. There was an inevitable parting of the ways.

Towards the end of the eighteenth century the heirs of the reformers lived and formulated a spirituality that was nothing if not Catholic, although it was the direct outcome of justification by faith alone in the grace of God in Christ alone, and of the Word of God as received in Scripture by a faith that was an intensely personal adherence. Or else, if they objected to the dissociation, they fell back into forms of spirituality that quickly lost all Christian or biblical character. And if they consented to neither the one nor the other, we find them with no spirituality to put forward at all; we find them suspecting all idea of spirituality and furiously rejecting mysticism itself—which is nothing else than the most pure and incandescent spirituality of the Gospels.

What holy souls Protestantism has produced among its great spiritual exponents, and what admirable teaching of the most genuinely Christian kind! And, let us say it again, the spiritual principles enunciated by Luther and Calvin were, and still are, the initial driving-force of their whole quest for God in Christ. Yet the quest was successful precisely in so far as it separated these principles from all the non-biblical elements that the reformers themselves had attached to them, and which had made the Reformation schismatic and heretical.

The conclusion of all this is undoubtedly that Protestants belong to the Catholic Church by what is best in them, and that what is most rightfully dear to them can only flourish in a certain and lasting way in her bosom, while the split between Orthodoxy and Catholicism is a misunderstanding, an absurd and scandalous nonsense.

But this is only half the truth. We must now add all the things that the Catholic Church has lost by the loss of the Orthodox and the Protestants, and all that Catholics still need to do to be reunited with them in the one Church.

There is a sense in which no division can cause the Church to lose anything that is essential to it. The separation between East and West does not prevent the Greek Fathers, nor the Eastern liturgies, nor the treasures of thought and spirituality accumulated by the Byzantine tradition and its heirs, from belonging for ever to the Catholic Church. And even the ruptures involved in the Protestant Reformation could do nothing to prevent the Word of God from being the great and incomparable richness of the whole Catholic tradition, or salvation from being for every Christian a grace that faith alone can grasp, or faith from being the starting-point of the most intensely personal relation of each soul with God in Christ. Whatever the schisms and heresies, every Christian in the Catholic Church can go on drawing life from all that . . .

But after the growing separation between East and West, what in fact did the Catholic West really and effectively know about the Greek Fathers and the liturgical and spiritual tradition of the Christian East? By concentrating on what was only a part of the traditional heritage of the Catholic Church, has not the West tended to bury itself in that and thus develop hardening of the arteries?

This surely was not the least of the causes that paved the way for the Reformation with all its jarring and partial characteristics. And who would be bold enough to maintain that after the Reformation the Bible kept or recovered the place that it should in principle hold in the spiritual life of Catholics? And similarly, did not the personalism of faith give place to a piety in which outward things and the social order played too big a part?

It is true that the Catholic Reformation (when not confined to a mere Counter-Reformation) largely reintegrated Scripture, the Fathers and the whole wide tradition of antiquity within Catholic piety. But was not this largely abortive, as is shown by the development of Jansenism and Quietism, either because it was wrongly confused in the Church with a concealed form of Protestantism, or else because, the problems raised by Protestantism not having been resolved but merely put aside, it slid once more into its errors?

And coming down to our own time when so many things are being rediscovered or restored to life in the Catholic Church (things which, had they always been of vital concern, would have forestalled schisms and heresies), can we truly say that we have solved the disastrous either-or of simple blind conservatism—which conserves one part of the truth only by neglecting the remainder—and those questionable systems of reform which only recover something of that remainder by losing something of the traditional basis and background?

The best lesson we can draw from the study contained in this book is to ask ourselves these questions. They govern the future of Catholic ecumenism and, even more important, of Catholicism itself.

One last word of thanks. We have already said how much we owe to Abbé Hasso Jaeger's work on Protestant and Anglican mysticism. Our thanks are also extended to Prince Serge Obolensky, M. Julien Green, the Very Reverend Fathers Christophe Dumont and André Scrima and Father Ion Goïa for their kindness in reading the manuscript and for their valuable comments. Finally we have often remembered the Very Reverend Edgar Milner-White, Dean of York Minster, while writing this book. We were responsible for the translation of his essay on Anglican spirituality thirty years ago, and he was one of our first guides . . . *ex umbris et imaginibus in veritatem.*

Abbaye de la Lucerne, 10 December, 1964.

INDEX OF NAMES

I. PERSONS

II. Places

Robert P. Scharlemann
THE BEING OF GOD:
Theology and the Experience of Truth
"A stunning theological achievement. . . . Here philosophical and confessional theology become one as a vigorous and compelling argument by its own inherent logic passes into kerygmatic witness, and the crucified God ceases to be the hidden God and becomes instead present as the ground of thinking itself." —Thomas J. J. Altizer
224pp

Anthony Battaglia
TOWARD A REFORMULATION OF NATURAL LAW
"In the present disarray of moral positions, just as much as in the present confusion of theological systems, the search for foundations is . . . surely indicated. . . . In his reading of the perennial point of natural law theory, Battaglia sees in it . . . confidence in reason and reality." —James P. Mackey
160pp

John Dominic Crossan
CLIFFS OF FALL:
Paradox and Polyvalence in the Parables of Jesus
"A sometimes difficult but very challenging approach to the familiar element of Jesus' preaching." —*America*
128pp

Langdon Gilkey
MESSAGE AND EXISTENCE:
An Introduction to Christian Theology
"Sound in theory and application, comprehensive in coverage, and skillful in presentation . . . one of the best books . . . on basic theory in recent years." —*Pastoral Life*

Pbk 272pp

Thomas J. J. Altizer
TOTAL PRESENCE:
The Language of Jesus and the Language of Today
"Altizer advocates a modern anonymity, an analogue of the apophatic way, which yields what he calls an eschatological faith and a total presence antithetical to classical vision and to biblical transcendence, both of which distorted primitive Christianity. . . . This controversial and thought-provoking book is highly recommended for large general libraries, and essential for academic and seminary ones." —*Library Journal*
128pp

Otto Kaiser and Werner G. Kümmel
EXEGETICAL METHOD:
A Student Handbook
(New, Revised Edition)
This indispensable reference work gives concise descriptions of all the critical methods used by biblical exegetes today, and clear directions for students to use these methods on their own.
Pbk 128pp

Thomas M. King
TEILHARD AND THE MYSTICISM OF KNOWING
"A philosophical analysis of a particular mystical experience. . . . A first for Teilhard. . . . A major contribution to Teilhard studies, the only truly philosophic study of his total religious thought."
—Christopher F. Mooney, S.J.
(author of *Teilhard de Chardin and the Mystery of Christ*)
192pp

Robert C. Neville
CREATIVITY AND GOD:
A Challenge to Process Theology
"Neville possesses a mind capable and willing to face the basic ontological and metaphysical problems that are the heart of any attempt to speak *rationally* of God." —*Best Sellers*
176pp